★ ★ ★ ★

Heroes of World War II from Florence County

BY BILL GISSENDANNER
WITH ANDY COLE
AND THOM ANDERSON

Cover: Sgt. Bill Gissendanner in Sicily with his dog, Daisy Mae.
Rear: Scene at the Florence National Cemetery.

2nd Edition

ISBN-13   978-0-97903107-0-6
ISBN-10   6-97900107-09

Printed by   Colonial Printing, Inc.
              Columbia, South Carolina

07 08 09 10 11 5 4 3 2

★ ★ ★ ★

ACKNOWLEDGMENTS

Those of us who have worked on *Heroes of World War II from Florence County* are grateful for help we have received from throughout the county.

It was encouraging to receive support and enthusiastic backing from veterans groups and from individuals all over the county. Among these were their families and friends of World War II vets.

Particularly, we thank the people who gave us information on Florence County veterans, enabling us to prepare entries on individuals. Sometimes their efforts to help us required that they overcome emotional barriers that made it difficult for them to relate their information. Their help is the backbone of the information that makes up this volume.

The Three Rivers Historical Society gave us permission to use their copyright list of county veterans they had compiled. Their list came largely from the efforts of government-related agencies that tried to place WWII veterans in jobs as they returned from the war. That enabled us to include the names of many veterans about whom we had no other information.

Harry Logan and Tom Kinard read the galley proofs and offered advice as well as corrections. Earle Davis of Colonial Printing in Columbia offered invaluable advice on page layout, type choices and picture placement as well as encouragement as we tried to finish the project.

Information on some of the subjects came from material published in the past, including from the Morning News of Florence and the Lake City News & Post.

Most of all, we are grateful to and inspired by the people from Florence County who served in World War II, some giving their lives for their country. To us, they are all heroes, and that is where the book got its name.

Draftees on Old Post Office building steps

★ ★ ★ ★

FOREWORD

I would like to thank each one of you for reading our book, *Heroes of WWII From Florence County.* A special thanks to Andy Cole and Thom Anderson, our co-authors, and Bill Gissendanner, the focus of the book, for their many hours of work and research to bring Bill's experience to us. It opened up many memories of his war experiences and his childhood. I thank them very much. This book is a project that I've wanted to undertake for many years, and it is a finally reality.

Bill was my Sunday School teacher for many years and I enjoyed hearing about his experiences in WWII. I encouraged him to put those experiences in a book so that others could read about them. I felt that it was important for future generations to know just what our veterans and this nation went through. Now it is done. Thanks again from my grandchildren, future generations and me.

The comments from our veterans have been outstanding and I will always remember this experience. Someone once said, "Life is memories." Through this book we hope our future generations can look back and remember what WWII was all about, the hardship, the death, the sacrifices made by the entire nation, and see what our ancestors encountered.

We are very fortunate to have memories, good and bad, of our past. We are privileged to have ancestors who fought and died for our freedom and prosperity. So many of our relatives, friends, and loved ones have already gone to the other side and are now resting in peace.

I am so thankful that we still have a large number of WWII Veterans in Florence County, so that they can share their memories and be recognized, not just for today, but forever. We are enjoying our lives full of tranquility because of who they are and who they were. We will always be grateful and will honor them forever.

To our Widows of Deceased Veterans, you have paid the ultimate price during the war and since the war ended. We know you have sacrificed greatly for many years and now it is time to be recognized for your contributions to us and to our country.

For the many Veterans that we did not meet, we are sorry we were not able to hear your stories. We wanted to let each of you know how special you are, and to recognize all men and women who are WWII Veterans in Florence County. You will always hold a very special place in our hearts. I hope you will remember the good times as well as the history that you helped to create. We are very grateful to you.

As we worked on this book, one thing stood out – our Veterans, male and female, white and black have contributed to what we are today. They were called on at a very critical time in history to do a job that required a very special dedication. I hope that this book will serve as a tribute to our Veterans and to Florence County. I hope this book will be in every school and library in our area and its history will be passed on to future generations.

I hope we can preserve our history about WWII, and that our future generations will remember our Veterans. It is sad that so many young people do not know much about WWII. My desire is to give them a way to study WWII in Florence County. I hope that our Veterans' families will obtain this book and place it in their homes for future generations to study so that we may keep our memories fresh and alive. This book is dedicated to the families of WWII Veterans in Florence County. I think Bill Gissendanner, Andy Cole and Thom Anderson did a yeoman's job in putting all of our information together in the telling of this story. Another special thanks to all of our Veterans who shared stories and pictures about their time in WWII. Without them and their efforts, this story could not have been told. I personally want to thank them for their contributions and their insight. This can be transformed into a deserving history lesson that shows what a great contribution our Veterans made. As President Roosevelt said when Pearl Harbor was attacked, this will be a date, "which will live in infamy."

I know that we have many more stories that are still untold and could be lost in history. I hope this book will motivate all Veterans to do their part in making sure their families are being taught about WWII. Do not let your WWII memories be lost or forgotten in history! There may be other books written on WWII, but I don't believe they will be written with more conviction and desire to keep this important part of history in our memories.

Our book is not designed to pick out one but all of the many heroes of WWII, and to tell the stories of as many of our heroes as possible. I know we have missed many and that their stories should have been told, but we really tried to capture as many as we could, and to get their names and stories if possible. I feature Bill's story because of the close relationship we have. He is my Sunday School teacher. There are many stories untold, but hopefully some-

how they will go down in history.

We received an overwhelming response to our request for information about our Veterans' WWII experience during the year and a half production. I would have liked to have included them all and have tried to capture as many as we could, and to include their names and stories. Maybe, there will be other stories we can write at another time. I hope that no one will be hurt because their story is not in the book. I will assure you that your information has been shared with many, and we really appreciate every one of you.

To the widows, children, grandchildren, and all relatives of WWII Veterans, you have a very special place in history and a reference book that will be used by future generations.

God Bless America and God Bless our Veterans of WWII and Widows of Deceased Veterans.

Billy Campbell
Producer - Publisher
Heroes of WWII from Florence County

19 June 2006

Bill Gissendanner
Veteran of WWII

Dear Mr. Gissendanner,

I read the article about you some time ago in *the Morning News* and my wife saw your ad soliciting World War II photos recently. I just wanted to write and sincerely thank you for your sacrifices long ago that so positively shaped the world. I'm a 40-year-old man who served in the peacetime Army and will likely never have experiences like you had, but I'm aware of history and have the deepest regard and respect for those once and now in harms way for our nation. Despite military service I'll never really know what kind of soldier I would have been under fire. I'm aware that there are many I can never thank but my gratitude extends to them with a realization for what they have done. Your generation came out of the Depression tough and resourceful and in many regards may have been our greatest generation as one writer recently stated. Philanthropy, service, education, and tenacity after the war is unquestioned.

I'd be honored if some afternoon this summer you'd join my family for a cookout honoring you and you can see some of the little babies that have benefited from the sacrifices of what <u>is</u> our greatest generation. I've got a daughter, 5, named Rebecca and two very young sons, Jack and David, who have surely been blessed by the outcome of WWII.

Thank you again, Mr. Gissendanner, for your sacrifice for us. God Bless you and all U.S. Veterans living and fallen.

Sincerely,

Chris Eaton

Chris Eaton

✯ ✯ ✯ ✯

CHAPTER ONE:

Florence, South Carolina at the outbreak of World War II

Sunday nights usually were lonely in downtown Florence. There were no Sunday movies, few businesses were open, so other than for window shopping, there was little reason to go downtown on a Sunday in 1941. But this Sunday night, the streets and sidewalks were packed with curiously quiet people.

It was Dec. 7, 1941, and stunned Florentines had just learned their country was at war.

About midday radio broadcasts reported that Japanese planes had attacked Pearl Harbor and the damage and loss of life was heavy. President Roosevelt would call it "a day that will live in infamy," and the next day Congress would declare war on Japan. A few days later, Germany and Italy would join the roster of enemies.

Many Florence people had the broadcast report interrupt their family dinners that Sunday. Others heard it on car radios. One family heard it when the radio of a car parked beside theirs at a drive in restaurant blared out the news. Telephone switchboards quickly were jammed.

Broadcast news (there was no television) was not what it is today, so many people headed downtown to try to find out more. Florence had two daily newspapers, and special editions from other cities would be shipped into town.

The Morning News was first on the street with an extra, and those papers were

Morning News employees that worked on the December 7, 1941 Extra review it 25 years later. From the left, Herbert Dudley, Pete Holland, Ernest Anderson, Willis Harper.

snapped up as the crowds increased in size. Other papers followed, and the Morning News did at least one other extra later in the day. Many local and out-of-town papers were sold on Florence streets that afternoon and night, and people gathered to discuss what they found in each new edition.

Some people went to church. Others just wandered in a daze, met and talked quietly with friends and wondered what it all would mean. Some lingered around the goldfish ponds that flanked the entrance to the Colonial Theater in the old City Hall.

Others gathered outside the Morning News office on East Evans Street as they often did when unusual events occurred. Some crowded into the newspaper office trying to see the Associated Press printers. Sometimes, they got in the way of the employees who were producing the extras and working on the Monday morning edition, which in the confusion would repeat the Dec. 7 dateline on the front page but

Soldiers parading at the corner of South Dargan Street and West Evans Street in downtown Florence. The U.S. military was still segregated during World War II, so the parades consisted of "Negro" units and White units.

had Dec. 8 on the inside pages.

Traffic was heavy, and drivers inched through the downtown. The sidewalks were crowded into the night. Some people absent-mindedly window-shopped.

Obviously, the country would want young men for the armed forces, and Florentines wondered which of their youths would go and whether or not they would come back. There

was much anger that night and anxiety, too, as they wondered what a major war would mean to them individually.

FLORENCE AT the time was still a relatively young town. The 1940 census counted 16,054 within the city limits, and the city area was a little more than three square miles in a circle with a radius of one mile from the corner of Front and Dargan streets.

In 1941 it was still a railroad town. The Atlantic Coast Line was the biggest employer, and most of the 3,485 families counted in the city in 1940 had a connection of one sort or another with the railroad.

Florence's population, according to the City Directory, was more than 99 percent native born, and nearly all of those were born in South Carolina. The foreign born white percentage was eight-tenths of one percent.

Of the native born, 58.1 percent were white and 41.1 percent "colored," meaning black. Florence and the rest of the South were rigidly segregated. There was a school system for whites and one for blacks. The main movie houses had seats for blacks in the balcony which were carefully separated from the whites, and there was one movie house for whites only and one for blacks only.

There were separate rest rooms for whites and blacks at public buildings and separate waiting rooms and rest rooms at railroad and bus stations. In stores, there were separate water fountains for blacks and whites.

There were two daily newspapers with combined circulation of 8,300 and the area's first radio station, WOLS, was about four years old, still the only one in town. There were three commercial banks and a building and loan. Florence was the retail and wholesale center for the eastern part of the state.

The downtown primarily was bounded by Darlington, Cheves, Coit and Ravenel streets. Surrounding that were tree-lined residential streets with growth tending toward the west and south. There were cultivated fields between the western edge of the city and Five Points, which was then a separate rural community.

THE STUNNED throng on downtown streets wondering what this war would do to their community and its members soon would see things happen.

There already were some Florence men involved in the European war that had started in 1939. A few actually had joined the Royal Canadian Air Force and were seeing action.

The local papers in the next few days carried reports on "Florence boys," as they usually identified them, who were in Hawaii on active military duty when the attack occurred.

The 263rd Coast Artillery, a Florence National Guard unit, had been called into federal service in 1940, as war clouds gathered, but about a year before the U.S. was at war.

They were to have served a year, but before their release, Pearl Harbor happened, and they were in for the duration. Some were sent to Ft. Bragg for reassignment, and others were sent into all branches, from the air corps to infantry, to artillery, to armor to airborne.

There were 145 men involved. Most served in Europe and saw combat. Some lost their lives, some were wounded, some made the army a career. Some were still living in 2007.

A news story said that the Navy recruiting office in Florence saw its busiest day ever on Dec. 8. That Japan had made the surprise attack while its envoys were in Washington for peace talks multiplied the outrage all over the country, and while many men immediately enlisted in the service, others who knew they were likely to be called began to put their business in order.

Draft calls soon came, and many young men of that time still have the traditional picture of themselves in a class of draftees posing

263rd Coast Artillary Reunion March 7, 1981

on the Post Office steps as they prepared to leave for boot camp.

Extra security was placed on federal installations, and Florentines read about beefed up security in Charleston harbor. The governor called out the Home Guard to protect the new Santee-Cooper dams in the lower state.

LATER, INTERNATIONAL supply lines having been interrupted by war and the military making heavy demands on the civilian economy, many consumer items became hard or impossible to get.

Women had to do without nylon hose. Young boys felt particularly victimized because cap pistols were replaced by hunks of plastic shaped like pistols but with no working parts. Even if one had a working cap pistol, caps were nearly impossible to get.

Meats, canned goods and many fruits were on the scarce list. Sugar became a luxury item, hard to get, and candy and soft drinks became scarce. People who had an "in" at a military PX sometimes showed envious friends and neighbors things they had gotten outside the civilian economy.

Meats and some other grocery items soon were rationed, and everyone was issued a ration book that entitled him to a certain amount of those hard-to-get items. Some local merchants occasionally offered a way around rationing in what was known as the black market.

Possibly the place where wartime demands imposed the most visible cutbacks were in the family auto. U.S. auto companies quickly shifted to military production, and after a few 1942 models made it to the public, there were no new civilian models available until after the war. The manufacturers were making tanks, jeeps and airplane parts.

In addition, gasoline was a high priority item and was rationed strictly along with tires. Drivers and autos got stamps in various categories with people like traveling salesmen who used their cars in their work getting approval

for more gasoline than the average driver. There was a popular song that said a plane was flying "on a wing and a prayer." Many family cars in Florence were running on tube patches, booted tires and prayers.

NOT AS bad as Pearl Harbor, but Florence got some unwelcome news just after the Japanese attack when it was learned that a bomber base Florence had hoped to land was going to Greenville, which local leaders noted, had more political pull.

However, they said there were still talks, and there were plans for more bases. Florence was still in the running for one. As it turned out, one located at the Florence airport, and Army improvements to the airport for use as a base enhanced it for post-war use.

Shortly after Pearl Harbor the first units appeared in Florence and set up tent encampments at the old YMCA grounds and Timrod Park. Later, the Army built structures at the airport and there were a large number of Army personnel from all over the country. Some brought families, and Florence children found classmates from other parts of the country, children who had come from military families.

Florence Army Air Field was a training base, and units would come here, train, then depart for action as units. There were several types of aircraft at various times with different outfits, but perhaps the most impressive was the P39, a sleek fighter plane.

Local organizations worked to help the young soldiers, and a USO was established. One result of young soldiers in town was suspension of the blue laws against Sunday movies. City Council approved matinees on Sunday and then an evening showing after theaters had closed a couple of hours. Apparently, they expected moviegoers to attend evening church services during the break.

After the air base went into full operation early in 1943, people became accustomed to seeing many more airplanes over Florence than

Florence began to look much like a military base at the outbreak of war. Above, the YMCA building in Florence became home to many soldiers stationed at Florence Airfield. Below, Timrod Park was turned into an Army camp for the soldiers.

ever before. There were tragic accidents when some base airmen lost their lives in crashes of Army Air Corps planes. One fatal crash was off Gregg Avenue near the present location of St. Paul Methodist Church. The plane had been seen flying over the city at a low altitude and apparently in distress. The pilot seemed to be looking for an uninhabited place to make an emergency landing. Neighborhood children were quickly at the site, worrying adults who feared they might get too close to the wreckage.

There were barracks on the base, but some married soldiers rented places in town and brought their families here. A few came with the Army and stayed here the rest of their lives. Among those were former New Yorkers Gene Lessmeister who became a local detective and Toufic Kirshy who became a Florence restaurateur.

The air base meant not only a payroll for local businesses to draw on, but Civil Service jobs on base for a number of local people. It also was a market for many local businesses and farmers to supply needs of the base population.

Presence of the base and rationing of gasoline led to success for a new city bus line oper-

ated by Pete Thornell. It reached around population areas and brought people into town in the mornings and took them home in the evenings. Another bus line ran between the city and the air base. When prosperity and end of rationing put people on their own wheels after the war, the bus lines shut down.

WHILE THE war action was far from Florence, the railroads gave Florentines a glimpse of it. Troop trains came through town crowded with soldiers moving to their next duty places. And military supply trains came through one after another, loaded with tanks, cannon and other war materiel. Trains were backed up on the lines leading into town, and the rail traffic was so heavy that the steam locomotives often filled the town's atmosphere with smoke.

Florence always had that kind of look at the nation's war efforts. It happened in other wars, including the Civil War when Confederate troop trains and supply trains came through. Florence was on the direct line between Charleston and the southern capital of Richmond.

Three new rail lines, the Wilmington and Manchester, North Eastern, and Cheraw and Darlington formed a junction here just before the Civil War and the station was named for Florence Harllee, daughter of the W&M president. The city and county eventually took the Florence name.

The village also saw some action when a detachment of Sherman's army came from the Cheraw area to destroy the railroad junction. A superior Confederate force happened to be on hand and after a skirmish chased the Union troops back through Darlington. The junction remained intact.

The Sherman detachment also had expected to free Union prisoners at the Confederate prison stockade that in 1864 was established south of town, but the prisoners earlier had been moved out. Thousands of prisoners died in the stockade and the Florence National Cemetery was established on the field where the northern soldiers were buried.

Other evidence of the war was what was called a "wayside hospital" which was established to treat wounded Confederates taken off of trains.

The tiny village around the junction got an economic shot in the arm from the southern war effort, and a number of Charleston people sought refuge here during the war. Some stayed afterwards and the village thrived. Businesses were established and professionals practiced. In the early 1870s, Florence was chartered as a town.

Railroad shops brought more money and business. The town developed into a trade center. The railroads had rebuilt and Florence thrived. The county was created by the Legislature in 1888, and Florence was designated county seat. Shortly after that, it was re-chartered as a city.

Tobacco came to the area farms late in the 19th Century. Much of the money that crop attracted wound up in Florence, and the business district grew. Possibly not much noticed was the beginning of medical practices and small clinics that treated patients. That was the beginning of the medical community that since has become the backbone of the local economy.

Florence had a glimpse of the Spanish American War and World War I efforts as sol-

An Army training plane flies over Florence Airfield during World War II. Florence became home to thousands of soldiers training at the field during the war.

diers and war materiel passed through on trains. Florence growth was strong and it moved up in the list of S.C. cities through the early part of the century until the Great Depression arrived early during the 1920s in a rural area like the Pee Dee and lingered until World War II.

A fine new Post Office, downtown hotels, department stores and the seven-story Trust Building that would be the city's tallest for more than 30 years were built before 1920, and Florence began to take on the look of a city. The Depression slowed the growth until after World War II.

AMONG THE local World War II efforts were some that involved children. The youngsters were excited and wanted to play whatever role they could in defending the country.

Schools had war stamp drives among the kids while War Bond drives were held in the larger community. Florence County bought millions of dollars in bonds to help finance the war, and children could fill books with stamps and exchange them for bonds.

The school children also got a chance to contribute by helping with the scrap drives in which paper, metal, rubber and other items were collected to be recycled by war industry. A kid could get promotions in the Junior Commandos by contributing various amounts of scrap to the drives. It was a thrill for a kid to be promoted in that junior organization while standing on the stage during his school assembly.

At the same time, teachers like Mrs. Kennedy Rutledge at Circle (McKenzie) School were trying to make sure that the children grasped the importance of the war. "You are lucky to live in such historic times and be big enough to remember it," she told her classes over and over.

She explained how Germany had been defeated in World War I but then Hitler had gotten control of that country, re-armed it and was seeking revenge and domination of Europe and the world. England and France

earlier had agreed to outrageous demands by Hitler, trying to avoid war, but when Germany invaded Poland and ignored an ultimatum from the allies, the war was on.

The Germans went on to swift victories, quickly over-running most of Western Europe. They were brutal. One incident in particular was heavy bombing of defenseless Rotterdam that did massive damage and killing, apparently just to frighten other countries.

Then Germany relentlessly bombed British cities in an effort to force a surrender without invasion. Although that failed, Germany turned on the Soviet Union, which had been their ally in partitioning Poland, and marched to the outskirts of Moscow, Leningrad and Stalingrad before bogging down.

The children were told of Hitler's and Mussolini's brutality and treachery, as in Germany's turning on the Soviet Union. Teachers did not know, so children did not hear about the Holocaust in which Hitler's brutality was magnified in an effort to "cleanse" Europe of Jews and some other minorities through death camps.

The children were told about Japan's effort to dominate eastern Asia and the Pacific, its invasion of China during the 1930s, its "stab in the back" of the U.S. at Pearl Harbor, and its brutality. Reports came in about Japanese soldiers torturing and killing Americans who were their prisoners of war

The war was about the effort of the Axis powers to dominate and the democratic powers' efforts to protect rights of people to determine their own destiny and live without undue interference from outsiders, she said.

AS THE war progressed, shortages of consumer goods were accompanied by wage and price controls that the government put in place to avoid great inflation as well as price gouging. One result was that many people had a store of unspent money at the conclusion to pour into the postwar economy.

Travel was a problem. As time passed, many private autos were not fit for long trips. Government and military personnel and military families had priority for transportation. Along with the trains carrying the men and implements of war, Florentines saw overcrowded trains pass with many passengers standing. Buses were similarly crowded.

Practice blackouts were used to train civilians to deal with air raids, however unlikely it was that Florence might be an air raid target. Many houses had dark window shades for use during blackouts. Air raid wardens prowled the streets during blackouts and knocked on doors and windows of houses that leaked light.

Something else new was prisoners of war. Some German POWs were housed at the Florence Army Air Field, and sometimes people saw them being moved about in the backs of trucks, wearing uniforms that designated them as prisoners of war. Many of them were sent out to work on area farms from which young men had gone off to war, and friendships were forged between some area families and the POWs that continued after the war.

The Monday Morning News disappeared. Many of the smaller city newspapers dropped that edition to conserve paper. It was a couple of years after the war before it returned.

As things looked better and better for the Allies, Florence became more comfortable with the idea that we were going to win the war. By 1944, much anticipated was an Allied invasion of Western Europe. One afternoon an usher in the Carolina Theater went to the stage as the house lights were turned up and announced that the invasion of Western Europe had begun. Many left the theater in excitement only to soon discover the bulletin was erroneous. A practicing teletype clerk in England had typed out a bulletin saying we had landed in Europe, thinking the machine was not on the network, but it was. It created a short stir, then people settled back to wait longer for the invasion.

The invasion finally came on June 6, 1944,

and Florence had special church services planned for it when it happened. People poured into churches that morning when they learned our troops were in France.

Although the war news was better and better for our side, there was devastating news for some local families even in the finals days of the war.

Word came through that some soldiers from this area had been killed, some were missing, and others were wounded. Family and friends rallied around those who had such losses, but as much support as families received, the loss and heartbreak could not be quickly repaired. Among those for whom we mourned was President Roosevelt who unexpectedly had died in April, just missing the end of the war that so many of us thought he deserved to see.

AS THE end neared, plans were made for special church services when the word came. Finally Florence learned in May 1945 that Germany had surrendered. Churches were packed and there was much thanksgiving, but Florentines reminded each other the job against Japan remained unfinished and we must not relax until that was done.

It finally happened in August 1945, when Japan, stunned by the atomic bomb drops, agreed to surrender. President Truman made the announcement at 7 p.m., and seconds after that, many heard a radio news show called Headline Edition start with the announcement, "The War Ends." Many who were in that quiet, stunned crowd downtown on Dec. 7, 1941, returned that night to celebrate.

This time, they were anything but quiet. They cheered, they patted each other on the back, tears of joy replaced the anger of 1941. Many didn't want that night to end. They stayed on downtown streets, cheering and generally acting out, until the town clock struck midnight and they let go a cheer that threatened to knock out store windows.

One of the features of the night was a

black man found marching along the middle of East Evans Street, proudly carrying a big U.S. flag. Florence Army Air Field soldiers picked him up and rode him back and forth through the downtown on the fender of their car. Others rode him through the main drag as the night wore on.

It was loud but orderly, but the Morning News reported the next morning that "unfortunately, some celebrated by imbibing intoxicating beverages." They had a chance to nurse hangovers because the next day was a holiday for local businesses and institutions.

Many people found time to attend crowded church services and then share the joy downtown. It was a wonderful moment but as they looked forward to return of our servicemen, their joy was tempered by remembering those they knew would not come back.

The next day the commanding officer of FAAF, told a ceremony at the air base, "This moment is ours." Representatives of the officers, of the enlisted men, of the civilian employees of the base, and the outside community spoke.

They expressed their relief and their pride in a job well done and looked forward to whatever else the future had in store for them.

✯ ✯ ✯ ✯

CHAPTER TWO:

Bill Gissendanner

Bill Gissendanner grew up like many children during the Great Depression. Growing up in Columbia, South Carolina, in a family with eight brothers and sisters, his father struggled just to keep them fed, much less send them to school. He worked two jobs to put food on the table, but there was little else left for clothing, shoes, or any of the other things that make life a little easier.

A hardworking man, with a tremendous sense of what was right and what was wrong, Walter Lee Gissendanner was faced with the struggles millions of Americans at that time were facing, but his struggles may have been more difficult than most. Little Bill was only 9 years old when his mother died.

"After the death of my mother, my father had eight children to care for. He tried very hard to keep us together and provide for us, but jobs were scarce and pay was low," Bill says of his father's attempts to keep the family together during such a difficult time. "He worked two jobs, a WPA job during the day, and a night watchman at night.

He had little time, and three young boys with torn clothes, worn out shoes who were constantly cited for truancy from school and for staying out late at night."

Working all the time, it was hard for Walter Lee to keep the three youngest boys, Bill, Emery and Tommy, in school. Wearing tattered rags, patched together by his older sister, the young Gissendanner boys just didn't go to school.

"We were poor, I mean really poor," Gissendanner says. "We weren't bad kids, that's not why we didn't go to school. We were just ashamed to go to school because we were so poor. It wasn't my father's fault, he tried to keep us in school, but there was little he could do. After several incidences of truancy, it was finally decided we could go to a boys school in Florence."

That school, the S.C. Industrial School for Boys, helped shape Bill Gissendanner. It was there that he was afforded opportunities few other children in his circumstances had.

Built in 1909 on a large tract of land donated by the Atlantic Coast Line Railroad, the Industrial School was set up as a reform school for boys who got into "trouble." Trouble back then was not the same as it is now. Boys who swiped apples from the market could be sent to the Industrial School. Truancy from school was cause for packing a boy up and sending him to Florence. But by the time of the Great Depression, The Industrial School for Boys had become a sort of refuge, a place for boys like Bill Gissendanner, boys facing such poverty that they were better off living as wards of the state than they were living at home.

Bill and his brothers were shipped off from Columbia to live in Florence, about 80 miles away. There they would live in relative opulence.

"We were rich," Gissendanner says of the school. "We had a huge farm there, we had dormitories and we even had a swimming pool. The campus was large and very beautiful, with many buildings and surrounded by a three-foot high, well trimmed hedge. The buildings included living quarters, and living quarters for employees. The buildings were designated as Company A through Company E, and the boys were housed according to their ages. Tommy and I were in Company C."

The Florence Industrial School for boys was a sprawling campus on the outskirts of Florence. Bill Gissendanner was sent to the school when he was 9 years old.

The Florence Industrial School for boys was a sprawling campus on the outskirts of Florence. Bill Gissendanner was sent to the school when he was 9 years old.

"The campus was practically a small city within itself. We had everything from athletic fields, a gymnasium, central dining hall, a large concert band with a band instructor. We had a voice instructor, a barbershop, a small hospital, laundry, a dairy, farmlands and electric and carpentry shops. The campus had its own water supply, and it had its own school through the sixth grade.

"Everyone was required to attend school through the sixth grade. Everyone could learn as many of the trades offered as they wanted to, but they had to take them one at a time. We had the run of the campus, but we had to be with our company whenever we went for meals in the central dining hall."

They were required to work at the various farming or industrial operations on the campus, but education was the most important aspect of the daily routine. After completing the sixth grade, they were allowed to make their own decision about continuing their education in Florence's public schools. Many opted to forgo a high school education to work at one of the Industrial School's many operations. But Bill knew that continuing his education was important. He had made good grades, and was convinced that he was going to leave that school with as much education as he could.

"After finishing the sixth grade, we had the choice of continuing in the trades offered at the school, or continuing our education in the public schools. I elected to continue my education as did many others. While going to junior high school and senior high school, we came and went as we pleased. We were quite popular in the public school, with the other students and teachers. Many of us were prominent on the athletic teams of Florence High School."

Bill was on the school's boxing team, lettering for two years, and played football, "although I wasn't very good," but he managed to score a touchdown the only time he was put in a game.

"The only time they used me, was in a game in Lake City. They were leading by three points, and there was about a minute and a half left. I was about the only player who hadn't played yet, and the coach told me to get in and play defensive back.

"The quarterback rears back to throw the ball, and he throws it right at me! I ran around their end, and 85 yards to a touchdown. The only play I ever played, I intercepted a pass and ran 85 yards for a touchdown."

Gissendanner also played baseball for Florence High School, a team of only ten boys who won the South Carolina Class "A" Championship in 1938. Bill played shortstop, right field and he was a substitute pitcher, a position he says he wasn't very good at, but James Blackwell, the team's pitching ace, had to have a back up.

"All I had was a fast ball. The catcher could put up his mitt and I could hit it with a fastball, but that was about all of my pitching ability. Still, I was the relief pitcher, and I had to take care of my arm. I was out in right field at practice one day and the coach was hitting fly balls out to us. We were supposed to throw it in to the cut-off man, but I shagged one of those fly balls and threw it all the way in to home plate. The coach just walked out there to me, really calm with that bat in his hands, and said 'if you do that again, I'm going to hit you over the head with this bat.' It's not that I was such a good pitcher, but I was all we had if James hurt his arm."

Bill's teen years were good ones. He threw himself into school life, both academically and socially, the way he would throw himself into adult life. He wanted to experience everything to the fullest.

"I knew practically every student in Florence High School, and their parents as well. I dated several girls during my school years, and went to a lot of parties. I graduated from high school in 1939, eighth in a class of 187, with a straight A average. I was a marshal in my class, a cheerleader, President of my homeroom each year, on the student council in my junior year and a member of the Senior Committee.

"The boys from the Industrial School who went to Florence High School were very popular with the Florence residents. We were invited to go to the beach with them and their families, we were invited to their parties, and we had parties at the Industrial School where we would invite girls from the high school."

A very important person in Bill's life was Mr. L.C. Morse, who was in charge of Company C. He and his wife, Mary who served as housemother for the boys, were surrogate parents to the boys, and took that responsibility seriously.

"They were two lovely people and I became very attached to them, all the boys in Company C were. Even after I was married, they would visit my family, and we would visit them. They had no children of their own, and I guess we were all their children. My children knew them as Aunt Mary and Uncle Lake.

I sat by their hospital beds as they were dying; first Uncle Lake, then Aunt Mary, and I held their hands. That's what they meant to me, even years after I left the school."

Another person at the school who helped shape Bill Gissendanner into the man he would become was G.W. Collier, the superintendent of the school. Bill reluctantly admits that he was Collier's favorite of all the boys at the school.

"I guess I was his pet," Bill says. "I was a good student, never got into trouble, and whenever Mr. Collier had to go speak to the Legislature about funding for the school, it was me he took to Columbia with him. He took me to show me off as an example of the kind of work they were doing at the school.

"So, whenever the other boys wanted to have a party, and wanted to invite the girls from the high school, they would chide me into asking Mr. Collier. 'You ask him Bill,' they would say. 'He'll do anything you ask.'

"So the Colliers would host parties for us at their home. They would provide food, refreshments and music, so that we could socialize with the girls from the high school."

With Bill's success during his nine years at the Industrial School, it was no surprise that Collier asked him to stay on when he graduated from high school. Bill was given a furnished apartment on the school's campus, and served as an assistant coach, and as a relief for other school employees.

"In 1985, Mr. Collier was dying of cancer, and he called and asked me to come see him. He was living at the beach and just wanted to see me," Gissendanner said of his surrogate father. "He died shortly after that, and at the funeral, boys from the Industrial School had come from as far away as Texas, Florida and Virginia to attend his funeral. There must have been a hundred or more there.

"He had only one daughter, Anne," Gissendanner said. "At the funeral she looked out at all of the people who were there, with all those boys who had looked at Mr. Collier as a second father, and said 'You know, my father only had one daughter, but he had hundreds of sons. Some have come and filled that section in the church to honor him and I appreciate that."

"People to this day constantly ask me what happened to so and so who attended junior high and high school. Some I know and tell them. Others I don't know."

★ ★ ★ ★

CHAPTER THREE:

Off to War

Three years after Bill graduated from Florence High School, he was working at the Industrial School. Life was pretty good. He had a good job, was well respected in the community, and he had a sweetheart, Edna Mae Streett. The two had been dating for some time, and Bill knew from the moment he met her, this was the one.

But the nation was consumed with World War II, and Bill, now 21 years old, was drafted in 1942.

"I actually got two draft notices," Bill recalls. "One had been sent to me earlier, but Mr. Collier intercepted it. I didn't even know about it. He went to the local draft board and told them that I was too valuable to him, and I couldn't be drafted. I didn't know about that, and I found out about it when I got my second draft notice. I went to him and told him not to intervene. I wanted to serve. You see, everyone was either enlisting or getting drafted. I would be in town, and people would ask, 'Bill, what are you still doing here?' They all thought that I would have been gone by now, so when I got that second draft notice, and found out that Mr. Collier had gotten me out of the first one, I was mad at him. I didn't want to get out of the second one.

"We had a lot of boys who had already left to serve, and it just wasn't right that I was still at home, while they were gone off to war."

The struggles of Bill's early life would seem minor compared to the next few years of his life. But he credits the Industrial School and its people, particularly Morse and Collier, for preparing him for what lay ahead.

Collier would eventually give up his position as superintendent at the Industrial School to serve his nation. Too old to serve in the military, Collier joined the American Red Cross as a volunteer overseas.

"He said that if all his boys had to be over there, then he needed to be there helping them," Gissendanner said. "That's how he felt about us. So many of us from the school were fighting in the war, and we were his boys. He just wanted to do what he could for us. He ended up in Europe working as a Red Cross volunteer for the rest of the war."

The example set by Collier would stay with Bill Gissendanner throughout his life, and particularly during the war. Bill would face some of the most horrible aspects of the war, and the strength of character built at the school by Collier, Morse and others would serve him well for the rest of his life.

"I entered the Army February 23, 1942 at Fort Jackson, South Carolina," Gissendanner says, rather formally, whenever he's asked about his service during World War II.

"I was on a bus with a lot of other boys from the area. They were from Marion, Mullins, Lake City, and some of them had been drinking some. I had never been a drinker, and I couldn't imagine going off to Fort Jackson and being drunk."

Bill and the other young men on that bus didn't know much about what they were in for at Fort Jackson. All they knew was that they were going off to fight the war. Some would end up in the infantry, others would end up being cooks, and still others would be singled out for special duties. Some would fight in the Pacific Theater, others in Europe, but none of them had any idea what would become of them.

Bill was one of those singled out for special duties. He wouldn't find out for some time what his special duty was, but shortly after arriving at Fort Jackson, he and a few other men were pulled out of the group of men he had arrived with.

"When we got there, we got our uniforms, then we were given a bunch of tests. It was about two or three in the morning. We didn't know what they were for, but the next day some of us were pulled out for more tests. We took tests all day long. Then the next day, this was about three days after we got to Fort Jackson, they pulled some of us out and told us to pack up, we were going to Savannah, Georgia to the air field there. We weren't told why, and we weren't told whether we were going to be in the Army or the Air Force, but you didn't dare ask any questions."

Though they didn't know it at the time, Bill and the others had been selected for a special new unit. Their training would revolutionize the way modern armies fought, and many of the things that unit did are still being done today.

They still didn't know why, but shortly after arriving at Savannah, they began learning to use radio transmitters, receivers and other communication equipment. Most of the training was done in classrooms. They learned everything there was to learn about the various communication equipment and the generators used to keep them running. Still not told why they were learning all about communication equipment, they quickly began to figure out that they were picked out for something very special.

"I had been at Fort Jackson no more than three days before going to Savannah, and had

started thinking 'what have I gotten myself into?' We didn't go through basic training. We didn't do the drilling that all the other soldiers did. We didn't do KP," Bill says. "We had it pretty good compared to the other soldiers. We weren't given any training on infantry tactics. We didn't do any marching, didn't do any of this left, right, left, right, right shoulder arms stuff. We weren't even given rifles.

"Some of the guys didn't make it through the school. It was really tough. We had to know all about the communication equipment. We had to take them apart and put them back together again, and we had to know how to fix anything that was wrong with them. Most of this training was done in classrooms. We actually did not physically do the work. We were given problems orally and had to respond either in writing or orally as to what we would do to solve the problem. We also had to take a lot of physical exams. They were always taking us to doctors who would examine us. One of those doctors told me my blood pressure was rather high. Well, I would imagine that quite a few of us had high blood pressure. It was a tough school, and we weren't told anything about why we were training like this.

"We were at Savananah about a month, and in April, I hitched a ride home to Florence when I had a weekend pass. It was Easter weekend, and that's when I married Edna Mae Streett. Back then you could hitch a ride anywhere in a skinny minute. People would go out of their way to take you where you were going.

"Edna Mae had made all the arrangements for us to be married by a friend of the family, a probate judge named Kenneth Grimsley. Well, by the time I got to Florence and we got married, it was after midnight.

"They had made all the arrangements. I had called from Savannah to talk to Edna Mae, and she told me 'When you come home, we're getting married.' I never asked her to marry me. We had talked about it, but she just told me we were getting married. That's how we ended up being married on Easter Sunday."

Newly married, Bill went back to Savannah for more training, only to be shipped off somewhere else.

"Shortly after that they put us on a train and sent us to Athens, Georgia. They put us up in a hotel, and we took up that whole hotel, two men to a room. While we were in Athens, we got the first inkling about what we'd be doing.

"They showed us some movies about the Germans' blitzkrieg, and they told us that was what we'd be doing."

In the years before the U.S. entered the war, Germany's army had rolled through neighboring countries, crushing their militaries with tanks, infantry and planes. This "blitzkrieg," or "lightning war," was highly coordinated, with dive bombers and attack planes supporting ground troops whenever they met resistance. The Germans used forward air observers placed in infantry and other ground units. These air observers were trained to use radios to call in air strikes against the enemy. It was a new way of waging war, using aircraft to deliver devastating firepower.

The Allies aimed to adopt this technique, but make it better. This is where men like Bill Gissendanner came in. He and his fellow soldiers were going to be a part of the 927th Signal Battalion, a newly formed unit that would use the very latest in communications equipment and apply them to winning the war. The 927th would be ground troops, but they'd be working with the Tactical Air Command. Though part of the Army, these specially trained soldiers would be a liaison between the troops on the ground and the pilots in the air.

Now the training they had received in Savannah started to make sense. But it would take a lot more than just knowing how to use the equipment. While many in the unit were anxious to get involved in the fighting, they understood that theirs was a special purpose, and someone much higher in their chain of command had something big planned for them.

"We were in Athens for three months," Gissendanner said. "We were getting more specialized training and we were being introduced to newer transmitters and other equipment. During the time in Athens we were able to go home for the weekends. Florence wasn't that far away, and it wasn't that hard for me to hitch a ride to see Edna Mae, which I did every chance I could.

"She came down to Athens to spend a week with me while I was in school, and it was wonderful. Of course, I took some kidding from the other guys about it. My wife was a very pretty woman, and when she came down there, some of the fellows teased me about how I ended up with such a pretty wife."

Though married only a short while, the love Bill and Edna Mae felt for each other was evident to everyone around them. It was this commitment to each other that would later help Bill get through the difficulties many veterans face when they come home from war.

Both of them knew that it wouldn't be long before Bill would be sent overseas, so they spent as much time together as they could. Bill would hitchhike from Athens to Florence every chance he got, and the week they spent together in Athens was the longest period they would spend together until the end of the war.

They didn't know how long they'd be apart once Bill went overseas. Unlike deployments in the modern army, soldiers during World War II were sent over for as long as it took to get the job done. They had no idea that once Bill got on a troop ship to head across the Atlantic Ocean, it would be nearly three years before he would come back. Of course, that was assuming he would come back. Neither wanted to think about it, but it's something that went through their minds. There was the real possibility that Bill could be killed in the war.

After training in Athens, Bill and his unit were once again sent to another location, this time for training that would be closer to the conditions they'd face in battle. Each phase of their training prepared them a little more for what they would soon be doing.

"When we finished the school in Athens, after we learned to use all of this equipment, we had to go out and use it like it was going to be used in battle," Gissendanner said. "We went to Montgomery, Alabama, and they put us up in a big hangar with cots. We were there about a week, when a sergeant came in and picked six of us who had drivers licenses. Not everyone had a drivers license then, you've got to remember, not every family had a car back then, so there were a lot of people who had never driven a car. This sergeant tells us to meet him the next morning outside the hangar.

"The next morning I get out there and he's there with a tractor-trailer. He said 'take me for a ride,' so I did, and when I was through he said, 'you're now a tractor-trailer driver.'

"All six of us were now tractor-trailer drivers, and he said 'tomorrow, you're going to take these trucks and trailers to Louisiana.'

"That's just the way it was. You didn't know where you'd be the next day, they didn't give you much warning when they shipped you out somewhere else, because they were being so secretive about it. We all knew we were being trained for something really big, but we had no idea what it was."

In August, 1942, the 927th participated in one of the largest "war games" to date. It was in Louisiana, though the men weren't allowed to write home about exactly where they were. They would write post cards and letters home saying "From somewhere in Louisiana."

In Louisiana Gissendanner and his fellow soldiers met other soldiers from the 927th who had been trained at Will Rogers Air Field in Oklahoma. They were under the command of Lt. Colonel Joseph P. Montague, who told them they would now be part of the 927th Signal Battalion, Tactical Air Command.

The 927th was divided into companies, each of which had a different communications mission. Bill was in A Company, which operated the transmitters so important to the front line troops. The company had teams, usually of five or six men, designed to be highly mobile. They would radio the information for aerial attacks back to the rear area.

Other companies in the Battalion had different jobs, but all related to the overall mission – providing communications to the Tactical Air Force for aerial support of the ground troops. The men in Company B for instance were telephone linemen. They would be farther behind the advancing troops, setting up and operating telephone systems. More reliable as a communications tool, but less mobile, the telephone lines would be set up once forward units advanced into and secured enemy territory.

In Louisiana they would get the first real look at how everything would fit together to provide a communications network. Each company would practice what they'd learned, with the added pressure of doing it on the move, with an enemy trying to kill them. Of course, no one was actually trying to kill them, but the huge exercise they participated in was a test.

During several days of training exercises, the men tested their training, their equipment and their abilities to work under the duress of war. There were scenarios thrown into the training that might actually happen during battle. Some of the scenarios were planned; other scenarios, like the cattle, weren't planned at all.

"We were training on farmland in Louisiana," Gissendanner recalls. "There were cows, and horses and crops, but that was how it would be in battle too, so it was realistic.

"The telephone linemen in Company B were busy, constantly running new phone lines back to the rear area, and they had miles and miles of telephone cables stretched out all over the place.

"Well, a lot of the lines ran right through pastures, and cows grazing in those pastures ended up chewing through a lot of that wire. No one had anticipated something like that happening, but that's what the training was for. That's something that could really happen when you're in a battle."

The training mission went well. The 927th and the other units working with them got a chance to try the new tactics and equipment they would be putting to use against the German army. The men had no idea where they'd be putting their knowledge and equipment to use, but they knew that they'd be doing it soon. There were rumors, speculation and a lot of discussion about where they'd end up, but none of the brass was saying anything, not even a hint.

When the 927th, newly formed with its different companies together for the first time, finished their training in Louisiana, they went back to Oklahoma.

"When we got to Will Rogers Field, the local newspaper had already heard about the training exercise. There was a headline that read something like, 'Despite hungry cows, training in Louisiana a success.'"

After the maneuvers, the entire battalion packed up and headed to Will Rogers Air Field.

"We were there about a week, then they told us we had a ten day furlough," Bill said. "I

headed home without telling my wife; she had no idea I was coming home."

It was a long trip of buses, trains and hitched rides before Bill arrived in Florence. But Edna Mae wasn't surprised to see him. Instead, she stood there crying, with a telegram from the War Department in her hands.

"It said 'Furlough cancelled. Report to Fort Dix, New Jersey immediately. She knew before I did that I was about to go overseas," Bill said. "Now, I didn't go immediately. I stayed there for the night with my wife. Then I spent the next day with her. And then I spent the next night. That would be the last time I would see her until the war was over."

She went to the train station with me. Her father also went, and I was glad. The train was about ready to leave; she walked to the train with me and began to cry. I put my arms around her, pulled her to me and said, "Angel, don't cry, I'll be back." She said, "I'll pray and I'll be waiting." She followed that train to the end of the passenger depot platform. I looked back and she was waving.

It would be over three years before I would see her again.

★ ★ ★ ★

CHAPTER FOUR:

North Africa

The Americans came into the war late, but they brought with them a massive industrial complex, and there was virtually no enterprise that was not converted to the war effort in some way. Automobile manufacturers began making tanks, jeeps and other military vehicles. Aircraft factories were churning out planes as fast as they could. Shipyards began cranking out the vessels to carry the supplies, machinery and men to the European and Pacific Theaters. The entire nation was dedicated to winning the war.

Bill Gissendanner was at Fort Dix, New Jersey with the rest of the 927th Signal Battalion. After months of grueling training, and months of wondering what their part in the war would be, the men of the 927th were about to find out.

"Most of the talk was about Europe, and we all assumed we would be going to England," Gissendanner said. "There was a lot of talk about an invasion, and there were a lot of American troops in England, so we all thought that may be where we were going."

But in the army you should never assume anything. The group would not find out where they were going until they were well under way.

"It wasn't long after we got to Fort Dix that we began assembling all of our personal equipment. This is when we were told that the equipment we had been using in training wasn't going with us. It was considered pure junk. They told us to forget what Midland Radio School tried to teach us. We were told that

when we arrived at our destination, we would get all new equipment, highly mobile equipment with the up to date technology that was fully capable of doing the job they wanted done. Everyone was busy loading those ships, and when we finally got everything loaded, we went on board."

The men spent their last night in the U.S. on a ship, which set sail in the dark. The next morning, anyone aboard that ship who didn't realize the scope of the mission they were embarking on realized it in the light of day.

"The next morning, we were at sea. We'd left at some point in the night, and when we got up, we could look out on the ocean and for as far as you could see there were ships. It was a massive convoy, and there was no land in sight."

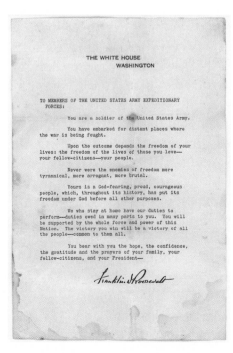

The note from President Roosevelt that the servicemen being deployed received.

After getting on board the transport ship, Bill was thankful for the fact that he was in the army rather than the navy. Every available square foot of the ship was filled with weapons, ammunition, food and equipment. That didn't leave much room for the other cargo, the men.

Living conditions aboard a troop transport were cramped at best. Men slept in bunks stacked atop each other, squeezed by each other in the passageways, and generally had to become accustomed to a lot less personal space than they were used to. They also had to contend with seasickness.

"Everybody got sick. I mean everyone. It wasn't just the rolling back and forth, but you could look out there and all you could see was water. It helped to look out at the horizon, but not much. I'd never felt sick like that in my life, and it didn't go away. Even when you threw up everything, you still felt sick, it just didn't go away."

A few days after leaving the shores of America, somewhere out over the Atlantic Ocean, Bill and the rest of the men found out where they were going, and it was a surprise.

"After we'd been at sea a couple of days, they told us we would be invading North Africa. Of course everyone had been keeping up with the developments in the war, and we knew that the British were fighting Rommel's army in North Africa, but we never thought we would be involved in that. We all assumed we were going to England.

"The British had the Germans on the run in North Africa, and our mission was to cut off their escape routes. We were going to rendezvous all of these ships at Gibraltar, and we would be hitting the beach at Casablanca. Troops from England would be invading Tunis and Algeria.

"The infantry would land first, then we would go in. We really wouldn't be any use to them until there were some air bases set up for the Tactical Air Force, so we wouldn't be going in on the first wave. I was thankful about that.

"Gen. George Patton talked to us while we were on our way to Casablanca. He told us he didn't know what kind of resistance we'd get, but he told us any resistance, regardless of who they are, had to be put down. They were worried about the Vichy French troops who were fighting in North Africa. We all knew many of them were forced to fight for Hitler, but no one really knew whether they'd surrender or fight us. Patton told us that any French forces who surrendered, we were to accept them and treat them as Allies."

The British Army and the Germans had been fighting viciously for some time. Rommel's army was made up of the best soldiers the Germans had to offer. They were tough, well equipped and experienced. But Montgomery's 8th British Army had them on the run.

Operation Torch, the U.S. invasion of North Africa began on Nov. 8, 1942.

"When we landed at Casablanca, it wasn't that bad. The infantry had already moved through, and we had an airbase set up, but Casablanca was relatively secure. We had air raids every night from the Germans while in Casablanca, but we weren't involved in any heavy fighting yet.

"We were in Casablanca only one day when we were introduced to that new equipment we were promised. Boy!! What a wondrous surprise. A field full of vehicles. Our name for them was 'Air Support Units.' From my memory, let me try to describe them to you. During the war even these changed from time to time."

They looked like a station wagon of the time. A cabinet was attached to each side for storage. It was highly mobile with a protected motor with double doors in the back. Inside, just behind the driver's seat was a huge transmitter that was almost as wide as the vehicle. The transmitter had two doors on top for changing the channel coils. There was a seat for the operator to sit so that he could control all of the dials and knobs. There was a padded bench for three operators with a counter top for three receivers with earphones to receive either Morse Code or voice messages. A whip antenna about 30 or more feet tall when fully extended was attached to the vehicle.

Each vehicle had a trailer with a Ford motor to power a 220 volt generator that was connected to the vehicle by a heavy cable. The generator had several plug-in places for either 120 volt or 220 volt lines. There was also space for carrying gas and water cans.

After looking at and entering these vehicles, we could easily understand that our old equipment was truly "junk". We had about six weeks with this new equipment before we left Casablanca, so we had to learn fast.

After the fighting in North Africa, things settled into a sort of a routine for a while. Living in a garage, the men were sleeping on the floor. That's when Bill would meet one of the best friends he would have during the war.

"We had a lot of idle time on our hands after the Germans surrendered. We could go into town, and there were bars there, and restaurants. And the people there were good to us. They were really glad the Germans were gone.

"Some of the guys in the company had gone out and gotten drunk in one of the bars one night. I didn't go out with them, and stayed back at the garage we were sleeping in. I was asleep, on the floor under a blanket, and I felt something on my neck. It startled me, because we had rats in there, and I thought a rat had gotten on me. I jumped up, grabbed a flashlight, and there was this tiny little French poodle puppy. She was not much bigger than my fist. I mean it was tiny. It turned out one of the guys had bought this poodle while he was out on the town. He had bought the dog on the spur of the moment, and the next morning, James Bugg said, "I don't need a dog, I don't care for dogs, I don't want a dog. Anybody who wants a dog; be my guest. Daisy Mae is yours. (That is what he had named her.)

"I vaguely remember that there was a beer and sandwich shop at Will Rogers Field. The owners had a little dog named Daisy Mae and the shop was called Daisy Mae's. James Bugg kept saying that he didn't want Daisy Mae, but nobody paid any attention to him. The soldiers, myself and even Bugg gave her food. We didn't miss the food; she only ate a little. After leaving Casablanca, James Bugg saw Daisy Mae with me and said, that little dog was no longer his responsibility. 'She belongs to you.' I guess that was final. She became the mascot of our crew."

Daisy Mae, a French Poodle that Gissendanner adopted, became one of his best friends.

Daisy Mae and Bill were nearly inseperable for the next 18 months.

"She was a really good dog. She would ride up in the cab of the truck with me, and she went everywhere I went. All the guys loved her, and she kind of became the unit mascot.

Everyone would get food from the mess tent, or give her some of their K-Rations. She just became part of the family."

She lived with Bill and the guys in their makeshift home, and when the unit was moving, she lived in the truck with him.

"What we didn't know was that the British were driving 300,000 crack German troops back on us. We left Casablanca about the beginning of February, and we were headed to the Kassarine Pass. That's where we had to stop the Germans. It was after we left Casablanca that we had our first casualty, a fellow named James Popson.

"It was our first night after leaving Casablanca. We bivouacked in a sort of an oasis, which had some palm trees. We were warned about the Germans leaving mines in the area. Popson stepped on a bouncing betty mine. He hit the trip wire, and it came up behind him. When that happens, you're surely dead, because you're getting the full force of the blast.

"That first casualty was the first real awakening we had that we were in a war. We took it really bad. Now you begin to realize that you're going to be shot at, this is no picnic."

And it would prove to be no picnic. The Germans were fighting their way to the coast, so that they could evacuate, rather than surrender. Kassarine Pass would be where they would be bottlenecked, choked off from the coast, and it was up to the American forces to take the pass.

Bill and his team began moving up to the pass.

"There was one road coming from the east, from the pass, and it branched off into three different roads toward the coast. There were tanks all over the place as we were moving up there, but there were troops moving the other direction.

"The U.S. soldiers were retreating. We went in to the west of Kassarine Pass, and the British attacked and drove the Germans back. When they drove the Germans back on us, it was our job to round them up.

"It came to be a stalemate there. It was winter, raining and cold, and there was mud all over the place. We'd bog down anytime we tried to go anywhere."

As the 45th and 36th Infantry Divisions fought, trying to gain the smallest advantage against the Germans, it became apparent that Hitler's forces would lose the battle to attrition. The Allies controlled the ports and the coastline, and there was no way for the Germans to get supplies. But they continued to fight, and thousands of soldiers on both sides died in the battles.

Some of the toughest fighting was done by the Army Rangers, Bill says. He'd worked with the Rangers, calling in air support when they needed it, and he'd gained an immense amount of respect for them.

"You can talk all you want about your Special Forces and all the others, but those Rangers were men, I mean, they were real men," Gissendanner says. "One of those Rangers was coming back from a patrol one night, and he tossed me this German knife in a sheath. It was a beautiful knife, embossed and engraved. He said he'd taken it off of a German officer, and said 'he won't be needing it anymore.'"

After Rommel smashed through their forces at Faid on February, 14, 1943, the Americans fell back to solidify their defensive position. Five days later, Rommel probed the lines, and the weakest point at Kassarine Pass, in the Tunisian Dorsal mountain range. Rommel drove the Americans back with his heavy Tiger Tanks, firing 88mm guns accurately.

The American forces had made several strategic mistakes, but recovered quickly from them. First, they fought Rommel's Afrika Corps tank-to-tank, while the Germans concentrated their fire. Another problem was inflexibility in the Americans' planning. Junior officers weren't given the ability to make real time, battlefield decisions. On top of these issues, the American M-3 Lee and Grant Tanks had 75mm fixed guns, which were inferior to the Germans' Mark IV and Tiger Panzers.

Over 1,000 American soldiers lost their lives in the battle, and hundreds were taken prisoner, not to mention a heavy loss of equipment.

But the Americans studied Kassarine Pass, and initiated quick changes, restructuring the command and control units, and coordinating devastating air assaults with ground forces. American forces quickly learned how to defeat the Germans and drove Rommel's forces back.

The fighting finally ended in North Africa when some 250,000 soldiers from Hitler's Afrika Corps surrendered to the Allies. Many of them would see South Carolina before Bill did.

"A lot of people don't realize this, but there were German POW camps set up in South Carolina. Many of those soldiers who surrendered in North Africa ended up right here in South Carolina. While they were POWs they gathered crops, and they were here for the rest of the war. A lot of them stayed here when the war was over, and made South Carolina their homes."

During "down time" in North Africa, Bill nearly died, not from enemy fire, but from something his own country had given him.

"I got really sick while we were in North Africa. I mean really sick, and the medics had no idea what was wrong. So they carted me off to the hospital on the coast. We had a medical unit set up there with a real hospital with beds and everything."

The army had issued anti-malarial drugs to soldiers because the threat was so bad. In fact, there were more malaria related casualties in the early days of World War II than there were combat related casualties. Because quinine was in short supply, the army issued another drug, developed ironically by the Germans. Soldiers were under orders to take the drug daily. But it turned out Bill was allergic to the drug, and it nearly killed him. His skin turned yellow and

for three days, he was fed liquids through tubes put down his throat.

"They pumped my stomach, and wrote orders in my medical records that I was not to take that drug anymore. If there was no quinine available, I was not to take any anti-malaria drugs at all. I ended up spending about six days there, and the unit sent some fellows up to the hospital to pick me up.

"Those jokers came and got me, and they had gotten a hold of some grain alcohol and some cans of orange juice. They decided that if they were going to get a couple of days to drive up, get me then drive back, they were going to have some fun.

"I ended up driving because they couldn't. We were driving along the coast, and when those jokers saw that beach they told me to stop. They stripped down to their underwear and jumped in. Now there were nurses there at the beach, and other soldiers, and the underwear they issued us was made of really thin cotton, so when they jumped in that water they might as well have been wearing nothing at all.

"Well of course the MPs showed up and these fools were making a lot of noise and splashing around. I told the MPs that if they'd help me get these guys back in the jeep, when I crossed a river on the way back, I'd throw them in and leave them there to teach them a lesson. They let us go on, but those characters cut up all the way back."

It was while he was in the hospital that another soldier made a big impression on Bill.

"I was in a bed next to a pilot who had lost both of his feet, or at least they'd both been mangled really badly. He had been shot up pretty bad while flying over the Germans. He said he had no idea how he got the plane back and landed it safely, because he had to use those feet to control the rudders. But somehow he had managed to get the plane back to his base and land it without crashing. That really hit me hard. I didn't know if I had that in me.

You think about things like that, wondering if you had what it takes inside of you, and hoping you'd never have to find out. I didn't know if I could do what he did, and I didn't want to know."

After a few months of down time, soldiers can get restless. Idle time is not good in the army, but that's the way it has always been. There was boredom, and some soldiers tend to get into trouble when there is boredom. They'll find the nearest watering hole, quench the thirst they've had for a long time, and then the MPs come and take them away.

One night Gissendanner went out with some of his buddies for some dinner at a local restaurant. There were soldiers from all over the area there, and a few of them started to get rowdy. No one was causing any serious trouble, but soldiers being soldiers, you couldn't tell where this was heading. Then the MPs showed up, bursting through the door.

"Alright, everybody get your ID out," this big MP yelled when he came through the door.

"I knew that voice right away, and when I looked up, it was a fellow from Florence," Gissendanner said of the 'what a small world' incident. "I don't recall his name now, but I looked up and said something about a big dumb guy like him coming in here and starting trouble. And he came over and said 'Bill Gissendanner! What are you doing here?' Well, he ended up leaving and didn't take anyone in that night."

There wouldn't be much more idle time. Just because the Allies had kicked the Germans out of North Africa, it didn't mean the war was over, and there was more fighting to be done.

"We were ordered to move back up to the coast, and when we got to the port, we began getting all of our equipment in order. There were LSTs (Landing Ship Tank) there, and we were all put in order. We were given numbers telling us when we were supposed to get on the ship, because they were loading us in the order we were going to be getting off. The last

The deck of an LCT, crammed with men and equipment, on the Mediterranean Sea. The ships would run aground, and the soldiers and equipment would unload.

vehicles getting on the ship would be the first ones off the ship.

While they were waiting for the orders to load up, there was again a lot of down time. Men waiting for something to do, anxious about what was next.

"That's the thing about war, you have periods of really intense fighting, where all you know about is what's going on within twenty yards of your position," Gissenedanner said. "You have these long stretches of sheer boredom. Waiting around on those docks was sheer boredom.

"I was taking a nap under our vehicle, which was in the hold," Gissendanner recalled. "My buddy Robert Lathrop from New Orleans was tugging at me, waking me up.

"He said 'Bill, Bill. You got any money on you?' Well, I did, and I asked him what for. He said he wanted to get into this dice game some of the fellows had going, and he needed fifty bucks to get in. He said we'd split whatever he won. Well, you don't really have much use for money on a ship, so I loaned him fifty dollars, and went back to sleep.

"Several hours later, he was tugging at me again. 'Bill, wake up. Let's split this up.' He had a wad of money, and started counting out my cut. When he was through, there was about twelve hundred dollars for me.

"I had to run around and find a place to get a money order, and I mailed that twelve hundred dollars back home to Edna, and she held onto it. She didn't spend any of it the whole time I was gone, and when the war was over we used that money to build our house."

It was shortly after Bill mailed that money home to his wife that the 927th, and thousands of other men were ordered to load up.

"We were assigned to LST 26, and I was in the second to the last vehicle to get on the ship, which meant I'd be the second one off the boat when it landed, wherever it landed."

An LST was a large cargo ship with a bow that opened like a set of jaws. The ship could take water into its aft bilges, making it ride high in the front. The ship would then run full speed at a beach, with its bow riding high. It would intentionally beach itself. Depending on the tides and the slope of the beach, the ship would either run right up to dry land, or it would end up farther out in the water.

This would be where the Navy's Sea Bees would come in. Sea Bees, who got their name from the abbreviation for Construction Battalion, or CB, were sea-going engineers. They were crucial to the war effort, establishing routes for supplies and equipment that landed on beachheads.

Pontoon bridges, built by Sea Bees, would form a causeway from the ship to shore. The ship would open its wide jaws, depositing tanks, jeeps, trucks and soldiers.

"There was another team from the 927th on that ship, but they got on early. My friend Howard Manness, from Greensboro, North Carolina, was number one, meaning his five-man team was the first to get on.

"They backed their vehicle onto the ship, then one tank after another backed in, and finally my number was called out. I backed my truck into that ship and one more vehicle began backing on. It was a tank with a large plow-like blade on the front. That blade was made to clear a path for the vehicles following it.

"When we finally got everyone on board, we went up several flights of steps to the sleeping quarters, then we went out on deck when the ship began moving out. The ship was carrying these pontoons lashed to the sides with heavy cables, and there were a couple of motorboats. We found out that there were Sea Bees on board, and their job was to cut those pontoons loose when we went in for the invasion. They would use the boats to pull the pontoon bridge pieces to the front, and create a bridge. They had to do this before we could get off the ship.

"Again, we had no idea where we were going. Everyone had their guesses, but we didn't know."

The entire convoy of ships, once loaded, moved into the Mediterranean Sea, and began sailing west toward Gibraltar. By now, no one dared to assume a destination. They knew that they'd find out in due time where they were going, but it was a Sea Bee officer who let them know they weren't going back to North Africa.

"We were standing on the deck, watching the coastline of North Africa, and some people were speculating about whether we'd be going back there," Gissendanner recalls. "This Sea Bee officer was standing there and said, 'ya'll take a good look at Africa, because that's the last you'll see of it during this war.'"

For several nights, the entire convoy would move toward the west, then turn around and go back.

"We figured they were keeping the Germans guessing," Gissendanner said. "They had planes in the air watching us once we got toward Gibraltar, but then we would turn around and go back to the same area we'd left."

Most of the men on these overcrowded war ships knew nothing about where they were going, or what they'd be doing when they got there. They anxiously passed time, standing watch over their equipment in shifts. There wasn't a lot to do as the convoy made its slow runs through the Mediterranean. Men would read, play cards, write letters to loved ones. Anything to ease the boredom.

The boredom was soon to be broken up. One night LST 26, along with hundreds of other ships made their nightly run toward the west, and like previous nights, the convoy turned back toward the east. But this time it kept moving east, past the port. That's when Gissendanner and the rest of the men on those ships found out where they were going. They would be invading Sicily, an island poking out from the tip of the boot that is Italy.

"The word was out, Sicily. We knew of course that an invasion was going to happen, but until then we only had a guess as to where.

"We ran into two bad spells of weather, with heavy rain and high winds. The boats were rocking furiously, and all of us were sick.

"Then one morning, about an hour before sunrise, we were told to go to our vehicles in the hold of the ship. We knew this was it." Invasion #2.

✮ ✮ ✮ ✮

CHAPTER FIVE:

Sicily

On the morning of July 9, 1943, the largest invasion fleet ever assembled began moving toward the shores of Sicily. Nearly 2,000 ships carrying infantry, tanks and equipment were about to invade the heavily fortified island. They faced an entrenched enemy, which had had years to prepare defenses.

Gissendanner and his crew would be landing on the beach near Gela, where some of the heaviest fighting would be. Gela was heavily fortified, and inland from the dunes on the beaches sat German artillery, on top of the hills. The German gunners had the perfect positions to rain down artillery fire on the invading Allied troops.

German tanks were pre-positioned to move quickly to fight off the invading troops. And German and Italian infantry were stationed in the most likely areas of invasion.

These were the conditions facing Bill Gissendanner and thousands of other British and American troops.

"My five-man team was sitting in our vehicle, ready to go," Gissendanner said. So was his loyal French poodle Daisy Mae, sitting between the two front seats of the Air Support Unit.

"Things began to happen pretty quickly. We felt that LST begin to pick up an extra burst of speed as it moved toward the beach. Then we could feel it as the ship ground itself and come to a halt. You could feel the vibrations and hear the noise of those pontoons being cut loose from the side of the ship, and then you could hear the Sea Bees motorboats as they moved the pontoons into place.

"About 45 minutes later the doors of the ship began to open. Those Sea Bees had done their job well, and there was a bridge from the ship to the beach.

"The Germans were ready for us. There's no other way to say it – all hell broke loose. The Germans were pouring artillery shells from the hills. A few German planes were flying over us.

"The noise was incredible, and there were explosions all over. There was machine gun fire, and the USS North Carolina was firing back at those German artillery emplacements in the hills. All the other ships were firing back too.

"The tank ahead of me, with its big plow blade, began moving off the ship onto the pontoon bridge, and I moved our vehicle in behind him. Our antennae went up and we began transmitting back to headquarters in Africa, letting them know what was going on.

"Other ships were unloading too. On both sides of us, infantry troops were moving onto the beaches and into the dunes. The tank ahead of me had reached the dunes, and we were on the beach. The tank behind us had just cleared the doors of the LST and was on the runway from the ship to the beach when someone yelled and pointed up the beach. About 200 yards up the beach a German fighter was coming right at us with his machine guns firing. He was strafing everything on the beach.

"My crew and I hit the ground and rolled under the vehicle. Our vehicle took some rounds, but they didn't cause any major damage.

"Above all the noise, I yelled at the crew to

stay put, and I rolled out from under the vehicle just enough to see what the plane was doing.

"He made a quick turn and came straight back toward us, but this time his machine guns were quiet. I watched him turn loose a bomb and my eyes followed that bomb all the way down. It fell right down the smokestack of LST 26 and exploded.

LST's unload equipment and soldiers on a beach during an invasion. Balloons tethered to the ships were designed to keep the enemy aircraft from strafing the ships as they unloaded.

"The whole ship was engulfed in flames, and nothing else came off the boat. My first thought was of Howard Manness and his crew. They were still on the ship, and there was no way anyone could have survived that explosion.

"The plane made another turn and was coming back for another run, but the anti-aircraft guns on all of the ships around us opened up on it and blew it to pieces.

"The tank ahead of us began knocking down the sand dunes so that vehicles could move inland. We crawled out from under the vehicle, and the fighting was intense. There were artillery shells exploding all over the beach, and as we were getting back into the vehicle to move out, I looked up and saw a general standing there as we were getting ourselves organized. He had two pearl-handled pistols on his belt. Was this Patton? I had never seen him before, so I wasn't sure, but

really, with everything going on I didn't even care that a general was standing there.

"He asked 'is everything OK?' I said 'yes sir,' and kept doing what I was doing. When I turned around he was gone.

"I followed that tank with the plow blade and as he continued, I slipped in between two high dunes and set up to start transmitting.

"We got in touch with our home base in Africa and their first remark was 'We thought we lost you.' We let them know that we were OK, but that we had lost the entire team number two. They asked if we were sure of that, and we told them yes, that there was no way anyone survived that explosion."

Years later, after the war, Bill Gissendanner would find out that was not entirely true. For years he had assumed that no one from Howard Maness' team had survived the blast on LST 26, but long after the war, he would see Maness again.

"We had a problem. The engine turning the generator for our transmitter was overheating. A hose from the radiator was leaking, and we taped it up as best we could. It slowed the leak, but didn't stop it. We only had one five gallon water can with us and our canteens, and at the rate it was leaking, it wouldn't be long before it completely drained out and quit working. We had to get some water, or we wouldn't be able to transmit.

"The fighting kept on all day. The Germans had moved some tanks to attack us, and Gen. Terry Allen's 1st Infantry Division was just ahead of us fighting them. It was infantry against tanks, and they were fighting them with rifles, bayonets, and sticky bombs. They would put TNT in a sock or some kind of sack, and then cover the sack with axle grease, which was sticky. They would slap that sticky bomb onto the side of a tank and blow it up. That's how brutal the fighting was; they were actually close enough to those tanks to stick bombs on them.

"We could see the 1st Infantry ahead of us,

they were that close, about 100 yards ahead. We were calling in air strikes against the tanks. The P-37s would come down, knock out a tank, and those infantry fellows would start fighting against another tank.

"But we weren't going to be able to keep calling in air strikes if we didn't get water for that generator.

"I remembered seeing the remains of a small farmhouse when we came across the dunes. I knew that it had to have some kind of pond for the farm animals. I told my crew that if I could make it to the farmhouse with the water can, I could get some water. We had a lieutenant from the 1st Infantry with us, acting as a liaison, and he didn't think it was such a good idea, but if we couldn't get water; we couldn't operate. Everyone of my crew volunteered to go, but it was settled. First of all, it was my idea, and I wasn't going to ask them to do something I wouldn't do myself.

"I told Elmer Neese not to let Daisey Mae follow me, because she would if someone didn't hold her back.

"We poured what little water we had left into a couple of helmets, and I grabbed the five gallon can and our canteens and started toward the farm house. I tried to keep the dunes between the Germans and me. There was artillery falling all over the place, but the sand was soft and the rounds would bury in it, so there wasn't much shrapnel. Sometimes I had to crawl, and sometimes I ran, but I made it to the farmhouse.

"Thank God, when I got there I found water. I filled every container I had as full as I could, and then headed back. About half way back to my crew, things really got bad. The artillery attack was getting heavier. I was on the ground, trying to keep from getting hit. I began digging a little trench with my helmet and that old German dagger the Ranger had given me in North Africa. I got down in it on my stomach. The trench wasn't big enough for my entire body, and my legs were sticking up

straight out of the ground. I remember thinking, 'I hope my legs don't get blown off by artillery.

"I was scared. I don't mind admitting. Anyone who tells you they weren't scared in a time like that is either lying, or they're crazy. God gives you fear for a reason, so I don't mind saying I was scared to death.

"There was a short lull in the shelling, and I got up and ran and crawled back to the crew. When I got back to the vehicle I collapsed, exhausted. Daisy Mae ran over and was licking me on the face, happy as she could be to see me."

The liaison officer said, "Your arms and legs were bleeding, but not bad."

"I had apparently taken some minor shrapnel or something, but the wounds weren't bleeding enough to worry about at this time. Alcohol and bandages from our first aid kit took care of that. I just lay there on my stomach, feeling like I could vomit. I had never been that scared in all my life. It took me a few minutes to regain my strength and recover, but I was all right very soon.

"The fighting continued into the night. We had enough water to keep the generator going, and we scrounged a radiator hose from a vehicle that had been hit on the beach and couldn't move, so we were in business and continued to call in air strikes against German positions.

"We could watch those big shells leave the USS North Carolina and watch them travel toward those hills, and you could see them hit. The sky was like a 4th of July fireworks display, only it was larger and the fireworks were coming from all directions.

"A parachute drop was planned that night. There was a full moon, and things kind of quieted down after dark settled in. We waited. And someone pointed up. We could see those planes with the paratroopers approaching from the east. The moon was shining bright, and suddenly the sky was full of parachutes. You could see them open as they left the planes. We couldn't see them land. They were too far away, but they were landing further inland from the beach.

"What happened next was very sad, and it wasn't revealed to the public until years later.

"After the planes emptied their paratroopers, they dropped down very low and began to turn back out over the sea, over the invasion fleet. They were flying so low we could read the numbers on their wings at night.

"The paratroopers had informed the higher ups about the drop, but the word had not gotten to everyone on the ships. Those anti-aircraft gunners had been busy all day shooting at German planes, and when our planes flew out over the fleet, someone opened fire on them. Once that started, all the gunners on all of the other ships started shooting, and within a matter of minutes, 32 of our planes were destroyed.

"We were under orders then to maintain radio silence, so we couldn't call to anyone to tell them to stop firing, and it probably wouldn't have done much good anyway, because it happened so fast. No one slept that night after that. They call it a 'friendly fire incident,' and twenty years later it would finally come out in *Look* or *Life* magazine.

"The next day we took Gela, and my crew moved in with the infantry. In Gela we saw some of the Rangers we knew in Africa. I asked about casualties, and I was told they had lost more people from falling through the roofs of buildings than they lost in combat.

"The paratroopers that had made their drop that night did their job. They had destroyed those artillery bunkers in the hill. They also stopped more German tanks from moving into the marshes near us.

"The beaches were clear and our headquarters outfit began moving in from Africa. The 927th headquarters moved inland. Meanwhile, Syracuse fell to the British, and Allied troops were moving almost freely across Sicily. We were called back to battalion headquarters for rest and reorganization. We had a good welcome back and had a few days of rest. We even saw a few movies while we were resting up. They had set up a couple of big tents under camouflage netting.

"But the war was still going on, and Patton had asked for a couple of portable signal units to move with him to Palermo. We didn't know it then, but Patton and Montgomery were racing to try to take Palermo first.

"Wendell Haye and I got the call to get our units ready to move out. We got our men and equipment together and went to the air strip to wait for two planes, C-47s, which would pick us up and take us to meet up with Patton's tanks.

"Wendell's team was on one plane and mine was on the other. One of Wendell's men was walking by our plane while we were loading it and said 'I sure am glad I don't have to get on that plane, I'm not sure they're going to make it.' We laughed and threw things at him, but little did we know how prophetic his words would be.

"We flew up to the airport near Palermo. The airport was supposed to be safe and clear of any enemy. Actually, we had bombed it ahead of Patton's movement.

"The first plane went in and landed, no problem. We followed, coming in low and all of a sudden, our right wing burst into flames. The engine stopped, and our left wing hit the ground. We skidded along that runway for about a hundred yards before coming to a stop.

"We were a jumbled mess. All tangled up with equipment and each other. Things happened quickly, Wendell's crew was there helping. Someone pulled the door open and someone yelled 'don't strike a match, there's fuel leaking.' Someone else yelled, 'run, run, don't look back.' They didn't have to say that twice, we ran stumbling and helping each other up, and when we got about twenty or twenty-five yards away there was an explosion. That plane was completely consumed with fire.

"Thank God. Everyone, including the pilot, got out safely. We all had minor cuts and bruises. I was bleeding from several cuts on my forehead. Blood was running down my face and I had badly twisted my lower back. We got all that taken care of with iodine and bandages from Wendell's first aid kit, and everyone was alright.

"Someone from Wendell's crew said they heard shots coming from the right side of the air field right before we landed, but I'm not sure of that. We ran into a lemon grove on the opposite side of the field, and spent the night there, sleeping on the ground. I remember there were chameleons and spiders all over the place.

"Wendell reported in and told the higher ups our situation. We had lost all of our equipment in the plane. We couldn't really do anything.

"There was an infantry company nearby which was not in the battle for Palermo at the time, so we joined up with them. We each got a blanket, and they had a field kitchen with them, so we had some hot meals while we were there.

"Palermo fell to Patton's armor, and he moved toward Messina, but we were told to stay where we were.

"Messina fell to the Allied forces on August 16, 1943, and the conquest of Sicily was complete. A short while after that a small plane came to the airport, picked us up and flew us to Messina, where we received all new equipment.

"About ten years after the war ended, I was living with my wife in Florence. One day someone rang my doorbell, and when I opened the door the surprise on my face must have been obvious. My heart went to my throat.

"Howard Maness was standing there, and said 'Hi Bill, you're not seeing a ghost.'

"I grabbed him and hugged him and pulled him into the house, calling my wife to come meet him."

Maness sat with Gissendanner and told the story of how he had survived the explosion that ripped through LST 26, killing the rest of his crew.

He was among the first crews to board the ship, meaning that he would be among the last to leave the boat. When the bomb hit, the blast knocked him to the deck of the cargo hold. He was knocked unconscious, and when he came to, was bleeding from the mouth.

There was fire throughout the hold of the ship, with the fuel from vehicles feeding the flames. Maness made his way to a ladder that went up to the top decks, and somewhere along the way his clothes caught fire. He moved up to the deck of the ship and found a rope hanging off the back of the ship. With his clothes burning, he slid down the rope, passing out as he hit the water.

"He said he was floating in the water, because he still had his life jacket on," Gissendanner said of Maness' story. "There were ducks, the amphibious vehicles that carried infantry to the beaches, running all over the water, trying to find survivors.

"They weren't able to pick up all of the bodies in the water, and were looking for survivors. One of the men on one of these ducks pushed him aside and he must have moved or something, because they realized he was alive. They pulled him aboard and treated him for his injuries. He was burned really bad, but they got him back onto another ship.

"Howard spent the rest of the war recovering from his injuries. He'd had severe burns all over his body, and he never fought in the war again. After the war he went back to Greensboro, North Carolina and went to work for an office supply company. He was in Florence on business and decided to look me up, remembering that I lived here."

✯ ✯ ✯ ✯

CHAPTER SIX:

The Invasion of Salerno, Invasion #3

The Italian people had become more and more disenchanted with the war, and even before the Allies invaded Sicily, arrangements were being made for the Italians to surrender, joining the Allies. Mussolini was forced to resign as the head of the government, and a new Italian government went through diplomatic channels to enter into direct negotiations with Gen. Dwight D. Eisenhower's representatives.

The Italians were in a tough spot. They wanted out of the war, but they were practically prisoners of the German forces in Italy. Distrusting the Italians, Hitler had reinforced his troops in Italy, making it even more difficult for a defection.

Rome had already been bombed once, Sicily was under Allied control, and an invasion of mainland Italy was the next logical step. The day before the Allied invasion, Eisenhower announced that the Italians had agreed to surrender, leaving the German troops to fend for themselves.

The invasion of Italy had more than one objective. Certainly, the main objective was to knock the Italians out of the war, and take the country back from German control. But forcing Hitler to commit troops to the battle in Italy would prevent those troops from fighting at the Russian front, or in the eventual Allied attack across the English Channel. Taking Italy would also give the Allies valuable airfields close to Germany and the Balkans.

The Allied attack on the peninsula of Italy would be as far north as the fighter aircraft based at Sicily could go, because all aircraft carriers were committed to the war against the Japanese in the Pacific.

The Strait of Messina was an important objective after Sicily fell to the Allies. The remaining German forces in Sicily had escaped the island across the strait just before the city fell on August 16, 1943. There was little time for rest for the weary soldiers who had already participated in two invasions. The Germans were on the run, and there was no time to waste. Two weeks later, on September 3, a British force under Montgomery crossed the Strait of Messina facing light opposition from the Germans.

"We had been flown to Messina from Palermo," said Gissendanner. "We received new equipment to replace the equipment we lost in the plane crash at Palermo. We also got some much needed rest, and very much needed hot showers and clean clothes. That didn't happen very often, getting showers. We'd go sometimes for weeks, or even months without a shower. Yes, we smelled really bad. We'd clean up by putting some water in a helmet and getting a little soap and a washcloth, but after doing that for a few weeks, or even a month, you got to smelling pretty bad. But everyone smelled bad, so it didn't bother us so much.

"They brought in flatbed trucks with shower stalls on them. You had to get in line, and they handed you a bar of soap, a towel and washcloth, and there were attendants there who would pull on the shower curtain to let you know your time was up.

"It was a short shower, but if felt good to get cleaned up.

"After getting some rest and getting cleaned up, we met up with some of the other teams from the 927th. We traded stories about what we'd done, and we got to relax a bit.

"But we were reminded that there was still a war going on. I was ordered to bring my unit to the docks. You guessed it...another invasion, our third since we left the United States.

"I found myself backing my unit onto an LCT (Landing Craft, Tank), but it wasn't loaded with tanks. It had a couple of small vehicles on it, and British infantry. We were to land with them to provide air support as we landed near Salerno, Italy.

"The LCT was much smaller than the LST. The front of the boat dropped down once it landed on the beach, which gave you a fast exit.

"One Navy pilot sat on a raised seat to drive the boat. Everyone wanted to know, 'Are you going to put us off in the water, and how much water?'

"He laughed and said 'This is a free trip fellows, and I'm not keeping you blokes on my boat any longer than I have to.' Now everyone laughed, because they knew he was joking. Then he explained how it would work.

"He said 'No fellows, this is all planned. My watch is set, and when it's time I'll catch a wave, and ride it in. I'm going to gun the engine, and you'll feel a lurch. When we stop, that door will drop and you'll be almost on solid ground.

"My unit was to go ashore with the British 10th Corps. It was the first and only time we worked directly with the British, when we were actually assigned to a British unit.

"The trip from Messina to the Gulf of Salerno was fairly short. During the trip, we met new friends, talked army talk and we talked about our families.

"The British lieutenant on the boat with us knew the plan, and he let us know what we were to do once we landed on the beach.

"We were to hit the flat beaches, and the plains beyond the beaches north of the Sele River. The American 6th Corps would hit the beaches south of the Sele River with the 36th and 45th Infantry Divisions. He told us the success of the plan depended on how fast we could take the beach and cross the plains to the heavily fortified mountains about ten miles inland."

The LCT cruised off the Italian coast until it came to a point near Salerno. The boat slowed giving other vessels the chance to catch up, and get into place for the beach landing.

"An alert was called," Gissendanner said. "It was dark, and we were told to stand by. The engines had slowed to a low purr. My stomach was full of butterflies, and I'm sure everyone else felt the same.

"But this was a different kind of fear. It's hard to explain. We were scared, but we also had a feeling of confidence. I think that everyone on that boat had made our peace with God, and we had the confidence that comes with that. Anyone who has experienced this feeling knows what I'm talking about, but it's hard to explain to someone who's never felt it.

"With the engines idling, we could hear the sounds of the small waves hitting the side of the small boat as we began to move in. We looked around at each other, smiled, nodded or gave a thumbs up.

"Then the engine roared and we felt the surge that pilot had told us about. We moved in fast and we could feel the boat wedge itself on the sand. Then the front of the boat fell, and we had no problem getting off that boat. That pilot did exactly what he said he'd do, and I don't remember seeing any water when we drove off.

"The Germans were well prepared, and they were waiting for us. It was no secret that we would be invading Italy. Just as the boat wedged itself into the soft sand, it was as if a switch was flipped, and all hell broke loose.

"One of my crew members yelled out, 'You can start the war now, we've arrived.'

"That kind of bravado broke the tension sometimes. Everyone on that boat was scared, but you could ease the pressure on everyone by saying something like that.

"The next few hours were pure mayhem. I have trouble keeping it all in order, the things that happened and when they happened, because there was so much going on at the same time.

"When you're in battle, you know basically what's going on right around you. Sometimes it's just twenty feet around you, so it's difficult to tell in sequence how things happened.

"As the boat landed, the British infantry were jumping over the sides of the boat to get onto the beaches as fast as they could. They weren't going to wait for us to get our vehicles off, they started charging the beach right away.

"The German artillery was bombarding us. I think they had every square foot of that beach covered with artillery. There was a small patch of woods between us, and the remains of some brick homes. The artillery was shredding through those woods, shattering the trees, and the air was full of falling stuff. Something struck me on the right side of my head, cutting me and damaging my ear. It was bad. It knocked me to the ground and I was bleeding from cuts, but in a minute or so I was O.K.

"Nazi dive-bombers were concentrating on our landing ships. Our broadcast antenna was up and we were asking for planes to aid us. We got an ok. Soon those planes were over us. Allied ships were giving us great support too. The USS Savannah was cruising up and down the shore, tossing shells over us into those German artillery positions in the hills.

"The arrival of our planes soon gave us control of the air over our heads. Artillery and tanks began to come in, which gave us another edge.

"In our initial briefing they said to take the flat beaches, and move on toward the plains as quickly as possible. Well, that's exactly what happened. The British infantry was magnificent. They moved in fast, and kept moving.

"We received word that the British commander, after a fierce and savage struggle, had taken Salerno. The Brits were closing in on the German airfield, which we needed badly for our own fighter planes. Our air strikes on Salerno and the German airfield had just about done away with the Nazi's air effectiveness, and we were in complete control.

"But the battle had a cost. The British casualties were great, both killed in action and wounded. But there was a lull, and we were breathing easy for a change.

"My crew was behind the walls of what had been several nice brick homes. British gunners had placed their .50 caliber machine guns in the windows, and they were pointed toward an open field, with a dirt road winding its way into some woods beyond the field. There had been some heavy fighting out there earlier, but for now all was quiet while we had our rest. We had lost track of time, but I knew it was afternoon.

"Our little rest period was interrupted by a British Lieutenant. He told us that we would be moving up for better contact with the advancing units, so that we'd be in a better situation to give them some help if needed.

"'OK, Sir,' I said.

"We moved out, and to my surprise, we were headed right down that road the British machine guns were pointing at. After a short while I asked the lieutenant if he was sure we were going the right way. He said, 'Yes, I have the map right here, just keep going.'

"I drove perhaps another 100 yards and began to see dead British soldiers all around us. I asked the lieutenant again, as I moved forward slowly. He didn't even answer me.

"I kept moving forward slowly. The road took a turn into the woods ahead of us, and as we made the turn, I saw two German Tiger tanks. I hollered at my crew, and we all jumped into some fairly deep ditches at the side of the road filled with briars and thorns and God knows what else.

"There was a burst of machine gun fire, and an 88mm shell went over our vehicle, landed in the field beyond and exploded. Then there was another burst of machine gun fire, and another 88mm round went over us, exploding in the field.

"Things got quiet then, and I looked around. There was a dead British soldier in the ditch and I was trying to use his body for protection. Then I realized that Daisy Mae wasn't there. I started out of the ditch to go look for Daisy Mae, and the lieutenant grabbed the butt of my pistol, stopping me. He asked where I thought I was going, and I told him I was going to get my little dog. He made it clear that he didn't think that was a good idea, but I pushed his hand away, and moved out of the ditch.

"I dashed out to the vehicle, and found her in the cab. Her collar had gotten stuck on something, and I got her loose, talked to her and ran back to the ditch. She followed me into those thorns and briars in the ditch.

"Just about then I heard the tank engines crank up, and they began moving away from us. I yelled at my crew to get the trailer unhooked and to swing it around heading back the way we came. I was going to turn the vehicle around, and I wanted them to hook the trailer back up to it quickly.

"'We're getting out of here,' I told them. Then the lieutenant decided it was time to remind me that he was in charge.

"'You were in charge,' I told him. 'Now I'm in charge, and we're getting out of here.'

"All of this took place in just a few minutes, and it didn't take long for us to get that trailer hooked up to the vehicle and go back down that road.

"We got back to the rear area, and we all just sort of collapsed. We were all cut up and scraped, probably from jumping into the ditches, and the infantry fellows bandaged us up.

"The British soldiers were all gathered around us, saying 'You blokes ought to be dead. What were you doing out there?'

"I pointed at the lieutenant and said 'We were following his orders.' And one of them said 'You'll learn not to listen to those lieutenants.'

"That lieutenant and I had some bad, bad words. He had almost gotten us all killed. But I took his word when he told me that at the briefing he had picked up the wrong map.

"We were all exhausted, and in spite of everything that had happened that day, we just passed out and slept. We were off the air and felt a sense of safety with all of those machine guns around us."

Two days after the landing, the Germans mounted a vicious counter attack, which threatened to split the beachhead that had been gained by the Allies.

For four days the Allies repulsed the German attack with quick reinforcements of ground troops, liberal air support, and relentless naval gunfire.

Germans began to withdraw, and patrols of the British Eighth Army arrived from the south to link the two Allied forces. Two weeks later American troops took Naples, gaining an excellent port, while the British seized valuable airfields near Foggia on the other side of the peninsula.

The Germans seriously considered abandoning southern Italy completely in order to pull back to a line in the Northern Apennines. But Field Marshal Albert Kesselring, the local commander insisted that he could hold for a considerable time south of Rome. He was right. The Allied advance would be slow.

Because the build-up for a cross-Channel attack, the main effort against Germany, was beginning in earnest, the Allies would send few additional troops or ships to Italy.

Bill and his men had been ordered to leave the British 10th Corps and cross over into the American 6th Corps' area. The only way over was to cross the river on a narrow railroad trestle bridge.

"We moved up to the trestle crossing. Other American special units had also moved up to the trestle crossing, which was shielded from the Germans by forest. The officer in charge of the crossing spoke to us, and explained that he didn't know whether the Germans were watching that trestle or not. He looked around and said 'Who's first?' No one spoke up right away. I was afraid, but in a matter of a few seconds I said, 'I am.' I looked at my crew and they all nodded. Don't get me wrong. I'm no hero, and neither were my men. We talked about it later, and we were all scared. 'Why?' they asked. I explained that I was playing the odds. Trees shielded that trestle. Not for a long way, maybe 100 yards or so, but if the Germans knew it was there, and if they were concerned about it, they would have blasted it to pieces long before now.

"So five scared American G.I.'s started out across that bridge. Bump, bump, bump, across the trestles. Others quickly followed. Thank God we all made it and as far as I know, that trestle bridge is still standing there."

The British 10th Corps, which Bill and his men had just left, had done well. Salerno was captured and the British had taken the German airfield, which was badly needed. U.S. and British engineers quickly got it in shape for Allied planes.

"God bless those engineers," Gissendanner says six decades later. "In all circumstances, they were just magnificent. The British had taken control of their section north of Sele River, which we had crossed to give air support to the 36th and 45th Infantry Divisions.

"The 36th Infantry Division, in their first action of the war, were to hit first in the American section at Salerno. That German artillery, the 88mm, was tough and had the 36th stopped with great losses. The veteran 45th Infantry Division was called in to help stop the German counter attack. It helped, but their losses were great also.

"Our tanks were finally getting off those LSTs and joining in the battle. We called in a good-sized air strike. The navy's big guns joined in, but we got word that the cruiser Savannah had been hit and had to retire from the battle.

"With all of those big guns going, and all of the other noises of war, our eardrums were about to burst. The noise was out of this world. But night was approaching fast, and things began to quiet down a little. Finally, the lull you hear about during war, those peaceful times after all of the chaos, began to take affect.

"I took this lull in the battle as an opportunity to refuel, check the oil and add water to our engine. While I was doing this, two of my crew were inside the vehicle checking the equipment, and two had found some protection and curled up for a little rest. Well, it was about this time that the Germans decided to say goodnight to us by firing another short barrage of artillery. Of course, our artillery had to answer back, and stuff began flying all around us.

"It didn't last long, but as I dove for cover something hit me in the nose and mouth. It broke one of my front teeth out. I was bleeding from my nose and mouth. There were scars on my upper lip, which disappeared over the years, but the one on my nose I still have to this day.

"All that didn't last but a few minutes and we had a peaceful night, if you can call a night like that peaceful.

"The next day or two, things began to go in our favor. Our artillery held the Germans in check and our air support was successful. The 26th and 45th, in spite of heavy losses, were moving inland.

"British troops that had made landings on the toe and boot of Italy were moving north. The Germans in turn were forced to withdraw from southern Italy. Members of the American

5th Army met members of the British 8th Army on September 16th south of the Salerno beachhead. The 36th and 45th and the British 10th Corps had suffered heavy casualties during their victory over the Germans at Salerno. They were pulled out of the battle lines and given a well-deserved rest. But not my crew.

"French troops were moved in to pursue and stay on the heels of the fleeing Germans. We were with them to give air support if needed. Our next objective was Naples, a seaport we really needed, but there were still many miles ahead of us.

"We passed through Battipaglia, a small town full of pretty and attractive houses before the invasion. We took it, lost it, and took it back again. Now, as we passed through, it was just a fantastic heap of ruins.

"In eight days the 5th Army advanced thirty miles against the solemnly retreating German Army. Ebrili was shelled by our artillery and was taken without a fight. Campagno was completely wiped out. At Lacerno, we just raced through. The 5th Army took many German prisoners, and gained some valuable information.

"It was at this time that I lost one of my crew. He wasn't killed or injured, but at his agreement, and the others in the unit, he was returned to Headquarters Company.

"The strain of the action, the noise of incoming and outgoing artillery, the mortar and machine gun fire, was all beginning to show on him. He had joined the army when he was in his 30's, and was an older guy. He was a good crew member, but the war was really taking a toll on him. We all discussed it, and realized that he needed to get back to the rear. No one held it against him, and he continued to serve, but he was in the rear with the headquarters for the rest of the war. Our crews were constantly losing men for various reasons, whether it was injury, or as in this case, it just got to be too much.

"We got a replacement. He was a hefty young Italian boy from Boston, Massachusetts. Gung Ho, and he spoke the Italian language perfectly. Al Grimaldi. He brought the nickname Spike with him, but I called him Al. He was a very likeable fellow, and we became great friends. Al was with me for the rest of the war.

"In some of the towns we were passing through, German rear guards were left behind to give us trouble. They had to be blasted out of the towns one at a time.

"The Germans were blowing bridges and roads, and leaving behind mines. All of this slowed us down from staying right on their heels. Everything was moving so fast that direct air support wasn't needed, but we were still in operation, sending information back to several units' headquarters.

"On October 1, less than a month since we invaded Italy, the 5th Army, my unit with them, entered Naples, our primary objective. But it was not before the Germans vented their rage on it.

"Remember, the Italians had surrendered to the Allies before the invasion. They turned their planes and ships over to the Allies, and then they declared war on the Germans. The citizens came out of caves and bomb shelters and greeted us hysterically. The Germans had evacuated their forces from the city, but not before they had torn the city apart. There was no water, no sanitation, no food, no fire protection, no electricity. The Germans had wrecked the docks, by sinking ships, and dumping rail cars and trains on top of the ships. The railroad yards were a mess and completely destroyed.

"All of this was reported to several headquarters, and immediate help would be on the way. I thought about Company B, which laid telephone lines, and the hard job they had ahead of them, putting all those lines back up."

But Naples had been taken, and Bill Gissendanner found himself there with his crew.

"Naples was a mess, but regardless of that, we had gained our first major port, which we badly needed.

"We were not in Naples long before we started back into our routine. We chased the Germans, caught up with them, then made them run so we could catch them again.

"In October the Italian rainy season began, and it turned cold. We were with the 34th Infantry now, and we faced a big problem – the flooding Volturno River.

"The Germans had destroyed the bridges, and damaged the roads. The Sixth American Corps and the British Tenth were temporarily stopped, but not for long.

"The great engineer units supporting the 34th went to work. Equipment had been brought up, and in spite of the weather and literally being up to their necks in mud, they built a bridge about 300 feet across that river. We were on the roll again.

"I've always had a great admiration for the remarkable American and British engineers. But then, engineers don't win wars by themselves. Nor did the Signal Corps. All those others, the infantry, artillery and tank soldiers who sometimes walked or rode with little or no sleep, eating short rations out of little cans and boxes. They deserve all the praise they get."

While the American and British engineers were building a bridge across the Volturno River, the Germans used the time to build another line of resistance. The Sixth American Corps was ready to tackle that. All fronts were beginning to advance, and Bill Gissendanner's team of the 927th Signal Corps was in the middle of it.

"We weren't really needed for air support, but we were kept busy sending messages back to headquarters, letting them know what was happening. We were also able to keep up with what was going on outside of our own area. That's one thing about war. When you're in it, you often don't know what's going on more than thirty yards away from you. At this time, we were hearing a lot about what was going on all over Italy.

"The 36th Artillery was giving support to the 45th Infantry. Casualties were high. The Third and 34th Infantry took Dragonia with little opposition.

"We gathered information from messages we were sending out, and we knew the whole front was moving forward. The Voltura River had been crossed with two more bridges, and our progress was dependent on how fast the engineers could work on the bridges. The war had become a war of roads and bridges, and the ever increasing rain and mud.

"There were two kinds of mud, the pouring kind and the solid kind. The solid mud would stick to your boots, and every step you took was like lifting fifteen pounds of mud with your foot. We used the pouring kind to wash off our boots. I can't say enough about the mud and how it affected everything. It was everywhere, in your boots, in your clothes, in your hair, in the food and water. You name it, and it was muddy.

"I saw one soldier demonstrate to another how to put his helmet next to a tree or truck wheel, then sit on it so he could lean back and sleep out of the mud.

"We had a problem keeping the mud out of gasoline, which could cause real problems because it would clog up the carburetor quickly.

"I remember one of my crew saying 'A good hot bath would really hit the spot right now,' and another crew member answering 'A good any kind of bath would hit the spot.'

"I was constantly worried about keeping the windshield clean so we could see where we were going.

"While we were crossing a bridge we saw some engineers in the mud on the banks of the river. They were up to their waists in mud, and someone yelled 'Does your mommy know you're playing in the mud?' Well that brought on a friendly mud throwing fight. That kind of thing could break the tension when you're so miserable covered in mud, tired, wet and cold.

"A second crossing of the Voltura was made by the 34th Infantry Division, and our forward troops were pressing the Germans closely. The German rear guard troops were either being killed or taken prisoner. Those being taken prisoner were giving lots of information, and they seemed to be happy to surrender. The injured prisoners were given much more medical help than they expected.

"The 45th Infantry Division had been in action since the invasion at Salerno, so they were pulled out to the Corps reserve for some much needed rest. But they were moved back up from the rear to support the 34th. Meanwhile, the weather got worse.

"The rain continued, and even though it didn't seem possible, the mud got worse too.

"German demolition teams and road destruction were meant to slow us down, but our engineers and infantry were working together. They took little time to get things moving again when they ran into obstacles. The Germans always took time to leave their dreaded little mines all around the area they were leaving. Our minesweepers had to be called in often as we moved forward.

"In early November the Sixth Corps crossed the Volturno River for the third time. The Volturno is a winding river and on several occasions when we were switched from one division to another we had to cross the river again. I lost count of how many times we crossed the Volturno.

"Wind and rain continued and it was cold. Military operations came almost to a standstill. The mud came up to the axles of our vehicle, and on many vehicles the entire bottom would drag through the mud as the soldiers tried to move forward. We were constantly trying to pull our trucks and jeeps out of the ditches. My vehicle and generator had to be pulled out of washed away roads constantly. Movement of men and equipment became slower and slower, and practically came to a stop. The Germans used this time to build a new defensive line, and it was almost impossible to fully attack this line, so we were told. But we did keep applying pressure.

"There was too much to be done to get our own lines in order. Bridges and roads needed to be rebuilt for us to keep moving on, but we did.

"As for my unit, we were basically useless. With the weather like it was, there was not much air support because the planes couldn't fly, so there wasn't much for us to do. And we were worn out. Just as infantry needs ammunition, food and new equipment, so do tanks and all fighting units. They also need rest, and that was the case for my team.

"So, while I was talking to battalion headquarters, I made the suggestion that we needed to pull back for a couple of weeks. We needed some maintenance on the vehicle and the generator needed some new parts, and the transmitter needed some new electronics. To tell the truth though, we were tired.

"I haven't mentioned it before, but occasionally we were pulled out of the front lines for short periods of times for various reasons. This was one of those times. After trudging through the mud for weeks on end, our equipment was worn out and we were too. Luckily, we had a good commander, and he told us to pull back.

"It turned out the vehicle didn't just need some maintenance; it needed a whole new engine. Not only that, but we needed a whole new generator too. Those things running constantly under those conditions can't last forever.

"We also got a nice rest, with folding cots, hot meals, a couple of baths and we got to see some movies.

"I also caught up on a bunch of back mail while we were in the rear. That's when I found out that my dad had died.

"He was 78 years old, and I loved my dad. He was a great and wonderful man. But I didn't find out he had died until weeks after, and there was no way I could go home anyway. That was how it was. Men found out their parents, or siblings or even their children died weeks after it happened, and they couldn't go home for the funeral."

Bill and his men were pulled back to the rear at Christmas time, 1943. The corps rear area had field kitchens and for Christmas Day, the men enjoyed a hot turkey dinner with all the trimmings. For the troops in the mountains of Italy, far away from the rear, meals were trucked to them, in big hot stack containers.

"It was good when I think about it," Bill says thinking back. "How did they do it? And those who carried all of it? All that was pure and wonderful – it really showed the love, respect and regard the American soldiers had for one another. Those men treated their mission of delivering a hot meal to the troops in the front as one of the most important missions they had."

Time passes fast when you're resting and eating well, but Bill and his men were not given much time to get used to it.

"After a couple of weeks, Captain Bearor told me to get ready to move out, so it was back to the front lines.

"It was January and the weather conditions had actually improved greatly. We had joined the American VI Corps. We were with the 34th and 45th Infantry Divisions again. All of the Allied forces were getting ready to attack the German Winter Line, heavily fortified in the mountain region. American artillery was throwing tons of shells into enemy positions and we were again calling in air support when needed.

"All the fronts were moving forward. The 34th and 45th divisions were moving too. Our assignment was to take the Minturno Gap that leads to the Liri Valley and toward Rome. This would give us access to Highway 6.

"We were told that Rome was our next objective. Rome was still a long way off and a lot of Germans were in between.

"The Germans fought hard to hold the Minturno Gap, and they bombed our positions, but we retaliated and our heavy artillery and the arrival of the American 5th Corps finally gave us an advantage.

"The information we got was that all along the British 10th Corps and the American 6th and 5th Corps, allies were advancing. We were with the 36th Infantry, and we were moving also.

"The American artillery was really bombarding the Gap and the mountains around it. This was soon followed by a parachute drop of airborne troops, which forced the Germans to withdraw.

"The enemy's withdrawal was orderly and very deliberate. Before they moved back, they would plant mines and booby traps to slow us down as we moved forward. But we moved through the Minturno Gap and through the town, and the German Winter line was no more.

"Days and weeks went by, and we kept moving forward toward Rome. But we were constantly reminded that the Germans were constructing another defensive line.

"The next German line of defense was built in a mountain range criss-crossing Italy at Cassino and blocking Highway 6 to Rome.

The Cassino Abbey was atop one of those mountains and had been taken over by the Germans. It was heavily fortified with German artillery. They also had the city heavily fortified and they controlled the entire area.

"Some infantry and my team moved right up under the overhang below the Abby late one night. We were not there long though, because the mountain hindered our transmission and reception.

"So at night we would move back out to our main attack group and we could transmit and receive.

"The Germans' artillery gave us a fit, but our artillery units responded in kind. From my understanding, Rome had asked the Allies not to destroy the Abbey, and the city, which was founded around 500 or 600 A.D.

"But it was decided that we had overcome all that the Germans and nature had thrown at us for all those months of fighting in Italy, and we certainly couldn't stop now, even if it meant blasting both the Abbey and the ancient city from the face of the earth.

"First, our planes came in and dropped leaflets telling the Italians to get out of the Abbey. I think it was three days later that our bombers came in. Wave after wave flew over and dropped some 500 tons of bombs.

"Next we followed the same procedure with the city. That done, we were again in control of Highway 6 to Rome."

By May, Bill and his team were moving toward Rome. The weather had turned nice, the cold rain and mud of the winter and spring had subsided, and moving was much easier for the troops. Then Mount Vesuvius, an ancient volcano, erupted.

"It lit up the night, and filled the air with volcanic dust which was everywhere, covering everything," Bill said.

"We kept moving toward Rome with medium resistance, and on June 4th, we rolled into Rome. The Germans had pulled out, leaving Rome without much damage. It was a great thrill to see our flag unfurled atop a high building in Rome. The people gave us a tremendous welcome as we rolled through the city."

Two days later, early on the morning of June 6, one of Bill's radios was tuned to BBC, and a bulletin came across from London. Allied troops were at that moment landing on the West Coast of France.

"One of my operators threw open the doors and hollered to me. I didn't waste any time spreading the news, and pretty soon we had a huge group gathered around the vehicle to hear what was going on.

"That was really a happy and rowdy time. Men were hugging each other, slapping backs and shouting hurrahs. As usual there were those one-liners, encouraging the troops too.

"The initial report said that it was the first Allied invasion on the European Continent, which really angered some of the guys, even though we were all happy that D-Day had finally come. We had been on the European Continent for a long time, fighting the Germans. 'The first invasion?' they asked. 'What have we been doing since we landed at Sicily?' But that didn't take away from the joy that this day had finally come.

"After D-Day, strange things began to happen. Our home base was moving up close to Rome, and I was told to join them, along with my crew, and other crews from the 927th.

"I understood the 3rd, 36th and 45th Infantry Divisions were pulled out of the front lines also.

"I followed orders, and when we got to the rear area, it was a happy time. We had a reunion with friends from other teams that we had not seen in months. We spent the rest of June just enjoying ourselves. In our jeeps, we really got a chance to do some sight seeing.

"We saw all of Rome on several trips. What a beautiful city. It was full of fountains, statues, parks, nice streets and beautiful cathedrals. We took a tour of the Vatican City and the Sistine Chapel, with Michelangelo's sculptures, and his paintings on the ceilings.

"We also saw the remains of the Colosseum. We visited the ancient city of Pompeii twice. We even walked up the side of Vesuvius, and watched the lava flowing down its sides from the eruption.

"I know that we had the opportunity to go places and see things that others didn't have the chance to see, because of Spike. Al Grimaldi in my crew spoke perfect Italian, and the Italian people loved him. He could get us into places that other people weren't able to get into. It was amazing, this young kid from Florence, South Carolina, touring Italy.

"But there was still a war going on, and we were reminded of it again. I was told to get my crew together, get our equipment checked out, and stock up on supplies. So off we went to join the 5th Army, headed toward Florence, Italy. Being from Florence, South Carolina, I really wanted to see the city. But that was not to be. I was later told to check off and head back to Naples to report to Allied Army headquarters.

"The trip back to Naples was faster, and a lot more enjoyable, than the trip from Naples to Rome. There was pleasant weather, no more rain and mud, and no more fighting, no more Germans every mile of the way, thank you Lord.

"What a difference a few months could make. Roads and bridges were repaired and two-way traffic was moving, so we just rolled along. But the towns and cities still showed that two fighting armies had passed through them.

"We arrived in Naples and I reported to General Patch's headquarters. Patch had taken over from Patton, who was now moving through Northern France after the D-Day invasion at Normandy.

"A captain took over and we started to work immediately. My operators, with some help, were setting up in one of the buildings. Al and I were taken to a park across from the seaport.

There was a road with trucks and other military vehicles loaded with all kinds of equipment moving fast in both directions.

"We picked a spot and started getting ready for remote line to be run in to us. Our operators were to be in one of the headquarters buildings and were to operate through us by remote lines.

"Our antenna was out fully, and we were in a cleared spot. Thank God. Our engine was running smooth at 220 volts. That big transmitter lit up, and began to hum. We both smiled and gave a thumb's up. The linemen had already arrived to start running remote telephone lines, and a hook up. We talked with the captain for a few minutes, and he gave us the frequencies we needed, and then he was gone.

"The captain had told us there was a field kitchen nearby, and we could eat there. There were also MP units in the park and all around us, so we were not alone. We had a jeep for transportation, so we had it pretty good there.

It wasn't too long before we tuned in our transmitter and told our operators by phone to go. Al and I both watched as those transmitter dials started moving. The operator on the other side called and said they were right on beat. Everything was A-OK. Al and I gave each other another thumb's up, as we always did when things were going well.

"We had a two-man tent with folding canvas cots, so we were comfortable. We also had a telephone by our bed and one inside our unit, so we could move around and not be inside the unit constantly. We were getting hot food, and we were getting a hot shower whenever we needed one. Only one of us could go at a time, because one of us had to be on duty at the transmitter at all times.

"The road between us and the loading docks was really alive with all kinds of vehicles, men and equipment. We didn't know it, but we guessed that something big was going to happen soon. Our operators from the headquarters would come by once in a while and they told us they were very busy sending messages in code to several other headquarters. Al and I knew this just by watching the dials on the transmitter jumping up and down. Thank God, with no fighting going on near us, we didn't have to sit inside constantly with those headphones on.

"Our biggest problem I guess was the Italian people, especially young girls and old people. Having Al there was great because of his perfect Italian, and the people just loved him. He kept me informed about what they were saying, but to my surprise, many of them spoke some English, especially the girls, some who were studying English. Quite a few older people also spoke English. Mothers wanted to adopt us, girls just wanted to talk about everything. Old men had relatives in America.

"They came in the early morning, and they stayed until early evening. They watched us shave, wash our faces, brush our teeth, or anything else we were doing. They asked hundreds of questions, and told us hundreds of stories about the Germans. But they all loved the Americans, and America, and they someday wanted to go there, especially the young girls. Sometimes the MPs patrolling the park would run them off, and sometimes they wouldn't. But it could be difficult to do our jobs when they were there, constantly asking questions. We couldn't forget that there was a war going on, and we had to put first things first.

"In early August, Al and I noticed that the big trucks going by, loaded with ammo and large equipment, were getting less numerous. More trucks with troops were moving toward the docks.

"Daisy Mae, my little black and white French poodle, was missing. I couldn't find her anywhere. Al and I searched the park and the surrounding area for a day and a half, but no sign of her.

"I had grown very close to Daisy Mae. She had been with me from North Africa, through battles in Sicily and on the beach of Salerno. She had also grown popular with the locals. The Italians who came by to chat always petted her and held her when they talked with us, so I was wondering if maybe someone just took her.

"I was pretty shaken up about losing her, but I didn't know what else to do. I'd looked everywhere I could, but Al and I couldn't go very far.

"Our captain came by and told us we would be closing down in a day or so, and our operators would be joining us soon. There was still a war going on, so Al and I began getting things ready for another move.

"Our operators joined us, and I was told to take the crew to a spot on the loading docks. I obeyed my orders and found myself backing into another LST. You guessed it, another invasion. Number four.

"But where? Other vehicles and supplies were being loaded into that ship. Soon the doors closed, and we moved away from those loading docks into Naples Bay. Rumors began

to fly. Operation Dragoon, destination, Southern France.

"We were once again assigned to the 36th Infantry Division to furnish air support.

"We found out some information from the work of our operators, who were at headquarters, that other invasion forces were being prepared at Salerno, Tunis and other ports in the Mediterranean. Orders had been going out through our transmitters to ports and airfields from General Patch's headquarters in Naples.

"On our ship we were briefed. All assault forces from several ports would come together at Corsica. Everything was finely timed. We would then move north to Southern France. We were also told that the soldiers were all seasoned veterans who had seen action in Africa, Sicily or Italy. We were on our way.

"As I stood on the deck of that ship on August 14th, and observed the invasion fleet of 900 ships sailing under their own power, carrying troops and weapons of war, and 1,500 smaller craft for assault troops, I gave little thought about what was going on above and around me. But now that I've read what history says about Operation Dragoon, I feel a lot of pride about having been there, and having had a part in it.

"History tells us about the invasion of Southern France. We needed a port in southern France so the 40 to 50 divisions on standby in the United States could join us in the fighting. Marseille would be that port. General Patch was put in charge of the 7th Army Assault Corps consisting of 80,000 men from the 3rd, 36th and 45th Divisions. These were highly trained and experienced men from the African, Sicilian and Italian Campaigns. These men would make the initial D-Day assault. My unit was assigned to the 36th Infantry Division for air support if needed. Another 33,500 men would land on D-Day + 4 to give aid.

"History also tells us that this time for soldiers on board ship was not a new experience.

Other invasions had taught them to relax, rest and wait, as well as how to fight. Ships in several ports were loaded with men and equipment before moving out. All ships were to rendezvous on the west coast of Corsica. Everything seemed to be timed perfectly and we were on our way. Bombers had passed over us during the night to bomb the beaches and German facilities.

"We arrived on the French mainland in the very early morning of August 15th, 1944 and were preparing to go ashore. Some of the assault troops had already landed on other parts of the beaches, but we and other boats in our vicinity had a short delay. After the delay, we began to unload on the beaches. All with little opposition.

"Early that morning, paratroopers had been brought in and dropped inland in Southern France.

"Bombs had been dropped inland on the roads leading to the French beaches. Our T.A.C. fighter planes, in a flight timed with the invasion, took off from air fields in Corsica to aid the paratroopers by strafing roads and bridges to prevent German reinforcements from reaching the beaches. They were also taking care of any German planes that might interfere. French glider troops were dropped into an area where Germans might plan a counter attack.

"As we unloaded with practically no resistance, word came back to us that paratroopers and glider troops had moved approximately 45 miles inland with very little resistance. Our transmitter antenna was up and we were receiving and transmitting all kinds of good information back to the Allied headquarters ship. Landing was on time, everything going well, light opposition, and many prisoners taken.

"Within just a few hours 2,000 or more prisoners were taken. Intelligence reported that two German divisions had been badly crippled. Allied troops were moving inland. French troops concentrated on Marseille and Toulon. American troops that we were with were headed toward Avignon.

"The Germans were fighting back, throwing everything they had at us, but we were still moving forward as fast as an army could move with their machinery of war.

"A special order of the day from Lt. General Alexander Patch, Commander of the 7th Army, came out to all the troops. 'Keep advancing. The enemy is perplexed and stunned and we have the opportunity for decisive results ahead of us.'

"I remember what I saw as we battled ourselves forward – German equipment and vehicles wrecked and burned, just piles of junk metal, on the sides of the roads. Supply depots burned and abandoned. Artillery positions bombed, and whole enemy convoys destroyed. At this time, the appearance of the German Air Force was almost nonexistent.

"Our bombers and T.A.C. fighter planes, along with paratroopers and glider troops certainly did their jobs ahead of us, and they did the job well. For that, I thank those fellows.

"As we kept on advancing, things became more difficult. There were rivers to cross and hills to climb. The artillery behind us kept the Germans off balance but some German troops were able to make hasty withdrawals and set up new defensive lines, always leaving their little booby traps and mines behind. In late August we ran into some heavy fighting.

"As we moved forward the civilian Free French fighters joined the Allied troops. They knew the towns, buildings, roads, streets and surrounding land, and they knew where the Germans would be hiding. They had their weapons and had been secretly fighting the Germans for years. The Allied troops were glad to have their help, and they were delighted to be a part of fighting the Germans. They probably saved a lot of Allied lives, with their courage, and fighting abilities.

"Allied troops continued to move north.

The 36th Infantry Division, along with the French 1st Infantry Division liberated Lyon. The French people gave them a terrific welcome.

"News came through that Allied forces were moving fast through all of Southern France. An all-French assault force entered Marseille less than two weeks after the landing. Fighting was fierce, but the French took Marseille. This was gratifying news to all Allied troops. We had our prize, a port in Southern France. Now those many divisions standing by in America could join the fight, and the French also took nearby Toulon.

"Those of us in the original assault force were in the thick of things, now fighting uphill all the way, with Germans looking down on us. In less than a month Dragoon forces linked up with Overlord forces, which came in across the English Channel in the D-Day invasion. We linked up west of Dijon, and we were now one big force. Dragoon forces had captured over 115,000 German prisoners and had freed all of Western and Southern France. Many towns and cities had been freed. Perhaps there is no happier sound than the noise created by a newly liberated town. The shouting, clapping, the thank yous, and the God bless yous. The happy tears, offers of wine, flowers and kisses. The response of a grateful people is hard to leave, but there was a war to be won, and we had to move on."

According to historians, Operation Dragoon, the invasion of Southern and Eastern France, was the best planned and timed invasion. The plan was put into action and carried out successfully with the best results, and fewer casualties than any other invasion. Thanks to General Patch and his associates. General Dwight Eisenhower said the real hero of the battle was the fighting man.

"He has surmounted heavily defended beaches and patiently fought his way into heavily fortified zones. He has endured cold, hunger, and fatigue. His companion has been in danger, and death has dogged his footsteps. He and his platoon commanders have given us an example of loyalty and devotion to duty. And courage that will live in our hearts forever, as long as we admire those qualities in men."
-Gen. Dwight D. Eisenhower

"Were my crew and I proud after hearing that? You bet. Proud to be a part of that operation and the part we had in it. Were you there? If so, push out your chest and be proud too, you deserve it."

"The German prisoners being brought in triggered discussions among the men about the quality of the forces we were fighting. They weren't the same fighting men we faced in Africa, Sicily and Italy. Some were in their early teens, and others were in their late 40's. This was not the same German army we faced in other battles. They weren't hard and trained. They weren't battle tested."

Some of the infantry battalions and armored units were being pulled out of the lines for a rest and new arriving units were brought in. Gissendanner's crew had been ordered back to battalion headquarters for a much-needed rest and for new equipment.

"I received a high voltage burn on my right hand during one of the skirmishes a few weeks back, the same as one I had gotten in Italy from the transmitter, and it usually took two to three weeks to heal. I was almost well but I needed some rest," he said.

"We got a little rest, but we were still working. This is one of those times when we would get called in to the rear, but we would be still operating, receiving calls from units still in the combat areas.

"The bad thing was that we could not be within two miles of the 927th headquarters or an air field. The telephone company, Company B, would run telephone and other remote lines down to us. Germans were always trying to find our location, but that was OK.

"Al and I had some very enjoyable times then, met some good families and good people. This time we were down a lane in a big clump of trees close to a farmhouse. The people around us were awful good to us, bringing us goodies. They brought cooked sausage and ham, fresh eggs and homemade cheese. We had a jeep, so we could go one at a time to eat hot meals. It was early October, and it was snowing lightly.

"We were there about seven or eight days, then we were off to the 7th Army headquarters. They were eastward, and they might need air support. We were really moving quickly, and didn't need air support, and we were seeing very few German planes by then.

"Most of their close airfields were already destroyed and their planes had been pulled back into Germany. Heavy fighting was going on at Aachen, and the Siegfried line. Rain and mud was another thing.

"We never got up into the lines where heavy fighting was going on. The situation and the weather was such that we were useless. The officer assigned to us kept us out of the heavy fighting.

"Times sort of get mixed up here, but I do remember we were ordered by the 927th T.A.C. Headquarters to move north of Aachen to the 9th Army. We did that, and we were assigned a new liaison officer.

"It was late October by then, rain and mud was awful. Again, we waited behind the lines. Circumstances and conditions sometimes ruled out close-in air support by low flying fighter planes and small bombers.

It seemed that the weather got worse, with more rain, more mud and even a little snow.

"This was one of those times. We could not be used. Aachen was taken and portions of the famed Dragons Teeth had been pierced, with some of the pill boxes of the Siegfried line being overrun.

"My unit was called back to the 927th T.A.C. headquarters. It was November and this time we were not in operation, just sort of loafing and enjoying hot meals.

"My captain came to me and told me he could give me a furlough for one of our so called 'vacation spots.' Well, this brought on one of those little spats that he and I got into sometimes.

"I said 'Only me?' and he said 'yes, only you.'"

"It didn't take long for me to respond, 'Thank you sir, it's kind of you to think of me, but if my crew can't go, then I don't want to go. We've all been under a great strain, and we all have plenty of back pay coming, and we're not needed here, why can't they go?'

"He just seemed to stare at me for a while, then he said, 'Let me think about it.'

"I snapped to attention, gave him a big salute and said 'Thank you sir,' turned and walked away.

"The next day he came to me and said, 'OK, you are all going.' I gave him a salute and said 'Thank you sir.'

"They took us to a town near Paris. Troyin was a town of about 88,000 people. We found a small hotel that could accommodate us, and we had a great time.

"The manager became our friend. He saw that our rooms were cleaned and fresh linens were put on the beds daily. He fed us good meals, things he scrounged and got off the black market. We saw some great live shows, dancing girls, skits and comics.

"We brought a lot of cigarettes with us, you know, trading currency. We got some gifts to send home, and we did some sight seeing. You know, we were in a different world. To us, for that brief time, there was no war.

"But the time came for them to pick us up to go back to the war. We arrived back at our battalion headquarters at night and went through routine check-in.

"It was December and snow and ice was

everywhere. Grimaldi had gotten himself into trouble, something not all his fault.

The captain had put him on duty tending to the officers mess, and taking care of their sleeping quarters. He had to take out the trash and keep their quarters clean. Al was the kind of fellow who, after a few days of that, was really getting teed off.

"The captain came to me and told me to check out my unit and get ready to move out. He and I had another one of those little chats, all about Al and his desire to go with me. The captain didn't want to send him, but I got another 'I'll think about it.'

"I did get Al, and after we found out my assignment, he still said 'I would rather be with you than doing what I was doing.'

"The captain gave me a map, marked the roads and circled a place where I was to meet General Patton's 14th Armored Division. We arrived and the officer assigned to us introduced himself. The Germans had just started their big offensive, the Battle of the Bulge, with everything they had. He told me our assignment, or objective. It was 35 miles behind the German lines, and we were to break up an enemy communications center.

"This place looked like something out of a western paperback novel. A few rough wooden buildings with overhanging roofs covering a dirt sidewalk. The road also was unpaved and the fields around us were loaded with tanks. There was infantry fighting going on about 150 to 200 yards away, where the road entered the woods. That tank outfit was new, just over from the States, without one day of combat experience, but they were gung ho.

"One guy said, 'Don't worry about us, we hit our target every time during maneuvers.' That's when one of my operators, O.L. Thompson said, 'The problem is, these targets will be shooting back at you.'

"As we were talking, a jeep pulling a trailer, with big red crosses on them pulled up. In the trailer there were dead soldiers. It stopped right in front of me. A soldier's arm was hanging over and dragging on the tire where there was no fender.

"I stepped out and as gently as I could, I folded his arm back over his chest. Then it really hit me. I was thinking, this is someone's son, or brother. He seemed so young. Before, it had been just part of the routine of war, just something you see everyday. But tears welled up and began rolling down my cheeks.

"My crew all stopped what they were doing and gathered around. They asked, 'Bill are you alright?'

"I said yes, and soon I was. This had never happened to me before, in all the time we'd been in combat. Before, it was an everyday routine. But at that moment, it all got to me."

✷ ✷ ✷ ✷

The Battle of the Bulge

The Battle of the Bulge was the biggest land battle of World War II, where 600,000 German soldiers, 500,000 American soldiers and 55,000 British soldiers, were locked in mortal combat. Well over one million men were fighting in the worst kind of weather imaginable. Mud, sleet, rain, and snow.

"Oh God it was cold," Gissendanner says. "Thousands of South Carolinians fought, died, were wounded and became heroes. But sadly enough, fewer than 60 of South Carolina's Battle of the Bulge veterans are alive today."

On December 16 the German Army struck in the area of St.Vith and Bastogne at night with 20 infantry divisions, 10 Panzer divisions and some 3,000 planes. The Allied Army was sort of caught napping. Christmas holidays were approaching. The weather was horrible with rain, sleet and snow, and the mud that created. The Allied lines were manned by troops fresh over from America with no battle experience.

The 99th Infantry and the 2nd Infantry were in the north. The 106th Infantry was in the center and the 28th and 4th Infantry were in the south. The German plan was to take advantage of this situation. Their main thrust was in the north sector, where they planned to quickly take St Vith and then in two days take the port of Antwerp, Belgium. This would split the Allied 7th Army and take away allied men and supplies. Then the Germans would fan out and retake Paris. Bully for the German plans. There was one ingredient left out of their plan, the bravery, ability and determination of the American GI's. There were thousands of heroes created during the Battle of the Bulge. In fact, all who were there are considered heroes. South Carolina had its share of heroes. One of those heroes I know.

✯ ✯ ✯ ✯

"At the time, 20 year old Claude "Bo" Scruggs of the 99th Infantry Division and fresh over from the States had no experience. The 99th Division, 395th Infantry, and 2nd Battalion took the full force of the initial assault.

"Outnumbered about 5 to 1, they stood and fought. Yes, they bulged but they did not break. Their casualties were great with the 99th, losing about 3000 men on the first day of the Battle. Bo's platoon was almost wiped out, with only 2 survivors. Bo was an Anti-Tank Gunner, which meant that he must be so close to the King-Tiger and Panther tanks that he would be able to get a clear shot at them. He was also a rifleman sniper and protected the rear when the situation required. Bo and the other GI's held their ground, and the Germans never got close to Antwerp. After some days, I think the 7th Armored Division as well as additional infantry came to give them help.

"Now the Germans are retreating. What a job those GI's had done. Let us not forget that other GI's over the whole area of the Battle of the Bulge were doing the same kind of fighting. Let us not forget Bastogne."

Bo Scruggs was a resident of the Bethea Baptist Home before his death due to Alzheimer's while this book was in production.

"Heroes don't ask for your pity" – just that you remember and truly appreciate what they did for their country.

✯ ✯ ✯ ✯

"Night came early in December, and those tanks began to come to life, pulling in line. Oh God, but was it cold! Raining, sleeting and snowing. Icicles were hanging from helmets. I was signaled in line between two tanks and we moved out on that road into the woods. The infantry had done a great job clearing the way for us. We had a little sniper fire, but no big damage. Snipers don't do much to men in tanks.

"We were traveling in darkness with only two little dim blue slits of light, about a half inch by two inches, in the rear of the vehicle ahead of us. Our biggest problem was keeping our windshields clear. Al kept punching me, saying 'Bill, you OK? You awake?'

"Our progress was slow, and we kept going all night. At early morning, we stopped and were told to rest and sleep. Immediately, all those who had been sleeping as we were moving unloaded and began setting up machine guns up and down that column. We were only about five miles behind the German lines at this time," Gissendanner said.

"We were awakened about 1 p.m. and told we were moving again. The word was passed that we would be encountering more opposition as we moved toward our objective. That was true. Scouts ahead reported a small town ahead. They also reported German infantry troops, but not much activity. The Germans had probably stopped to rest.

"A couple of well placed shots from our tanks brought some stiff response. They had some anti-tank weapons, and made good use of them. For about an hour, things got hot and heavy. We lost a few tanks and some men. But their losses were bad in both men and equipment. As I remember, the Germans decided to pull back and run, leaving machine guns, a few vehicles and some small artillery and ammo. We cleared that little town out and moved on.

There were lots of little skirmishes after that, but nothing very big.

"We had almost reached our destination later in the afternoon. The 14th commander decided to wait and hit it the next morning. No one slept much that night, with German sniper fire all night long.

"The next morning, as we moved out, was just like other mornings, a couple of rifles with bayonets sticking in that frozen ground and blankets covering dead G.I.'s

"We hit that German communications center fast and furious, but to our surprise, there was no opposition. The Germans had destroyed most everything and moved out.

"Things were getting sort of muddled. Allied troops were pushing the Germans out of the combat areas and were pretty well in control of things. The Germans were in retreat leaving behind tanks, trucks, artillery and other war equipment.

"Our scouts had reported a prisoner of war camp ahead. We joined an infantry group headed in the same direction. After a few well placed warning shots overhead by our tanks, we just moved in without any opposition. The guards just raised their hands in surrender. We didn't find any GI prisoners, though, just a few French freedom fighters and a whole lot of Polish freedom fighters. The Polish prisoners had to be held back. They wanted to get to those German guards. There was a report that one of the prisoners grabbed an infantryman's rifle and shot one of the guards before they could stop him. I can't confirm that, but I understand it was just a flesh wound in the guard's right side."

"The Germans were pulling quickly out of the bulge they had created in the lines, and they were leaving lots of equipment behind. They also left snipers behind to slow the Allied advance while they retreated.

"We left the infantry and moved on. It was late December and I was still with the armored boys. We were moving sort of fast and still in France. We weren't seeing a lot of bad fighting now, but that could always change quickly.

"Time passed and the situation changed quickly. My crew had been moved to an infantry outfit, and we were in Alsace. It was early January and still very cold. Alsace had about an equal number of Germans and French people. The French took over after World War I, but the Germans said it really belonged to them. But if we were going to keep our plan of going on to Germany, then all of Alsace was in our way.

"This infantry outfit and others with air support hit it so fast and furiously that the Germans left so fast they didn't have time to take anything with them. Some left their meals uneaten, still hot on their tables.

"We were at a standstill for a while. The infantry I was with had settled down for a rest. Others were still on the go. Alsace is not quite as big as our state of Connecticut, and it is located between France and Germany. The Germans mounted a small counter-attack, and they were pushing our troops back.

"My crew was moved up to the tanks again, and with us calling in air support, we were on the move again. It was very cold and everything was frozen. The Germans pushed us back some in their locality, but we just fell back, composed ourselves, and we began pushing back. We had some casualties, but that is expected.

"We fought our way across Alsace through January and February, but all of the Allied armies had their eyes on the Rhine River and Germany. The talk was that for Hitler and Germany, the war was over, but they continued to defend something that was already decided and lost.

"The weather turned in our favor, and my unit was back with the infantry and artillery. Our planes were in the air and we were giving air support when needed. Heavy artillery fire had been going out, but there was very little coming in. Being right there with it, the noise was terrible, and my ears were ringing, feeling like they would burst.

"It was early March, and good news came in. American troops had captured the bridge at Remagen in good shape. The 1st Infantry I was with was headed toward Germany.

"We got inside Germany, up past the Dragon's Teeth and the Siegfried line. March was full of action, all in favor of the Allies. One American general voiced the opinion that the German soldiers we were facing now, were not of the quality of the soldiers we had faced in the past.

"All Allied forces were moving fast. Air support was not needed. We were over the Rhine.

"The following is a letter I wrote to my wife:

April 12, 1945

We are a good distance into Germany, but just how far I can't say. We entered and liberated a P.W. camp a couple of days ago. The prisoners were really glad to see us too. Had a little of everything in it, Americans, English, French, Russians, Slavs and others. Some of the French and English had been prisoners for five years or more. The Russians, Slavs and some others wore huge grins and saluted every man or vehicle that passed them. The first thing they did was to loot the Nazi store houses and officers homes. They wanted to get all the food they could find. To me, they looked pretty well fed, but some of the British said the food was very bad for the last few months. One British Sgt. came up to me as we came in and said, 'Man we're jolly well glad to see you blokes. We knew you'd get here.'

After seeing a little of this it kinda makes you proud to know that you're part of something like this, and you're helping out a little. Of course, you have already read about this in the papers-Gen. Patton's son-in-law was one of the prisoners. I was told this later.

"Thanks to my wife for keeping that letter.

"It was early April and we were really moving. One of the officers remarked, 'If war can ever be fun, then this is it. We're on wheels and cruising.'

"We'd run into a little trouble, and hit the ditches. Take care of that, and keep rolling. Prisoners were trying to surrender everywhere by the thousands. They said they'd rather surrender to Americans than to Russians.

"This was the time to get scared, and be alert and very careful. Some die-hard snipers might want to take a shot at you, kill an American. At this stage of the war, you don't want to be one of the last casualties of World War II."

★ ★ ★ ★

CHAPTER SEVEN:

The Children

How do I tell the story of the children of war?

Someone should, and I guess maybe I should try.

Every town we came to, from Sicily through France and Germany, children would come out to greet us. Those who had lost their parents and families through bombing raids, fierce battles or other tragedies of war, need to have their stories told. There were those who slept in caves, burned out and bombed out buildings, with no food, no clothing, no place to call home. Just a few mementos and memories.

When combat troops had a chance for a hot meal, the children came. They came out from everywhere and surrounded us. What are you going to do about a little girl, barefoot with matted hair and ragged dirty clothes covering her body? Yet, with a smile on her face, she pushes her bucket, pan, tin can or whatever she has toward you, asking with her eyes for your scraps or some of your food. What are you going to do?

I'll tell you what you're going to do. If you're an American G.I., you're going to smile and divide your meal with the four or five little ones around you. You watch them motion a 'thank you,' and watch as they quickly eat it with dirty little fingers. You might even feel a tear roll down your cheek. But you're not

alone. Other G.I.'s are doing the same thing all over. Yes, the tough, hardened fighting G.I. has compassion too. Especially for the children, the elderly and for pets.

When you think "I can go through that long chow line and get another slice of Spam and fixings, or a small can of hash or spaghetti from the C-rations or crackers and cheese from the K-rations," you know you don't have it too bad. It's not hard to give your meal to a hungry child, in fact, it's hard not to. As harrowing a time as most of us had, these children of war had seen the worst.

I've often thought about what happened to those children I saw. Over the years I've often wondered about how they ended up, whether they ever found their families, if they survived the war, or if they even grew up. It's something that has haunted me.

Many G.I.'s remember these times through Italy, Southern France and into Germany. Thank God the news of the children's condition was always sent back to the rear echelon headquarters, and troops with food, water, clothes and other necessities of life were quickly sent on their way to help the children.

Engineers would be dispatched, and it was absolutely amazing how quickly those fellows could put a city back in working order.

--Bill Gissendanner

✩ ✩ ✩ ✩

CHAPTER EIGHT:

The End of the War

"It's early May 1945. My crew and I had been ordered to leave the infantry unit we were with and report to Army Headquarters in Salzburg, Austria. We were surprised at the order. We were in Germany. The German people were friendly and waving and actually seemed glad to see us. Would you believe it, those rough tough G.I.'s were shouting friendly remarks to the frauleins, and they were waving and shouting to the G.I.'s.

"The German troops were absolutely demoralized and were making every effort to reach the American troops so they could surrender. What a war this had turned out to be. Everything was in turmoil.

"But my crew had been ordered to Salzburg for whatever reason, so we had to go. Our route went through several small villages on an unpaved road, across small rivers and over to the Autobhan. We were held up several times by groups of German soldiers with white flags, and by MPs trying to get them loaded onto trucks to be taken to processing centers. We moved on and out of sight of all this. Then there was an American soldier standing in the road waving at us to stop.

"I noticed some soldiers with rifles and machine guns standing and lying in small trenches at the side of the road. I pulled up and stopped. It was then that I noticed he was a Lt. Colonel," Bill said.

"Where are you headed sergeant?" he asked.

"We've been ordered into Salzburg, Sir," Bill said.

"So have we, but we've run into a little problem. There are German soldiers in that creek basin, and around that bridge ahead. On occasion they fire some mortars in our direction."

It was late afternoon, and he said in a joking kind of way, "You can keep on going or spend the night here with us."

"About this time a few mortar rounds went over us and into the woods beyond. Everybody scattered for cover. The colonel and I raised up at about the same time and I said, 'Sir, we're tired, and we will gladly accept the offer of your kind hospitality, and your offer to spend the night.' This was with not a little humor, and we both laughed," Bill said.

The night passed quietly with nothing happening and they were all up and moving around early. The colonel approached Bill and said "Sergeant, I have good news and bad news. I've sent patrols in and around that bridge and creek and there is no one there, just abandoned equipment. The other thing is that a messenger was sent up with orders for us to turn and go into another town to assist the MPs with processing prisoners. We won't be going on to Salzburg. Sergeant, I can't give you advice, but if it were left up to me, and with all the talk of the war's end, and all the German soldiers surrendering, and the fact that they have abandoned their equipment, I would say it is safe to go on. But do it safe and carefully."

"I turned and walked to my crew, praying silently, 'Lord help me make the right choice.' We talked, and I said, 'You know the situation, what are we going to do?'"

"They were brave men. How do you praise such brave men? Their remark? 'We're ready, you're in charge, tell us what to do.'"

Bill turned back to the colonel and said "We're going to Salzburg as ordered, sir."

"That colonel was great. He was a career Army man, close to 40 years old. He took my right hand in his and put his left hand on my shoulder and said 'You guys are great. We'll see you cross that bridge and as far as we can see you before we move.'

"Those infantry guys were great, hugging us, patting our backs and saying 'you guys will be ok,' and giving us the thumbs up as we left.

"We crossed the bridge and traveled about a quarter mile. All I saw was beautiful mountains, sloping green hills and fresh plowed fields. It was early May, and this part of Austria had been spared the ravages of war, but rain coming down off the hills had washed away about two-thirds of the roadway. I tried to maneuver around it in low gear, but had no luck.

"Our trailer carrying the generator and the rear of the vehicle began to slide and took us right down into a lake of mud, slush and weeds.

"We unloaded and were standing there trying to figure out what to do. Suddenly there was some movement in the woods beyond us, and 200 or more German soldiers (we didn't bother to count them) were coming towards us with their arms raised over their heads.

"My first reaction was to slowly move my hand towards my pistol. Then I got a great surprise. The German soldier in front said in perfect English, "Sergeant, you won't need that pistol. We are looking for someone to surrender to."

"My heart, which was in my throat and beating fast, began to slow down and slid back where it was supposed to be.

"The soldier and I shook hands and gave each other a hug, to the delight of all the other German soldiers who responded with clapping hands and nodding 'ja, ja.'

"I asked him about how he learned to speak such good English, and he told me about studying English in school, saying that he had studied at Harvard for three years before we got into the war. Then in 1941, he came home to visit his parents. He was still a German citizen, and they drafted him into the army.

"We spent well over an hour together. He, the German, English speaking soldier, introduced me to two Germans who I think were minor officers, but all the Germans seemed to have put him in charge. He explained everything to them and he in turn explained to us."

All of the German soldiers seemed to be asking their leaders a question that Gissendanner knew before he asked, "Do you have any American cigarettes?"

"We each got a carton of cigarettes a week, but none of us smoked, so we kept them because they were good for trading, either with other American soldiers, or with the locals.

"I said yes, and told my crew to bring some out and we passed them around. In a minute we were having a lighting and smoking party. You would have thought we were passing out hundred dollar bills.

"We needed to do something, because we were supposed to be in Salzburg. We were talking and pointing and some of the Germans asked their leader what was going on. He explained to them the problem. They pointed to a house about 200 yards away and told him that the man there had a big tractor, which could pull our vehicle and trailer out.

"He told me he would send one of his men up to the house, but one of us would have to go with him because the man would not let his soldiers have the tractor. One of my crew immediately said, 'I'll go with him.'

So up the hill they went, and a few minutes later, down the hill they came, one German soldier, and one American soldier riding on a large tractor with the farmer on the driver's seat.

One of the crewmembers remarked about the tractor's label. It said "Made in the U.S.A."

Gissendanner shook hands with the old farmer and he smiled and immediately hooked his winch onto the front of Bill's vehicle. Then through the interpreter, he said to put the vehicle in low gear and press lightly on the accelerator as he put the tractor in gear. In just a minute the vehicle was free of the bog and back on the road.

"Now to get the prisoners on their way. They had no weapons, having thrown them in a nearby lake, they said. I gave them a small camper's axe that we carried on our vehicle and told them to cut a stick from the woods, at least six or seven feet long. They did, and looked for a piece of white cloth to tie on the pole. I really don't know how we found something white, but we did.

"I told the English speaking fellow to carry that flag up high at all times, and when they saw the first signs of American MPs to raise their arms to show surrender. I also told him it would be best if he walked beside the one carrying the white flag.

"We passed out some extra cigarettes and matches and said goodbye. I told them to go in the direction we had come from, cross the bridge and turn right, and continue on until they met the MPs. They started out, went a short distance and turned and waved. We waved back and watched them until they crossed the bridge and turned right.

"We tried to give the farmer some money, but he refused. He tried to make us understand that he was proud to help. One of my crew offered him a cigarette, and he accepted, asking for a light. Seeing this, I told someone to hand me a carton of cigarettes and I quickly handed them to the farmer before he could refuse. After looking at me for a moment he smiled and said repeatedly, 'Thank you, Thank You' in German.

"We loaded up, he started toward his home, and we gave each other a goodbye wave and parted.

"I've often wondered if he ever told his children and grandchildren about that meeting that day, and how he helped the Americans. I hope he did."

After about eight miles or so they arrived at the Autobahn, drove on it and headed toward Salzburg. It was a relief for the crew to see country that the ravages of war had hardly touched. Everything seemed peaceful and beautiful.

"We arrived at MP headquarters in Salzburg about two days late. They wondered what had happened to us, but after having explained everything that happened, they thought it was funny and they were amused by our adventures.

"We were sent there to help process prisoners, but they had plenty of help so we were told to just stand by if needed. Salzburg was a beautiful city and surrounded by gorgeous scenery.

"One of my crewmembers was in the unit with a receiver tuned to BBC in London. Suddenly the door flew open and he was standing there shouting, 'It's over. It's over. The war is over, Germany has surrendered.'

"Soldiers started coming out from every direction to see what was going on. We could hear chimes, church bells and people shouting on the radio.

"I can't tell you exactly what happened with us, but I'll try. The realization of what had happened hit us all at once. We started hollering, patting backs, hugging each other and yes, crying with joy.

"Then all of a sudden, things got quiet, and soldiers and civilians were going to their knees and silently praying, thanking God. The nightmare was over.

"A minister stepped up (Yes, there were ministers present throughout the war, God bless them. Where there were soldiers, there were ministers, even in harms way.)

"He read from the Bible and prayed for those of us who had survived and those who had paid with their lives for this moment.

"The next hours were filled with talk of home and families. Yes, of mothers, fathers, brothers, sisters, sweethearts, wives and children, and how great it would be to see them all again.

"Although the war was over, I'm not so sure everyone slept well that night. Minds were being filled with home, family and good and happy things to follow.

"The next morning we were up early. It was May and it was a beautiful day. Salzburg is a beautiful place untouched by the horror of the war and destruction. Forests and orchards were tall and green, homes and buildings were not destroyed. In the valleys and hills we could see just a normal day in May.

"We had radio receivers in our unit and one was tuned to BBC in London. It was giving the news of London and what was going on in the United States. Many soldiers not on duty were gathered around us listening. We had our transmitter tuned to the 927th battalion headquarters to receive orders. This isn't difficult because we've done this a hundred times during the war.

"We were told to stand by. One of our officers was talking to each unit one at a time. My time came and it went something like this:

Hello, Sergeant.
Hello, sir.
Sergeant, how's your crew?
We're real tired and sort of beat up, but principally, we're OK, and glad this war is over.
How's your unit Sergeant?
OK sir, a few holes and minor damage, but mechanically OK. We can travel.
What are you doing?
Nothing, sir. We have been just standing by since we arrived here in case we were needed.
That's good. Check out with headquarters there and come on home. We are in Darmstadt, Germany, across from the park. The MPs will give you directions when you get here. We'll be waiting and happily looking forward to seeing you.
Thank you, sir.

"We spent the rest of that day getting our equipment together for travel, and getting plenty of gas and water and a few extra C-rations and K-rations. Darmstadt, Germany was a long trip from Salzburg, Austria.

"We had a good trip with a few delays from army convoys and road blocks. It was a pleasant trip and we were looking forward to being back at our battalion headquarters and seeing the other guys. We had been gone since the middle of December, 1944, and had not seen any of them since then.

"We arrived and had a great reunion. It was happy, but also sad. Some of the guys we knew were gone for various reasons, and others we did not know had moved in to take their places. Everyone was talking, telling of their experiences. Some funny, some sad, some exciting and full of action.

"Two days later, we removed all of our personal stuff from our vehicles and turned them over to an ordnance company. It was a kind of sad occasion. Some of us sort of patted their vehicles and made remarks, others didn't . As they took them out of sight, we realized we would never see them again, and part of our lives was gone forever.

"I don't know how long the 927th Signal Battalion stayed in that place. I was there seven or eight weeks or more before I was transferred out with others to the 322nd Signal Company to start our journey home.

"We spent these days and weeks just loafing. No assignments, just doing what we wanted to do. We had transportation and did a little sight seeing.

"The park across the street was very nice, and very pretty. It was spring, and the weather was great. The park was partially lighted and we spent a lot of time there. We met a lot of nice and friendly German people. Believe it or not, they sort of looked at us as liberators. They were glad the war was over and they had gotten rid of Hitler and his gang. I well remember them talking of children dying because there was no medicine to treat their illnesses, and of the soldiers returning with tuberculosis, after fighting on the Eastern Front.

"But they also talked of good things and hoped that Germany would recover and be a great friend to America.

"During that time, those of us who were scheduled to leave the 927th were each called in to have a one-on-one talk with our commanding officer. Colonel Montague was a career army officer and rather difficult to figure out. Sometimes you liked him, and sometimes you didn't. He wanted to be a general, and sometimes he put himself before the welfare of his men.

"I don't remember everything about our meeting, but the important part went something like this. I knocked, the door opened, and I stepped in and snapped to attention and saluted. He said 'At ease, sergeant, and have a seat.'

"It was evening, and we had a little small talk. He asked if he could fix me a drink or a cup of coffee. I told him coffee would be fine, so we both had coffee. There was more small talk, and then he asked, 'Sergeant are you leaving the service completely, or are you planning to reenlist?'

"I said 'No sir, I have a beautiful and wonderful wife, and she has assured me that after three years of separation, that when that train arrives in Florence, South Carolina, she'll be standing there full of joy and happiness to welcome me.'

"He smiled and said 'You're a lucky man.'

"'Yes, I know,' I told him. He handed me a copy of the Unit Citation from the 12th Tactical Air Force."

"That is the kind of thing I like to hear about my men," he said. "Keep it and be proud of it. You and the others were a part of it."

"We walked to the door, I came to attention to salute, and he moved his hand toward mine and said, 'Relax sergeant, you men don't owe me a salute, I owe you men one.'

"Then he said, 'Sergeant, you have a happy and wonderful life.' I said, 'You too.' The meeting was over. This time, you had to like him.

"Finally, our day came, and in late July we were transferred to the 322nd Signal Battalion to start our journey home. Just a few of us made this transition. Others were sent to other locations and outfits. Our battalion was breaking up. I, and others with high points were picked up and brought there by plane. We were back in France, about 80 miles from Paris, and thirty miles from Rheine.

"It was August, and I'd had a few trips to the dentist. During one of my physicals the doctor asked me how I got those scars on my lips and the bigger one on my nose, and the broken tooth. I told him and he sent me to the dentist. The dentist was great. He pulled the fragments of that broken tooth and checked for other damaged teeth. He told me that the scars on my lips would vanish over the years, but the one on my nose was deep and probably would be there all my life. He also told me that I had to come back after my gums healed to let him make arrangements to replace the tooth.

"In this outfit, we all had jobs. We were called the "Army of Occupation." I, and another sergeant named Jerry, had a wonderful job, and we loved it. Some of the other men envied us. It goes like this: We leave here tonight, for Luxemburg. We arrive there tomorrow. After a 24-hour layover, we come back. Then we rest 24 hours, during which time we work for eight hours. Then it's back to Luxemburg again, and so on. We are carrying documents and messages. Luxemburg is a beautiful city and strangely enough, most of the people speak English.

"The commanding officer of the 322nd Signal Company was a great guy. He kept us posted on when we'll be going home. It seemed we had a low priority rating and he was working on it. He told us that if our colonel in the 927th had not put us in the essential rating and wanted to keep us with him, we might already be home. All shipping was being used to get materiel and men to the Pacific for the war against the Japanese.

"It was August 23rd. I spent three hours that day in the dentist chair. He cleaned and checked all my teeth. Checked the roots around my missing tooth, and prepared the tooth next to it to support an insert. Then made an impression. He told me it would take a while to be made and to come back. If it weren't ready, he'd send it to my home in South Carolina. It didn't get back before I left, but he did send it to me. I took it to my dentist when I got home, and he slipped it in place. A perfect fit. My dentist at home praised the army dentist. His remark, 'He certainly knew what he was doing.'

"It seemed like the war in the Pacific would soon be over. Things were really improving. Our colonel had gotten our priority moved up to nine, and that was good, but he said he was working to get it up higher.

"In the last days of August, the 28th I think, I had been checking and rechecking my records. They were now in the hands of clerks for final check. We had also turned in surplus clothes and other equipment, our pistols, ammo, etc.

"The weather was awful rain, rain and more rain, and the nights were cool. Our colonel had brought us some real happy news. He said he would guarantee that by the end of September we would be well on our way, or already home.

"He also told us we would be moving up to, or be very close to Paris the next day. He said we would probably be there less than ten days, then we'd be sent to ports of debarkation and on our way home.

"I wrote to my wife telling her not to write anymore letters because I wouldn't get them before I left for home. This was my last letter to her from Europe.

"I don't know how long we were in Paris. We saw the many interesting sights, and part of

Paris, and several good stage shows, including the famous Follies.

"I remember we stood in line for the second show. The soldier in front of me turned around and said 'It's a long wait.' It was then that I saw his Chaplain insignia. The show was very good, beautiful costumes and various headdresses. The chorus girls were great with dances, skits and songs. They were well-dressed with bare arms and legs. Racy stuff in 1945. It was good entertainment to relieve the pressure of war.

"My thoughts were not of Paris, or what it had to offer. My thoughts were centered on that boat and getting back to Florence, South Carolina. I don't remember how long we were in Paris, but it was only a few days. We were broken up again, and sent to different ports. I was sent with others I did not know well, to Antwerp, Belgium. I was the only one from my outfit going to Antwerp. I was told this was done to designate where we would be landing in America. There was a large group there waiting for us and that boat.

"We were in Antwerp one or two nights. I really don't remember. We were kept busy. We were given physicals, our records and I.D.'s checked. We were also given a list of things we could not take on board with us. Animals, reptiles, plants, weapons, ammo and many other things. They also told us our I.D.'s and barracks bags would be checked again at the boat. They did let me keep the souvenir dagger given to me way back in Africa. My thoughts went back to Daisy Mae, and I was glad that I would not have to leave her on that dock when we left for home.

"All of that taken care of, they told us to report for boarding at the docks. We were staying only a very short distance from that ship. It was a liberty ship. Our bags and I.D.s were checked and we were settled down below decks on stacked bunks.

"We wandered around below and above decks for about an hour or so. Then we felt that boat move away from the docks, and head into the English Channel. We let out shouts of joy and happiness that could be heard in England. As we glided along toward the open Atlantic, we could see a faint outline of what we thought was England. My thought was 'Hello England, goodbye England. Sorry but glad I missed you. We're on our way home.'

"But there were lots of miles and water between us and America. It was September and we soon found out about weather in the Atlantic. The first of the journey was OK, except for seasickness. But I expected that. Then we ran into terribly high winds and hard rain that was horizontal to our ships. No one was allowed on deck, but then no one wanted to be on deck because they would have been blown off in ten seconds or less. That boat was being tossed about like you couldn't imagine. Those waves were hitting us broadside, and the noise was deafening. It seemed that the next one would tear the ship to pieces. We were praying. I remember saying, 'After all we've been through, Dear Lord, please don't let it end here.' And the Lord didn't.

"I don't remember how long that continued, but it was many hours. The worst was over and the ocean began to calm down. This also took many hours, but the rain kept coming. Through all of this some fellows kept bringing us food and pills and almost pushing it down our throats. One in particular kept coming to me and saying 'Eat it, put it in your stomach, even if you don't keep it down. But in a short time, it will give you strength.'

"I don't know how many times he came, but soon I was able to sit up, and even walk around a little. Soon the rain stopped and the sun came out, and we got cleaned up a little.

"We landed at Fort Patrick Henry in Virginia. As we unloaded we knelt down and hugged and kissed mother earth. A last, we had arrived, not home, but on American soil.

"The people there had received advanced notice of our arrival. They had long lines of telephone booths set up and gave each of us 15 minutes to make calls. They also had telephone directories. I knew my number, so I got a booth right away.

"I remember I had no way of telling my wife I was on my way before we left Antwerp, so I assumed she was working, and that I'd be talking to her mother or father. Also, my mother-in-law and father-in-law had a son in the service named Bill.

"I dialed the number and a woman answered. I said, 'Hi mom.' She said, 'Who is this.' I said, 'This is Bill.' She said 'Bill who?' I said 'Bill Gissendanner, mom.'

"I heard an 'Oh my God,' then I heard the receiver hit something, and roll. A neighbor picked it up and said hello. She told me my mother-in-law was looking for keys, saying she had to get the news to Edna. I told her to get my mother-in-law back on the phone, I only had a few minutes left. That done, she apologized for getting so excited, but said Edna was so worried because she had not heard from me. I told her to listen closely. I told here we had just arrived at Fort Patrick Henry, and that I thought we would be leaving soon for Wilmington, and then on to Fort Bragg, and to tell Edna I would call as soon as I could. She understood and about that time, someone was knocking on the booth telling me my time had expired.

"We got a quick shower, clean clothes and went on to Wilmington, but I really don't remember why or for what reason. Then it was on to Fort Bragg. We were not exactly received with open arms. We all felt that the ones checking our I.D.'s and records and making notes were either tired or felt we were intruding on their time. They asked us many questions and then made remarks of their own. There were many arguments at many desks in that room. The doctor gave us good physicals. Mine said he was making a note that my blood pressure was pretty high, but due to the circumstances, he was going to let it pass. He asked me about my teeth and scars. I told him the story and that the dentist in Paris had taken care of that.

"All that over with, we went through the ritual of discharge, received back pay, pay that was due us, discharge papers and train tickets home.

"I had called and found out the train schedule. I called Edna and told her I would arrive in Florence around 1 or 1:30 a.m.

"About 15 of us were taken to the depot because our train was scheduled to leave shortly. Soldiers were taken to the depot according to departure times, and where they were going. Our destinations, South Carolina, Georgia and Florida.

"Then another problem came up. Seems as if we had already had our share of problems, but the conductor refused to let us on the train. He said it was full, no more room. The soldiers and combat nurses already on the train started hollering, 'Let them on, we'll make room.'

"You know, soldiers solve their own problems. This one we did. A soldier stepped up and pushed the conductor aside. I don't know who he was, or where he was going. I just know he was one of us.

"He said, 'OK, fellows, give me your ticket and get aboard.' This taken care of, he turned to the conductor, handed him the tickets, and said, 'Do what you have to with them.'

"The conductor, realizing he was beaten, smiled a big smile, gave the engineer, the 'All Aboard,' and we were on our way.

"As I remember, the conductor turned out to be an alright guy. Told me I would be first stop, first off in Florence. He said there would be a 15 minute stop in Florence, to give others a chance to get gum, drinks, snacks and whatever was available. Everything worked fine. We took turns standing and sitting, everyone willingly cooperated.

"As we sped through the night, my thoughts were of another time. It was September, 1942. I had just said 'Goodbye Angel, I'll be back,' to my beautiful little wife who was crying. I was going east, out of Florence, into the unknown. Three years was a long time. Now it was September 1945, and I was going west back into Florence. The Unknown Accomplished.

"I knew that pretty little wife would be standing on that station platform with tears of joy in her eyes. With tears in my eyes, I would say, 'Hello Angel, I'm back.'

"We were a happy group that night. The air was filled with talk, laughter and discussions about what was to come. The only time we gave thought to the train we were on was when we passed through the Pee Dee, and the tracks in the swamps. Our train was almost at a halt, and moving very slowly. Our conductor told us that the tracks were actually under water from the storms off the Atlantic. We made it through OK.

"Before that train reached the Florence depot, I had retrieved my barracks bag and was standing on the steps of that passenger car. When I tell of what happened next, I still get watery eyes and tears on my cheeks. This is as if it's happening now.

"It's about 2 a.m., and I can see that one lone little figure is standing outside the depot. That train finally comes to a stop opposite of where she's standing. I step off, drop my bag and start toward her. She comes running toward me and literally propels herself several feet into my arms, nearly knocking me down. I sorta mumble, 'Hello Angel,' but that's all, because she keeps saying over and over, 'Oh, thank God, you did come back, just like you said you would. You did come back.'

"The others had gotten off the train and had crowded around us clapping and wishing us well. Someone was trying to give my wife the shoe that she had lost running toward me. But she didn't seem interested in that shoe at all, and kept hanging on to me.

"My father-in-law came out of the depot. He had brought Edna, and stayed with her to meet me. The Red Cap had my bag and my wife had her shoe back.

"We waved to the others getting back on the train. We walked through the depot to my father-in-law's car. Edna and I got in the back seat, and my father-in-law put my bag in the front with him, then offered the Red Cap a tip. The man refused. 'I'm not taking any money for helping our soldiers getting home from that war,' he said.

"I was home. Everybody was still up to welcome me home, even a few neighbors. We did manage to get a little sleep that night. We lay there with our arms around each other. My thoughts went back to my meeting with my colonel when I told him of my wife. He had said, 'Sergeant, you're a lucky man.'

"Yes sir, I know.

"I was very tired. I had been through a lot the last couple of days and had lost a lot of sleep. I guess I just dozed off. The next morning, she was propped up on her elbow with her head in her hand looking down at me. She said 'Good morning love.' I said 'Good morning, Angel,' then she smiled and kissed me. Three years was a long time.

"My mother-in-law had a great breakfast that first morning.   Grits, homemade biscuits with cheese and jam, fried eggs over light and ham, orange juice and fresh coffee and fruit. That was the best and most relaxing meal I had had in a long time. I really loaded up.

"My wife and I had a very happy, wonderful and loving life together. We had three beautiful children. First a beautiful and wonderful daughter, followed by two handsome and wonderful sons.

"Later in life, Edna contracted colon cancer, and she had an operation. We thought it was successful, and for four years it was great. Then the cancer returned in the sacrum. The doctor said it was terminal. She wanted to die at home if I could take care of her. I told her I would, and I guaranteed that she would die at our home. She was bedridden for six months,

and died peacefully in her sleep on December 23rd, 1985. Two days before Christmas, in her home. We had almost 44 years of happy life together."

★ ★ ★ ★

During his service overseas, Bill, like all other service men, made use of the V Mail system to stay in contact with his family.

Bill also made arrangements with Talley's Flower Shop in Florence to deliver flowers and letters to Edna on their anniversary each year he was overseas.

Bill added, "I had three brothers in the service with me. My brother George Gissendanner was in the Air Force in India. He was a Maintenance Staff Sergeant on big bombers. I don't know of any particulars about him. He entered the service before I did and saw little if any combat service.

"My brother Emery Woodrow entered the Army in 1941 with the Coast Artillery from Florence. He later transferred to Glider Troops. He was a career Army person. He later transferred to the Air Force until his retirement. He was a Staff Sergeant but didn't see any combat duty.

"My brother Thomas, the youngest of us, entered the Marines and saw intensive duty in the Pacific. He was badly injured by Japanese machine gun fire. He recovered but took some of that lead with him to the grave because it was too close to his spine to be removed. He received the Purple Heart and other Medals.

"They are all dead and I am the only survivor today."

✮ ✮ ✮ ✮

CHAPTER NINE:

Individual Information and Memories

Florence County people at war brought back many stories.

Florence men were quick to sign up, and as youth came out of high school, many quickly enlisted before being drafted. An often-told story was about one Florentine who weighed a pound or so too little to be enlisted, so he went off, ate a stalk of bananas, came back and was accepted. There were others who now tell the story of having used phony birth certificates to get into the armed forces before they really were old enough.

During the research for this book we met many people who spoke proudly of relatives, now gone, who had served during World War II. Many of them had nothing more than photographs as memories. They didn't have a history of their loved one's service, or any stories the veteran shared with them.

These are some stories and photos of Florence County's Heroes of World War II.

✮ ✮ ✮ ✮

ANDREW AKERS

ARCHIE ALFORD

Archie Alford served as a Staff Sergeant in the Army from 1942 until 1945. He was stationed in England, France, Germany and Belgium.

✮ ✮ ✮ ✮

ELLIS JOHN ALT

Ellis John Alt of Florence flew B17s, C54s and B29s during World War II. He served as a flight officer at Blackland Flying School in Waco, Texas, and flew as pilot of four-engine missions overseas and later served as an instructor at the USAF C54 schools. He rose to the rank of captain.

BILLY ANDERSON

★★★★

CHARLES APPLEBY

In summer 2006, Charlie Appleby of Florence made his second trip to Normandy.

His first visit was more eventful. It was two days after D-Day, and he was a third class Navy ship fitter and top gunner on the front deck of the USS Atlas. They were there to repair damaged landing craft.

During his 2006 visit, he went to the American cemetery and recalled on his first visit seeing dead 18-22-year old men stacked like cords of wood. Like many veterans, Appleby avoided talking about it for 62 years and says that probably was a mistake.

★★★★

JAMES R. BAKER

James R. Baker was a Corporal in the Army from 1943 until 1945.

JOHN BANKS

John Banks was a command pilot on a B17 Flying Fortress. He served with the 95th Bomb Group, 334th Squadron, which was based in England at Horam.

★★★★

THOMAS J. BARFIELD

Seaman 1st Class.

★★★★

FRANK BARNWELL

One of Florence's most colorful characters, Frank Barnwell served as a lieutenant during World War I. Then he went into the National Guard and became a major by the time World War II loomed.

In January 1941 his Florence Guard unit was called to national duty and assigned to coastal artillery defense of Charleston Harbor at Ft. Moultrie.

He commanded the Ft. Moultrie operation

until the threat of invasion, which never was great, passed and Barnwell served at several other places briefly before receiving a medical discharge.

According to Nick Zeigler's biography of Barnwell, he blazed a trail through those posts and probably was not soon forgotten.

Near legend is the story of the day Barnwell was returning to Ft. Moultrie from Charleston and found an underclad sentry at a bridge, shivering in the cold. Barnwell had the car stopped and left his overcoat with the sentry who was instructed to turn it in to his commanding officer when relieved.

When Barnwell returned to civilian life, it was as a colonel.

✯✯✯✯

DR. ALBERT BAROODY

When America entered World War II, Albert Baroody of Timmonsville had finished medical school and a year as an intern in Charleston.

He went into the Army Medical Corps in 1942 and served until April 1946.

Baroody was a medical unit commander and served on Guadalcanal, the Solomons and Philippines. He received the Bronze Star and the Philippines Liberation Medal with Bronze Star as well as other decorations and was discharged as a major.

He practiced as an OB/GYN in Florence and his portrait hangs on a wall at the Women's Pavilion at McLeod Regional Medical Center.

✯✯✯✯

B.J. BAROODY

B.J. Baroody of Timmonsville went into the army as a lieutenant and served in medical research, largely at Black Mountain, N.C.

One of the fruits of his research was a plan for diagnosis and treatment of a tropical disease,

schistosomiasis japonica, which afflicted many U.S. servicemen who served in the Pacific during World War II.

It became known as the Baroody Method and was adopted as the army method of treating and diagnosing the disease.

He delivered papers to medical societies on his research, and as a result was admitted to the Royal Society of Tropical Medicine in London.

✯✯✯✯

WILLIAM BAUKNIGHT

✯✯✯✯

WILLIAM A. BEATY JR.

In April 1942, William A. Beaty Jr. went through radio operator and B17 mechanics training. After that he was promoted to corporal and went to the army's first radar school at Boca Raton, Fla.

Then Beaty was accepted for officer candidate school and was commissioned as a second lieutenant. He became communications officer for the 329th Searchlight Battalion, but that unit was disbanded before shipping overseas.

He attended Officers Mule Pack School at Ft. Riley, Kan., for 18 weeks training, then in 1945 was shipped to the Philippines where he was when the war ended. He returned to the States in March 1946 and was discharged as a first lieutenant.

★★★★

GEORGE ARTHUR BEAUMONT

George Arthur Beaumont went to school in Florence and in Clemson, then went into the Navy air service and served as a radioman.

Beaumont put in several years during World War II in Africa and returned home after the war.

★★★★

ROBERT M. BEAUMONT

★★★★

BISHOP A. BELL

Bishop A. Bell enlisted in the Navy on Oct. 1, 1942 and went through PT boat training before going off to assignments that eventually would give him an unusual glimpse of events that brought World War II to an end.

Bell said that he had been stationed on Okinawa with PT boat Squadron Ron 31 for several weeks when the atomic bombs were dropped on two Japanese cities, and soon the Japanese put out word through neutral countries that they wanted to talk about ending the war.

He and his crewmates were keeping up with reports on the radio and knew that some Japanese officials were to go to the Philippines to talk with Gen. Douglas MacArthur.

One afternoon they looked up from their Okinawa base and saw two twin-engine Japanese bombers circling the base. They were painted white and black cross marks were painted on their wings, fuselage and tail fins.

They landed at a nearby airstrip and were transferred to a U.S. transport plane that took them to meet MacArthur in the Philippines. "At the meeting MacArthur told them to carry word back that the only acceptable terms for ending the war were unconditional surrender - no strings attached," Bell said.

The Japanese government agreed to unconditional surrender, and on Sept. 2, 1945, documents were signed in Tokyo Bay aboard the battleship Missouri.

Bell had taken a long route to Okinawa. He had boot camp and a "storekeeping" course before volunteering for PT boat service. That training was in Rhode Island and on Lake Pontchartrain at New Orleans.

Then they took a long voyage from New Orleans to Miami and through the Panama Canal to the Solomon Islands with stops along the way.

"There were 15 boats in our squadron, so this required three oil tankers. (The tankers) were loaded with fuel for the war zone, and we were just hitching a ride. The voyage took 18 days, and we were all glad to get to our destination. I would advise anyone against ever accepting even a free cruise on the steel decks of a loaded oil tanker," Bell wrote after the war.

There were about 300 men in his squadron, and his boat included two officers and nine enlisted men, which included gunners, torpedo men, motor machinists and a navigator. A tender was assigned to the squadron.

He went to the northern coast of New Guinea, the Palau Islands, the Philippines and finally Okinawa where he was when the war ended. About a month and a half later, he was home.

★★★★

VERGOL RANDOLPH BELLFLOWER

★★★★

QUEENE ELIZABETH BOWERS

Queene Elizabeth Bowers of Olanta became a pharmacists mate second class in the WAVES. She enlisted in November 1944 and

was discharged in April 1946. She served Stateside, including Long Island and Washington, D.C.

★★★★

LANFORD BRACKETT

Lanford Brackett, was a sergeant in the Marines and served from 1940 to 1945.

He served in the South Pacific and was in the initial landing on Bougainville in November 1943 with the 3rd Marine Division. He won a Silver Star there.

Brackett also served on Guadalcanal and other engagements in the South Pacific. He is another Marine who wound up in literature. He was included in John Monk's book, "A Ribbon and a Star," which was a history of the 3rd Marine Division.

He later moved to York County and spent time lecturing school classes on the war.

★★★★

SAUNDERS BRIDGES

It says a lot about the horrors of combat that Saunders Bridges considers himself "lucky" to have been severely injured.

After just 39 days of combat at the Battle of the Bulge, the young 2nd Lieutenant had his leg blown open by a 20mm anti aircraft round.

"The only way you got out of the infantry was to get killed or to get injured badly enough to be evacuated," Bridges says. "I was lucky, I got wounded and evacuated."

That was March 3, 1945. Bridges, an

infantry platoon commander in the 78th Infantry Division, had been in France since January 3. Though his time in combat was limited to just 39 days, the experience is still vividly recalled.

"It seems like it was yesterday," Bridges says. "All of the horror is gone, but I remember everything as if it just happened.

"When I got online, the division was already in combat, and in contact with the Germans. We were taking patrols out every night, and we had contact with the enemy every day. The Germans were still alive and kicking and putting up a fight. You woke up in the morning and the war was all around you. If you weren't in a bombed out building, you were in a hole, or you were patrolling. It was a present threat from the moment you opened your eyes in the morning. It may be German artillery, or it may be their infantry trying to pick you off with their patrols, but it was a constant threat."

Saunders Bridges and his wife Elise.

Like most veterans of World War II, Bridges recalls the humorous moments.

"You always remember the funniest stuff," Bridges says. "In the middle of the fiercest firefight, someone will say something funny and everyone breaks out laughing. It's a psychological parachute we have.

"Headquarters called up and told me to bring some of my men back to the rear area for a shower. They had set up a massive shower room, and you would take off all your clothes except for your boots, and throw them into a pile. You'd go through the showers, and on the other side they'd issue you new clothes.

"After I got my men in the shower, the water ran out, but a sergeant there told me to go down the road to this little yellow house where they had a bath tub. It was the general's headquarters, but he wasn't there at the time.

"So I get there, and there's a guy in the tub drinking a bottle of champagne. I didn't know what rank he was, but he said, 'Come on in.' Turns out he's a lieutenant colonel, and he's through with his bath. He said the water was still hot, and he got a bath every other day, so I could go ahead and use the water.

"So I got my clothes off and got in the bathtub, and I was drinking that bottle of champagne. This guy walks in and all I saw was the star on his uniform, so I jump to attention in that bathtub, stark naked, and salute.

"He asked who I was, I told him, and then he said to sit back down and finish my bath, 'But give me that champagne.'"

On one of his patrols, Bridges and his platoon ended up capturing 70 German infantry troops.

"We were to move out and meet with two other platoons, but when we got there, there was no one on either side of us, so we kept moving. One of my men got shot, but wasn't hurt seriously, then a German came running at us, and one of my men shot him. We then captured another German, and realized that we were surrounded. They were sending soldiers at us to see how we would treat them if they surrendered to us.

"The problem was, we were behind enemy lines, and they wanted to surrender. There were 70 of them, and only 30 or so of us. So, we decided to unload all the German's rifles, but they would put us in the middle of the group, as if we were the prisoners, so that if Germans stopped them, we would be allowed to pass. Then when we got past the Germans, and back across the lines, we would switch up.

"We made it back to the American lines, and turned our prisoners in. That's how my platoon captured 70 prisoners."

Bridges' injuries were serious enough to keep him hospitalized throughout the rest of the war. He was sent first to a hospital in Paris, then London, and finally back to the U.S.

"My knee got jammed badly just before I got hit, so I had the knee injury and I had my leg blown open. I was in Liverpool, England in a hospital on V-E Day, and I was at a hospital at Augusta, Georgia on V-J Day.

"While I was recovering, I would send my wife the V-Mails, but instead of writing letters, I'd draw cartoons on them. I still have several of them today. She saved them, and we've even framed some."

★★★★

THE BROCKINGTONS

Four Brockington brothers served in the armed forces during World War II, and all of them came home safely.

Keels Brockington, who later operated a funeral home in Lake City, served aboard the USS Goodhue and sailed into Tokyo Bay aboard that ship three weeks after fighting ended.

Paul Brockington was a commander aboard the USS Hornet. On April 30, 1944, on the island of Ulithi, Keels' and Paul's ships were anchored near each other and Keels got permission to use a landing craft to visit his brother, and there he had dinner and met the ship's captain.

David Brockington was a lieutenant stationed at Manila Air Base. When Keels' ship was in that port, he went to visit but learned his brother had just left for Japan. His also learned his brother had just been promoted to first lieutenant and wrote him a congratulatory letter.

"Needless to say, he was surprised by my congratulations letter," Keels Brockington said.

Bill Brockington, the oldest brother, was a doctor with Patton's 3rd Army in Europe and was with them during the Battle of the Bulge.

Keels Brockington's ship, the Goodhue, was commissioned in 1944 and went to the Pacific as a transport ship. It sailed to New Guinea, then took troops to Okinawa for that invasion.

On April 2, 1945, it was target of a kamikaze attack when suicide pilots hit the Goodhue and two other ships. The Goodhue attacker hit the ship's mainmast and fell to the rear of the ship with bombs exploding and fires set. There were 27 dead and 117 wounded.

Brockington said he worked through the night with the wounded until they were sent to hospital ships and helped sew bodies of the dead into body bags for shipment home.

He particularly remembered passing time the night before the attack with a fellow crewmember. "The evening before the attack on our ship, which was the evening of the invasion on Okinawa, I was talking with a guy from Tennessee.... I sewed his body bag the next day," he told the Lake City News & Post.

On the Goodhue's first visit to The Philippines, Brockington recalled attending a USO show, which featured Irving Berlin and his musical revue, "This Is the Army." Berlin, in a World War I uniform, asked about 3,000 troops in the audience on a hillside to light matches or cigarette lighters, and he then sang his "God Bless America."

"I can still see it like it was yesterday," he said.

In the kamikaze attack the ship was not badly damaged, and after repairs it went back into action. It landed troops on Le Shima later in April and then made a round trip to San Francisco to bring more troops to the war zone.

The ship was in The Philippines training for its next mission when the war ended. Brockington said the captain then opened the ship's sealed orders which then were not in effect and found they had been scheduled for the invasion of Japan which was avoided after the atomic bombs were dropped.

After the fighting ended, the Goodhue sailed to Japan and delivered occupation troops, then picked up Allied troops who had been prisoners of the Japanese. They were nearly starved, he said, and the Goodhue crew enjoyed feeding them all they wanted.

"Those were the most marvelous periods I ever lived," Brockington said of moving the former POWs from Japan.

★★★★

LE ROY BROWN

★★★★

RUSSELL S. BROWN

PFC Russell Samuel Brown of Friendfield served from Oct. 20, 1942 to Feb. 5, 1946. He was a rifleman with the 98th Infantry Division. He spent time in Hawaii and then with occupation forces in Japan.

WILLIS BARNWELL BROWN

Willis Barnwell Brown was a T/Sgt. in the Air Force from 1941 until 1945 in the Pacific.

★★★★

CARTER BYRD

At first Carter Byrd thought the noise that had awakened him was some kind of weekend training exercise, but it lasted too long.

It was Dec. 7, 1941, and he was in the Army-Navy YMCA in Honolulu. There was no training exercise going on. Japanese planes were bombing the U.S. naval installation at nearby Pearl Harbor.

Byrd noted later that when he turned a radio on, there was a program in Japanese on one of the Honolulu stations, something that was not unusual in the islands but seemed ironic just then.

Byrd kept a diary of his early days in the Navy that included detailed accounts of his activities and thoughts just before and after the United States suddenly found itself at war.

He had volunteered for a Navy program

that because of his skill as a stenographer gave him a Yeoman/4 rank. He figured that was a better deal than being drafted, paying about four times as much with the possibility of some special privileges. Restless in a Charleston assignment, he figured Hawaii would be a nice change of scenery and volunteered for duty there.

His diary describes a nice train trip across the country to board a ship in San Francisco. Sailing to Hawaii from there, he became very seasick and said he was glad to have a Navy job skill that probably would keep him on shore.

He was stationed at the naval base but received a per diem that allowed him to find housing in the city, and the YMCA offered a nice room at a low rate. So for then he was calling the 'Y' home.

Going down to the street during the attack, Byrd found chaos, and emergency vehicles were running around. A bomb fell about a half-block from where he was. He heard later that a man had been killed by the blast, but smoke was too heavy for him to see much down the street.

Commandeering a taxi, he went out to Pearl Harbor. Judging from the smoke he saw rising, he believed bombs had hit the big fuel storage tanks at Pearl Harbor, and he expected to find the place a wreck. However, it turned out that the smoke mostly was from ships, and the base was damaged but not nearly as extensively as he had feared.

He reported to the intelligence unit where he worked and told of being too busy to remember many details of the day. One thing he remembered was parts of Japanese airplanes that had been shot down being brought in. One was a generator with labels that showed it was made in East Orange, N.J.

One thing he recalled was being unable to make a phone call to tell his folks he was all right, but finally, he managed to send a cable that told them, "Am perfectly safe. Don't worry any." The cable message was published in the Morning News a day or two later.

Gunfire was heard often for a few days, and once at night, the people in his unit hid behind desks when shooting started again. It turned out it was U.S. guns shooting at U.S. planes. There was such fear of another attack or invasion that people were trigger-happy.

Until the attack, Byrd wrote in his diary, "we had held the controlling hand in matters in the Pacific, but with the blow that had been given us, the (Japanese) then held the cards."

There was a large Japanese population on the island, and one fear was that they might help an invasion. Another fear was that the water might be poisoned. Once a day or two after the attack, he ordered water with his sandwich but was warned that it might be poisoned and drank Coke instead.

The "shock of an American city under attack and in fear" was the main thing he recalled feeling in the first days after the attack. He also heard rumors that one Navy pilot had reported seeing a Japanese plane near Pearl Harbor two hours before the attack but the report was not acted upon.

One man on Maui apparently did not believe any of it was real. He thought it was another staged production like Orson Welles' "War of the Worlds" broadcast that had panicked much of the nation a few years earlier.

For a time after the attack, Byrd said he did not believe anything he heard on the news. He knew the Japanese reports were propaganda, and he knew enough about the American news reports to know reality at Pearl Harbor differed from what the newspapers said.

A few days after the attack, Byrd accompanied an officer of his group on a tour of the harbor. "I saw the damage that had been done, and it was simply horrible," he wrote.

He told of two destroyers "completely wrecked" in dry dock and the dry dock extensively damaged. On Battleship Row, he saw the sunken big ships, "either on the bottom or there was just a little of the ship sticking up." At the Naval air Station on Ford Island, he saw "just about the whole lot" of planes destroyed on the ground.

Later, he visited the Army Air Force's Hickam Field where a direct hit of a barracks killed many airmen. Many planes were destroyed on the ground and all of the hangars were hit except one that housed no planes. He took failure to hit the empty hangar as evidence of splendid intelligence available to the attackers.

Summing up, he expressed outrage over politicians in Washington placing blame for the attack after they had failed to prepare the country for war. He also showed prescience when in January 1942 he commented that he did not think the battleships were that important to the coming war effort.

DOC M. CAMPBELL

Rev. Doc M. Campbell went to Florence schools, graduated from Florence High and was a drummer in Ed Turbeville's band.

He served in the U.S. Army in 1945 and 1946 and went into insurance briefly before going to Anderson Junior College and later becoming a Baptist minister. He served as pastor of Ridgecrest Baptist Church in Florence among other churches.

He died in 1970 of injuries in an auto accident.

LEAVY H. CARTER JR.

Leavy H. Carter Jr. was a Signalman with the Navy in the Pacific Theatre from 1943 until 1946.

★★★★

R.L. COCKFIELD

R.L. Cockfield of Lake City had his education at The Citadel interrupted when in 1943 he joined the Marines. If he had to go, he wanted to have the best training, and that was what he expected at Parris Island. In fact, he stayed long enough to become a drill instructor.

Then he shipped to the Pacific where he was in island-hopping action as U.S. forces moved toward Japan. His unit was training to be part of the invasion force on the Japanese home islands when the war ended. "I was thrilled. I knew that meant I was coming home," he said.

A memorable moment for Cockfield came when he and 15 other Americans went to a small island to see that the Japanese there were following surrender orders. It was an anxious moment as they approached the island, wondering for one thing whether the Japanese garrison there even knew about the surrender, and for another thing, whether they planned to respect it.

When they approached, he said they found about 150 Japanese in formation on the beach. The Americans, he said, took down the Japanese flag, folded it and presented it to the Japanese commander, then raised a U.S. flag, and everything was all right.

Cockfield returned to school and later received a doctorate. He served in the public schools, finally as Florence District 3 superintendent, and was mayor of Lake City.

★★★★

JAMES RUTLEDGE "COTTON" COLEMAN

James Rutledge "Cotton" Coleman was a captain in the Army with the 68th Signal Battalion. He went into the service in December 1941 and was discharged in December 1945. He served in the Luzon Campaign in The Philippines.

★★★★

RAYMOND W. COLEMAN

Raymond W. Coleman served in the Army from July 31, 1943 to June 15, 1946. He was a captain at discharge and an antitank unit commander with the 116th Infantry Regiment, 29th Division in Normandy, Northern France,

the Rhineland and Central Europe.

Coleman received the Combat Infantry Badge, Bronze Star, Purple Heart, European-African Middle Eastern Campaign Medal, with four battle stars, World War II Victory Medal, Army of Occupation Medal and Presidential Unit Citation. After fighting ended, he operated a leave center for vacationing soldiers in Denmark.

★★★★

BILL COLLINS

Bill Collins of Florence went into the Army Air Corps in February 1943 and, after training in Florida, Georgia, Illinois and California, went to England as part of the 8th Air Force, 466th Bomb Group, 786th Bomb Squadron.

Collins spent the war there, helping send B24 bombers over to attack Germany. "We lost a lot of planes," Collins said of his unit, which was based about 100 miles from London. Crew members needed 30 missions before they were eligible to return home, but many did not make it.

The base was bombed on one occasion, and Collins remembers German V-1 buzz bombs passing. "You heard their motors, and if the motor cut off, you'd better duck," he said.

After Germany surrendered, he was training to work on B29s and serve in the Pacific when Japan surrendered. He was discharged in New Mexico in September 1946.

SIDNEY M. COOK

Sidney M. Cook attained the rank of Staff Sergeant during his service with the Army in England, France and Germany from 1942 until 1945.

★★★★

THEODUS ROOSEVELT COOPER

Theodus Roosevelt Cooper served as a Corporal with the Army Quartermaster Corps in Germany from 1945-46.

★★★★

MALCOLM CRAVEN

Malcolm Craven was a young Florence man who wanted to do his part in the war. He joined the Army, and ended up in the infantry in Europe fighting the Germans. He's another veteran of that war who doesn't like to discuss it much.

"It was bad," Craven says. "You see that much death and destruction again and again, and it has an affect on you, it would have to affect you."

After Normandy, Craven began his march across France, toward Germany. It was tough going, but through it all, Craven said he gained a profound respect for the men he worked with. Like many veterans of war, Craven had a special bond with the men around him.

"It's true what they say, that you become a band of brothers," Craven said of the camaraderie men at war develop. "It's a special bond that you don't get in any other relationships."

★★★★

H. LEWIS CROCKER

H. Lewis Crocker flew bombing missions in B26s in Europe during the war. He considered himself lucky to have come through it all without wounds. On one plane he flew aboard,

there was a patch with his name on it because it was over a flak-made hole that was very close to where he had been.

78

BAILEY WILLIAM CURRIN

Bailey William Currin served as a PFC with C Co. of the 23rd Infantry from 1944 until 1946. He saw action in Ardennes, Rhineland and Central Europe.

JOHN PRESTON DANIELS

John Preston Daniels was a Private in the Army from 1943 until 1946. He was involved with the invasion at Normandy and was stationed in Northern France.

RICHARD CLARENCE DAVIS

Richard Clarence Davis of Florence became a sergeant in the Army. He spent part of his time at Ft. Jackson teaching reading to some of the other soldiers. He got out in 1945.

FRANK A. DOUGLASS JR.

Frank A. Douglass Jr. was a Seabee with the Navy in the South Pacific from 1945 until 1945.

★★★★

JULIAN DUSENBURY

When Julian D. Dusenbury graduated from Clemson College in 1942, it was just a few months after Pearl Harbor had plunged the United States into World War II.

He had been a U.S. Senate page, having been appointed by Sen. E.D. Smith before going to Clemson. Then he was a leader among the Clemson cadets when it was still a military school. When he went into the service, it was as a Marine lieutenant.

Dusenbury was stationed for a time at the Marine base at Quantico, Va., where he was an instructor in officer training. He had some well-known students in the classes of officers he trained. Among them were movie stars Tyrone Power and Sterling Hayden.

Later he went to the South Pacific where Marines saw most of their World War II activity.

He won his first big decoration, the Silver Star, in landing on and taking Peleliu Island, a controversial project that saw heavy Marine casualties. By that time, he was a captain, commanding Company A, 1st Battalion, 5th Marines, 1st Marine Division.

The Peleliu landing was reported to have been opposed by Admiral Bull Halsey, but it went ahead with heavy Marine casualties.

Dusenbury led his company in the action on Sept. 15-16, 1944, and he was cited for having ignored heavy Japanese fire to lead his company in repulsing two attacks by enemy tanks.

According to the citation, "Under intense artillery, mortar and machine gun fire, (he) led his assault company across 1,400 yards of open airfield and, although severely wounded by shell fragments after reaching his objective at the far side of the airfield," continued until ordered by the battalion commander to the rear for treatment.

Besides the Silver Star, he received his first Purple Heart in that engagement, and the division received a Presidential Unit Citation.

He soon recovered from his wounds and returned to command his company. During the Pelleliu campaign, he also ran into Arthur M. Parker of Lake City, also a Marine officer and a classmate of Dusenbury's at Clemson.

Along the way he made a famous friend in newspaper columnist Ernie Pyle, who was with his outfit for part of the Pacific campaign.

Pyle was possibly the most famous of the newspaper columnists who wrote about individual GIs in Africa, Europe and finally in the Pacific, leaving major reports on campaigns to the wire services. Pyle and Dusenbury became good friends, and Dusenbury was named in some of his columns. Pyle was killed by enemy fire on Okinawa during the closing weeks of the war.

It was on Okinawa that Dusenbury had his biggest moments. There, he won the Navy Cross, the next thing to the Medal of Honor.

He was credited with braving intense enemy fire to keep his unit moving toward their objective as Marines attacked strongly fortified Japanese positions.

"When one of the platoon commanders was seriously wounded during a critical phase of the assault, he reorganized the platoon and, in the face of intensified enemy fire, led it in continuing the attack," said the citation.

He moved about under heavy fire to coordinate the advance of the troops with supporting tanks, and he directed the fire of the tanks to soften Japanese positions.

"Although painfully wounded during the initial stages of the advance, he refused to be evacuated and continued to direct the attack until Japanese resistance was broken," the citation, signed by Secretary of the Navy James Forrestal, said.

On Okinawa, Dusenbury's company ran short of ammunition at a critical point, and he went through Japanese lines in rain, mud and fog to get and return with machine gun ammunition to keep their attack going.

Mattie Brunson, a friend in Florence had sent Dusenbury a Confederate battle flag, and after they captured Shuri Castle, a Japanese stronghold on the island, he raised the Confederate flag. That proved to be a controversial action, and it has been argued that he might not have been have been recommended for the Medal of Honor for that reason.

After the U.S. forces had won most of the island, Dusenbury was on a ridge looking over the field of fire when a Japanese sniper hit him. The bullet shattered his spine and damaged his kidneys and other organs. He spent the rest of his life in a wheelchair. He was treated at Bethesda Naval Hospital and was discharged as a major.

After the war, he served two terms in the S.C. House of Representatives from Florence and ran for the state Senate. He was one of the early leaders in formation of the S.C. Republican Party.

★★★★

BARBARA F. EADDY
AND HENRY EVANDER GOODWIN

Barbara F. Eaddy was a McLeod Infirmary nurse who in March 1942 joined the military and became a second lieutenant. She served most of her time in a military hospital in southern England and saw many results of the battles raging in Europe.

She recalled seeing German and Allied planes flying over the area. A German V-1 buzz bomb hit her hospital and she received injuries that she called "minor," but she received a Purple Heart because of the wounds.

"There was an onslaught of patients after D-Day," she recalled. There was no time off and all hospital personnel worked long, hard shifts. She made first lieutenant over there.

Henry Evander Godwin was in the 256th Artillery and fought through Northern France, the Ardennes and Central Europe. He was a PFC who won the Bronze Star and also had a brother, William Godwin, who was killed in action in Italy. Before returning home and after fighting stopped, Godwin got time off and went down to Italy to visit his brother's grave.

Eaddy and Godwin were married and raised five daughters after the war.

PAUL J. ECONOMY

Paul J. Economy served in amphibious forces of the U.S. Navy during the war. In the Pacific, he said they helped clear the way for forces landing on Okinawa and Le Shima, spraying rockets onto the landing areas. Late in the war, he had a chance to seek an appointment to Annapolis but returned to South Carolina and graduated from The Citadel in 1948.

EDWARD JOSEPH EDGERTON

Edward Joseph Edgerton of Rt. 1, Florence, went in late in the war, April 1945. He served until November 1946 and became a tech sergeant. He served with the 22nd Ordnance Med. Maintenance Co. of the 8th Army.

★★★★

THADDEUS JACKSON EDGERTON SR.

Thaddeus Jackson Edgerton Sr. went into the Navy on June 7, 1942. He wound up with the USS Euryale, a submarine tender, in the South Pacific. He was a third class torpedo man at the end of the war. Among places he served in were Australia, New Guinea, the Galapagos, Society Island, Admiralty Island, Guam and Pearl Harbor.

E. CARTER ELLIOTT

After finishing Florence High School in 1943 Carter Elliott went into the service and to The Philippines.

He received a direct commission and served with the 4th Infantry Division and the First Cavalry in the South Pacific. Among decorations for valor and service are the Purple Heart and Silver Wings of a master Army aviator.

He remained in the service as a career and served in the occupation forces in Japan and Germany. He also served in Korea and Vietnam.

Elliott retired as a colonel in 1968 after 25 years service.

★★★★

DR. NORMAN DOUGLAS ELLIS

After an internship at the Naval Hospital in Charleston, Doug Ellis briefly served as a Marine recruiter in Raleigh, N.C., and then went to flight surgeon school in Pensacola.

In 1943-44, he served as flight surgeon in Corpus Christi, and then served as flight sur-

geon on a carrier and at Rudyard Bay in the Pacific.

In 1945 until early 1947, he was medical officer at Jacksonville, Fla. He was released from service as a lieutenant commander.

★★★★

WILLIE J. "BILL" EVANS

Bill Evans was a PFC in the Army from 1943 until 1947. He was stationed in the Pacific.

★★★★

WYLIE LOUIS EVANS

Wylie Louis Evans was a Corporal in the Air Force from 1943 until 1945 and was stationed at Alexandria, Louisiana.

SAULS B. FILYAW

Sauls B. Filyaw served as a Sergeant with the Army Air Corps from 1941 until 1945. He was stationed in the Panama Canal Zone as well as Italy.

★★★★

GLORIA WILDER FITCH

Gloria Wilder Fitch of Lake City was a Marine PFC who went in March 1944 and was discharged in December 1945. She served at U.S. bases and at Pearl Harbor.

JOHN PRESLEY FITCH

John Presley Fitch of Lake City was in the Marines from Jan. 1, 1942 until Oct. 10, 1945. He received three Bronze Stars and a Presidential Unit Citation while serving in New Zealand, Australia, New Guinea and New Britain.

★★★★

WILLIAM CARLTON FITCH

William Carlton Fitch was from Lake City and served in the Marshalls, the Gilberts, Saipan and Tinian. He was in from Jan. 1, 1942 until September 1945.

★★★★

CHARLES B. FLOWERS

Charles B. Flowers served in the Merchant Marine starting in 1944 and served in the Atlantic and Pacific War Zones. He received a Coast Guard discharge after the war and remained in the Merchant Marine until retirement in California in 1973.

WILLIAM LEE FLOWERS

William Lee Flowers became a corporal in the Army. He served from August 1945 until June 1947. He was in France and the occupation of Germany.

★★★★

FRANK WILLIAM FLOYD

Frank William Floyd of Olanta went in on Sept. 29, 1943 and was discharged Dec. 28, 1945. Floyd served in France, Belgium, Luxembourg and Germany and was wounded in action on June 18. 1944.

JACK HICKS FLOYD

Jack Hicks Floyd of Olanta went into the Marines in 1942 and served in the Pacific area, Ellice Islands, Gilbert Islands, Okinawa, Tarawa among others. He was discharged Sept. 22, 1945, after nearly three years in combat zones.

★★★★

JAMES FLOYD

James Floyd served as a Captain with the Army in Europe from 1941 until 1945.

PAUL FLOYD

Paul Floyd served in the Corps of Engineers and became a Tech. 4.

He received a Bronze Star and Asiatic Pacific Service Medal. He also got a Philippine Liberation Medal, World War II Victory Medal, Meritorious Unit Award and Good Conduct Medal.

★★★★

VERNON EPPS FLOYD

Vernon Epps Floyd of Olanta was in the Army from January 1944 until May 1946. He served in England, France, Luxembourg, Holland, Belgium, Czechoslovakia and Germany.

SAMUEL VICTOR FOSTER

1st Lt. Samuel Victor Foster on Nov. 15, 1944, led the lead platoon on an assault against a heavily defended German position. He led the group across an open area under mortar and machine gun fire and supervised cutting of hostile barbed wire, and then led an assault that overwhelmed the German position.

The record also credited him with "gallant and courageous leadership." He received a Silver Star for that action, and he also received a Purple Heart.

★★★★

HAROLD GAINEY

Harold Gainey served in Normandy, Northern France, the Rhineland and Central Europe. He received a European Campaign Medal with four Bronze Service Stars.

ROCKY GANNON

In the 11th grade, Roland J. "Rocky" Gannon took a test on which he made a score that qualified him for Army Air Corps pilot training, so he left school and went into the Army.

He finished and qualified in the B17 and was about to ship out to Europe when Hitler committed suicide and Germany surrendered. Then he trained and qualified in the B29 and was on the way to the Pacific when the atomic bombs were dropped and Japan surrendered.

He has often said that he ended the war because each enemy surrendered when they heard he was coming. He's kidding about that.

One problem he encountered was that he not only had no college work but also had not finished high school, so they could not commission him. They made him a flight officer, a grade that was eliminated after the war. Then he was made master sergeant pilot.

He later served in Korea and Vietnam where he said he had 387 missions. He finished college work and was commissioned before retirement.

WILLIAM HERBERT GIBBS

With Co. A, 334th Infantry William Herbert Gibbs served as a military policeman in the Rhineland, Ardennes-Alsace and Central Europe.

He went in on June 1, 1943 and was discharged on Dec. 29, 1945.

Gibbs received the Bronze Star, EAME Campaign medal with three bronze stars as well as the World War II Victory Medal and Army of Occupation Clasp.

✯✯✯✯

ALBERT KEELER GODWIN

Albert Keeler Godwin of Lake City was an Army major. He was killed Dec. 15, 1944 when he was aboard a Japanese prison ship that sank. He was in before Pearl Harbor and was reported missing in action on April 3, 1943. He served in the Philippines.

SIDNEY A. GODWIN

Sidney A. Godwin served as a Private with the Army from 1942 until 1943 and was stationed at Camp Breckinridge, Kentucky.

CHARLES E. GOFF

Charles E. Goff enlisted as an aviation cadet and trained at four bases before he received his wings and commission. He then went to Harvard AAFB in Nebraska and met his other crew members for a B-17 Flying Fortress.

In November 1943, his 447th Bomber Group planes flew to England while some of the crews went on the Queen Elizabeth.

When they arrived, crews flew 25 missions before being assigned to other duty, but that was raised to 30, which Goff flew. He received the Air Medal with four clusters and the Distinguished Flying Cross. Later he operated the Sundae House in Florence, remained in the Reserve and retired as a major.

CHARLES EDWARD GRAHAM

Charles Edward Graham of Olanta served from May 1945 until December 1946. Part of his time was in the occupation of Japan.

JAMES MALORY GRAHAM

James Malory Graham of Olanta went in May 28, 1943 and was discharged April 27, 1945. He was on Guadalcanal and the Solomon Islands. He was a Navy pharmacists mate third class.

LUTHER B. GRAHAM

Luther B. Graham served from May 11, 1945 until Dec. 15, 1945.

ERNEST STEWART GREGG

On Dec. 30, 1943, Ernest Stewart Gregg joined the Marines along with John Carson Brunson of Florence and trained at Parris Island before shipping to Camp Pendleton, Calif. Then they went to Guam where they were to be replacements, but after standing by off-shore for two weeks, they were sent on to Guadalcanal.

Having been trained on antiaircraft guns, they were assigned to the 14th Regiment of the new 6th Marine Division. Brunson then volunteered for the Peleliu campaign.

Gregg's division landed on Okinawa in the seventh wave on April 1, 1945 and with the Marines 1st Division, they secured the north end of the island but were sent to the south end as reinforcements.

They were then on Guam but were getting ready for the expected landing on the Japanese home islands when the atomic bombs forced a Japanese surrender. "Thank God for Truman's order to drop the bombs," Gregg said.

The day after the Japanese surrender was announced, Gregg's division was shipped to North China to spend seven months disarming and shipping Japanese troops to Japan. Gregg and Brunson returned to the States and were discharged at Camp Lejeune May 3, 1946. "Nothing in my life compares to my training, travels, exciting and frightening experiences, but I would not want to repeat it," Gregg said.

BOBBY GRIFFIN

Robert Perrin "Bobby" Griffin of Florence brought home two Bronze Stars, a Silver Star, four Purple Hearts, Combat Infantryman's Badge and European Theater Ribbon with three campaign stars.

General orders of the 26th Infantry Division describing the incidents that won his decorations read like something out of a movie. On Dec. 11, 1944, 2nd Lt. Griffin organized and led his battalion's reconnaissance patrol unit. Leading this group through a mission, "oftentimes under enemy fire, while working under adverse climatic conditions and over difficult terrain," valuable information was gained for U.S. forces. The order notes Griffin's "courage, initiative and devotion to duty reflect the highest credit upon 2nd Lt. Griffin and the Armed Forces of the United States."

A second general order reports on Griffin's "gallantry in action." On Dec. 30, 1944, German troops approached his company positions under the pretext of surrendering, and then suddenly produced weapons and hand grenades to attack. He organized his company "into a skirmish line and personally led his men through a wooded area to clear out the enemy and capture many prisoners."

Then more Germans supported by four tanks approached, and Griffin ordered his men to hold fire until they were within 75 yards. The U.S. gunfire took out all of the enemy soldiers. But the enemy tanks continued to approach and opened fire. Griffin took a radio and radio operator across open terrain, under fire, and called in U.S. artillery, which drove the enemy tanks away.

He and the radio operator again crossed open terrain under fire and radioed for mortar fire that compelled the entire enemy force to withdraw. "His heroic action enabled the company to hold its positions and inflicted many casualties on the enemy. The Army noted his courage under fire and aggressiveness in action against the enemy."

Griffin became company commander and led his unit in the first contact with German troops in the Ardennes campaign of 1944. He also fought in the Battle of the Bulge and the Rhineland and Central Europe campaigns.

Griffin was a 1943 graduate of The Citadel who went into the Army shortly after graduation. He was stationed at Camp Croft and Ft. Benning and soon found himself a second lieutenant assigned to Patton's 3rd Army. He landed in Europe 21 days after D-Day and quickly found action. He was promoted to first lieutenant on Christmas Day 1944 and finally was discharged as a captain.

Shortly after the action that won him high decorations, Griffin was captured in Luxembourg. He must have given the Germans some bad moments, because he escaped twice but was re-captured before he could make his way back to Allied lines. His brother, Tommy Griffin, knew little about his escapes. "He didn't talk about them, and I didn't ask him," his brother said.

First, his parents, Mr. and Mrs. Bob Griffin of Florence received a telegram saying that he was missing in action, then word followed that he was a prisoner of war. That information came from Gene Tomlinson of Olanta who called to tell them that his son, Capt. Ryan Tomlinson, also a POW, was in the same camp as Griffin. It was the Moosburg Camp near Munich.

After that, Griffin's parents received a letter from him from Le Harve, France, saying that

he was headed back to the U.S. He returned to Camp Kilmer, N.J. and shortly after that came home on 60-day furlough. He had wounds that left him with leg problems from which he never completely recovered. Upon his arrival in the States, he was pictured in Newsweek along with several other wounded former prisoners of war. He was quoted in news reports speaking highly of the Red Cross, saying, "Without a doubt, many of us would not be alive today without the Red Cross food packages." Upon leaving the Army, Griffin's service was not complete. He served as commander of Florence VFW Post 3181 and as State VFW commander.

After the war, he was an auto dealer, was one of the original owners of the Darlington International Raceway and served on its board. He entered the first car in the first Darlington Southern 500 in 1950.

Griffin "served our country with great distinction and honor," Sen. Fritz Hollings said in a memorial he inserted in the Congressional Record after Griffin's death. Hollings told of Griffin's having been a Senate page before his college days. He was appointed page by Sen. E.D. Smith of South Carolina. He served for the maximum of three years from 1937 to 1939, part of it as chief page for Vice President John Nance Garner. He graduated from the Page School in Washington before going to The Citadel.

Bothered by his service disability until the end, he died in 1994 at the Dorn Veterans Hospital in Columbia where he had a suite in the nursing facilities.

★★★★

DR. JOE GRIFFIN

After going into the Army in January 1943, Joe Asa Griffin II, departed for Europe in June 1943 in what he believed was the largest convoy to cross the Atlantic.

He landed on Omaha Beach on D-Day

plus 16 as a sergeant in the Engineers Corps. He was commissioned second lieutenant at Fontainebleau, France, and served as a platoon leader in Patton's 3rd Army, 94th Division, 376th Infantry.

When the war ended, he was in Vodnany, Czechoslovakia, where they met the Russian army. He received four campaign stars for Normandy, Northern France, Central Europe and Rhineland.

After the war, he went to Peabody College, then the University of Tennessee dental school. He married Allene Williams and they came to Florence in 1953 where he practiced dentistry for 38 years.

★★★★

TOMMY GRIFFIN

Thomas C. Griffin of Florence was working for the Atlantic Coast Line Railroad when the Japanese attacked Pearl Harbor, and by April 1942, he was in the U.S. Army. "I was sworn in at Ft. Jackson on April 1, 1942, and they told us this was no April Fools joke." It wasn't.

They sent him back home, and the most memorable thing about the time before he returned to duty was a visit to his old working place at the ACL Railroad station. "I was down there when President Roosevelt came through," Griffin said. "He was on the way to Bernard Baruch's place at Georgetown, and there was lots of security."

Griffin was sent to St. Petersburg, Fla., for basic training and on to Gulfport Field in Mississippi with the Army Air Corps where he trained to work on B29s. Then they sent him to Detroit to study B29 engines at a Chevrolet plant and on to Great Bend, Kan., where he trained further on B29s.

The B29 program was designed to create a bombing force that could strike heavy blows once island-hopping U.S. forces got airstrips close enough to Japan for long-range planes to make the round trip.

His unit moved forward as Pacific Islands were captured and set up the bases from which the big bombers could fly. Griffin was on ground crews that worked steadily to keep the planes airworthy, and he became a crew chief and a sergeant. "We had about 800 B29s on those islands," he said.

"Lots of times, we had to work through the night on the planes because the sun made the metal too hot to touch during the daytime. It would burn your hands badly." At nights, they had elaborate light towers they called "Christmas trees" to provide the light they needed to work during darkness.

They knew something big was up as the war neared its end. "I saw leaflets that we had printed up to drop on Japanese cities that might be atomic bomb targets. They didn't tell them what was up but told them they should leave the cities. I saw some of the leaflets," he said. Nobody knows how many Japanese heeded the warnings and missed the atomic bomb attacks. Before the atomic bombs, he said, Japanese cities had been devastated by U.S. air raids when U.S. planes dropped incendiary bombs that started fire storms that leveled huge areas and killed many.

Griffin said they heard something about a big bomb having been dropped but still were pretty much in the dark when one night a general dropped by their work site and told them to just take off and take it easy. The Japanese were surrendering.

One memorable day came when Griffin was on Saipan before the invasion of Iwo Jima. "We got a red alert, which meant we were under attack, and we sure were. About 17 Japanese Zeroes came in on a suicide raid."

Griffin said he got under a truck just as the Japanese planes strafed his area. They made several passes. "When they came over, they were so close I could see the pilot sitting up in the cockpit looking down at us. I could hear the bullets hitting the ground all around, and some hit the truck I was under."

It happened that all but a few of the B29s in that unit were away on a mission to Japan. The Japanese hit about three planes that were on the ground, but all of the Zeroes were destroyed.

Griffin went on to spend a few weeks on Iwo Jima, and then shortly after the war ended, he was on the way home. "I came on the carrier Independence, and we made a stop at Wake Island on the way back," he said. "The Independence later was one of the surplus ships that were sunk in a hydrogen bomb test at Bikini atoll.

"We came back in to Pier 26 in San Diego," he recalled. "That was the pier I left from to go to the Pacific. I had always felt like I would come back but didn't know it would be to Pier 26."

Then came a long troop train ride across the country. "We lost a lot of men along the way. We would have a stop, and some would just disappear." It was unclear whether they got off partying and just missed the train or they were close to home and couldn't wait.

"In New Orleans we had a layover for several hours, and a lot of them didn't make it back to the train that time." Anyway, the train was a lot less crowded at the end of the trip.

"I got home on Dec. 22, 1945. I walked from Palmetto Street to my mother's house. They were looking for me, and it was a big party."

JAMES H. GRIMSLEY

James H. Grimsley was with Troop D, 92nd Armored Recon Squadron. He finished war service in Germany.

★★★★

RAY GROOM

Ray Groom served as a radio operator on the crew of a Lancaster bomber with the Royal Air Force. He was in the 115th Squadron, RAF Bomber Command. The plane, which had a crew of seven, was based at Witchford, Cambridgeshire, England.

WILLIAM FREELAND HAM

William Freeland Ham of Timmonsville was killed in action at Davao, Mindanao, Philippine Islands, on April 28, 1945.

He had entered the Army on Dec. 7, 1942 and had become a sergeant. Ham served at Pearl Harbor and New Guinea before the Philippines action.

Four Hayes Brothers served in the Army.

ANDREW J. HAYES

Andrew Jackson Hayes served in the Army until retirement.

EMERSON HAYES

Emerson Hayes joined on Dec. 11, 1942 and served until Aug. 13 1945.

GEORGE WILSON HAYES

George Wilson Hayes was a corporal with Btty. B, 321st Glider Field Artillery Bn., 101st Airborne Division and was in the D-Day landings in 1944. He was with the 101st at Bastogne during the Battle of the Bulge.

He served in France, Holland, Germany, Belgium, Luxembourg and Austria. Hayes went in on March 4, 1942, and was discharged on Nov. 17, 1945.

ROBERT VIVIAN HAYES

Robert Vivian Hayes went in March 16, 1944 and served until he was killed in action on March 6, 1945 in Belgium. He also served in England, France and Holland with Co. E, 217th Bn., 67th Regiment.

★★★★

PETE HENRY

BUBBA HICKEY

William Edward Hickey Sr. went into the Army as a second lieutenant and was shipped to Europe in January 1944.

He landed on Omaha Beach on D-Day, and his son said he believes Hickey was on the front line when the German surrender was announced. "I believe he was in the second wave on D-Day," he said.

He fought across Northern France, the Ardennes and Rhineland and wound up a captain. He had been a company commander at Clemson.

Hickey won the Bronze Star with Oak Leaf Cluster, the Combat Infantry Badge and campaign ribbons with five stars. In addition, he brought back a distinguished unit citation and meritorious service award.

His son said that Sarge Frye, a sergeant from South Carolina for whom the baseball field at the University of South Carolina is named, was in his company. Despite the strong rivalry between Clemson and USC, they remained close friends the rest of their lives.

Like many WWII vets, Hickey did not talk much about it, but one story he told was of awakening from a nap in a tent in France to find Ernest Hemingway there. The famous writer signed a map of the area and Hickey brought that home.

HOUSTON HICKS

Houston Hicks went in on Feb. 14, 1944 and was discharged on April 11, 1946. He served in the Army in the Rhineland and Central Europe and became a staff sergeant.

★★★★

NOBLE J. HICKS

Noble J. Hicks of Timmonsville went into the Army on Nov. 6, 1941, nearly an exact month before Pearl Harbor, and was discharged on Oct. 6, 1945. He served in the Philippines.

TONY L. HICKS

Tony L. Hicks went into the Navy May 25, 1945 and was discharged May 18, 1946.

★★★★

L. GORDON HILL JR.

After attending the University of South Carolina for two years, L. Gordon Hill Jr. entered the Army in December 1942 as a buck private. He went to Officers Candidate School and was commissioned a second lieutenant.

He served during World War II as an artillery officer and held several commands in coastal artillery during the 1943 to 1945 period.

Hill became a career officer and also served in the Korean War and Vietnam War in various artillery commands, advancing in rank and finally retiring from the Army in 1980 as a major general.

When Gen. Creighton Abrams was chief of staff, Hill was appointed chief information officer of the Army, a position now called chief of public affairs of the Army. His last assignment before retirement was as head of the Armed Forces Staff College at Norfolk, Va., for three years during which he reported directly to the Joint Chiefs.

Earlier as an 11-year-old, he delivered the Morning News and later Roy Graham, who was sports editor and associate editor of the paper, took him under his wing. Graham also was a

World War II veteran. Through that relationship, Hill became interested in journalism and later as a sophomore at the University of South Carolina, Hill was editor of The Gamecock, the student newspaper. He was the youngest editor of that paper, which usually was edited by a junior or senior.

He received his BA in journalism from the University of Wisconsin and a masters at George Washington University. He was Phi Beta Kappa.

Hill, who had three children, died in 1990. His widow, Helen, who is 85, lives in Fairfax, Va. She still plays golf and has a 26 handicap.

★★★★

LUCIUS F. HILL JR.

Lucius F. Hill Jr. was 16 in 1941, so his parents had to sign for him to enlist. He served in both the Atlantic and Pacific war zones and was discharged on May 28, 1945.

WILLIAM MAXIE HINDS

Going into the Army in 1941 as a teenager, William Maxie Hinds served until September 1945.

In 1942, he went to England, then to Africa where he was involved in the Battle of Kassarine Pass. In Algiers, he contracted spinal meningitis and was hospitalized there, but he recovered and returned to duty, seeing action in Sicily and Italy. He particularly recalled the children caught in the war, eating from garbage cans and begging.

After his automatic weapons battalion was disbanded, Hinds served in a training cadre for combat engineers.

Among his medals were the European-African-Middle Eastern Campaign Medal with three bronze stars, World War II Victory Medal and Army of Occupation Medal.

LOUIS C. HITE

Louis C. Hite Jr. served in the Army until Feb. 10, 1946. He was in the Quartermaster Corps and attached to the Air Corps. He served as supply officer at Harlingen Army Gunnery School, Dodge City Army Air Base and in Lubbock, Texas.

WILLIAM HENRY HOBBS

William Henry Hobbs was with the Military Police and served until 1949.

★★★★

TID AND EARL HOLLOWAY

Tid Holloway was a dietician aboard the USS Dogwood, a hospital ship, and she made several trips across the Atlantic bringing wounded servicemen back from England. She said the worst wounded patients were from the

Battle of the Bulge. There were many amputations - there had been much frostbite - and many psychiatric cases.

After several of those trips, the Dogwood was sent to the Pacific where they were to treat the many casualties expected from an invasion of the Japanese home islands. While there she ran into Julian Dixon of Lake City who was an Army officer.

Word of the surrender came when her ship was in Manila Bay preparing to receive casualties from the invasion of Japan, and she said there was not a great deal of celebrating. "Everybody just started counting points." There was a point system for combat time and various types of service, and when a member of the armed forces reached a certain total of points, it meant a quick trip home.

Tid Holloway's husband, Earl Holloway, also was in the Pacific as part of a unit that followed island-hopping invasions, cleaning out Japanese garrisons that had been left behind. He ran into Lake Citians R.L. Cockfield and Jim McElveen in the Pacific.

★★★★

ROBERT T. HOOK

Robert T. Hook was in the Army from June 12, 1944 to Nov. 21, 1946. He served on Bougainville, in the Philippines and in the occupation forces in Japan.

★★★★

BILL HORNSBY

Bill Hornsby of Timmonsville was among Florence County men who were wounded in Europe. He was hit by shrapnel and wounded after he had fought through France, Belgium and the Netherlands into Germany. He was hospitalized in England for four months, then until the war ended trained troops who were on the way to action in Europe.

Hornsby had gone into Normandy shortly after D-Day with the 30th Division, an outfit of men mostly from the Carolinas, Georgia and Tennessee. His was one of the units that fought through the famous hedgerows of Normandy that he said, were "perfect for defenders."

His unit also was victim of a major war mishap when Allied bombers mistakenly dropped some of tons of bombs intended for Germans on his division's troops. "Because so many were killed, they had to replace the officers and made me a sergeant," he said. He became an educator after the war.

★★★★

CHARLES HOWARD SR.

Charles Howard Sr. served with the 36th Infantry Division in southern France and Italy. He was in combat against German troops in Salerno and Cassino. On Aug. 15, 1944, he landed in the invasion of southern France.

In France, he suffered frostbite and was in a hospital in England for a month, then assigned to limited service with the Army Air Corps.

★★★★

CHARLES HUBBARD

Charles Hubbard of Florence "saw Ike and (Bernard) Montgomery (the British general and later field marshal) when they came around to visit with us, " before D-Day he said. Hubbard didn't actually meet either, but he saw them during their visits.

He was part of the 3rd Armored (Spearhead) Division. They were in England training for six months before that, and "they told us a lot of us were not going to come back." He lost his best friend in the Battle of the Bulge.

"We were the first division unit to cross the German border, first to take a German town in this war, first to breach the Siegfried Line, first to shoot down an enemy plane from German

soil, first to fire an artillery shell on German soil... and first invader of Germany in force since Napolean," Hubbard said.

His unit liberated prisoners at the Nordhausen Concentration Camp, and "they were so thankful to see us."

"We landed in Normandy on D plus 12 (12 days after D-Day)," and they fought through the infamous hedgerows of Normandy. "We lost a lot of men."

He still has a German helmet that he brought back as a souvenir. He also brought back five Bronze Stars, the Combat Infantryman's Badge, a Purple Heart and a Good Conduct Medal.

★★★★

JAMES H. HUMPHRIES

James H. Humphries became a radioman, third class during his Navy service between 1942 and 1945. He served on Guadalcanal among other places during the U.S. drive across the South Pacific.

★★★★

PETER D. HYMAN

Peter D. Hyman went from Florence High School into the Navy on June 24, 1943 and served in the Asiatic and Pacific theaters.

He was discharged on Jan. 18, 1946 but was called back to active duty as a member of

Btty. D, 713th AAA of the National Guard. He was released from that tour on Aug. 1, 1950 and graduated from the University of South Carolina Law School in 1954.

Hyman remained in the Army Reserve and became a brigadier general. He also served several terms in the S.C. House of Representatives from Florence County and was a key political figure in establishment of Francis Marion University.

BARRY JONES

Serving in the Army in Europe, Barry Webb Jones was involved in the Battle of the Bulge, recalling long after the war the cold the troops endured.

He was wounded in action and had a very unusual aftermath to the wound. He saw the German soldier who shot him during close combat. The U.S. troops won the skirmish and took the disputed ground, then brought in vehicles to transport wounded men back for treatment.

Jones said he was put into a truck with other wounded and found the German who had wounded him among the other patients in the truck. He would have liked to resume the fight on the truck.

Later, when he was returning to the United States on a transport, he did not know what port they would go into, but as they neared the U.S., his group was asked if there were any men there from South Carolina.

Jones and one or two others were, and they were told, "Well, you're in luck. We're going into Charleston." It made it easy for his parents to come immediately to visit him.

DONALD F. JONES

Donald F. Jones was a Staff Sergeant in the Army from 1943 until 1946 and served in Italy.

DR. EARL JONES

Dr. Earl Rivers Jones practiced medicine in Florence from 1951 to 1981, but before that, he was an infantry officer commanding the 1st Platoon, Company B, 232nd Regiment, 42nd Rainbow Division, attached to 3rd Army and 7th Army.

He and the rest of the junior class at Clemson were drafted in 1943, and he went through Ft. Jackson, then officers candidate school at Ft. Benning. From there, he went to the 42nd division and landed at Marseilles, France, and went into combat in November 1944.

"My men were excellent soldiers, very brave and totally dedicated to their miserable tasks. Most of the men were only 18 years of age and risked their lives every day in combat," Jones said.

He was in frontline combat until counterattacking German forces on Jan. 18, 1945 surrounded his platoon.

They were taken prisoners and sent to Hammelburg, Germany, and held from January 1945 until March 27, 1945 when a 3rd Army unit overran the camp but were unable to hold it and withdrew. Jones and several other POWs walked away from the camp in the confusion and made their way to American lines.

They wanted to rejoin their units, but due to severe malnutrition, Jones was shipped back to Camp Kilmer, N.J. After recovering, he was reassigned to an infantry company, which he commanded at Camp Joseph T. Robinson in Little Rock, Ark.

He was awarded the Bronze Star and Purple Heart and several campaign ribbons. After the war he finished Clemson and went to the Medical University of South Carolina in 1946 and graduated in 1950. He married Polly A. Catoe in 1949 and lived in Florence until his death in 1990.

★★★★

FRANCIS MARION JONES

Francis Marion Jones served as a Staff Sergeant in the Army from 1943 until his death in Luxemburg on February 9, 1945.

JOSEPH EZRA "JOEY" JONES

Joseph E. "Joey" Jones graduated form Elim High School in 1938 and attended the University of South Carolina before serving in the Army during World War II.

Jones was a staff sergeant with the 108th Chemical Warfare Division on Guadalcanal.

He received a Bronze Star, World War II Victory Medal, American Campaign Medal, Asiatic Pacific Campaign Medal and Good Conduct Medal.

★★★★

JOHN KASSAB

John Kassab was one of the draftees called up in the nation's first peacetime draft before World War II. He came down to Ft. Jackson where he was assigned to a cavalry unit and actually rode and cared for horses.

That was much different from his circumstances when the war ended. By then, the outfit had changed from 102nd Horse Cavalry to

102nd Mechanized Cavalry. In Europe they rode in tanks instead of horses and in between had spent some time on motorcycles.

He was in Columbia on Dec. 7, 1941 with discharge in hand, getting ready to go home from his draft hitch. Then the news of the attack in Pearl Harbor broke. Discharges, like leaves, were cancelled, and he was in the Army for the duration.

In June 1942, his division shipped out for England, and he believed they were the first unit to arrive over there.

The 102nd spent nearly two years in England, training and waiting to take part in the D-Day invasion. During that time Kassab got the chance to visit London, and he was there during the Blitz when German aircraft were bombing the city every night.

Finally in the spring of 1944, the invasion of Western Europe was at hand, and he recalled boarding ships on June 4 for a planned June 5 landing in France. Weather delayed things, and thousands of troops spent nights on rocking ships. Seasickness probably was more the norm than the exception.

The next day, Gen. Dwight Eisenhower made the difficult decision to go ahead despite doubtful weather conditions. Meteorologists said there should be a break in the storms the next morning long enough to make the landing. He feared a longer delay would enable the Germans to figure out Allied plans and better prepare to beat back the invasion.

So the morning of June 6, 1944, Kassab's 102nd Mechanized was aboard ship waiting to land on Omaha Beach. He told of larger British ships being just behind them so that when those ships took part in the barrage of German shore batteries, they fired over Kassab's LST.

During what seemed like a long wait to go ashore, Kassab who had worked his way up to first sergeant and the others in his armored unit saw craft with infantry come by and saw the torrent of fire that greeted them when they landed on the beach. They went up the beach

not only under heavy fire but among land mines that from time to time blew. "I don't see how anyone could get through alive," he said years later.

Finally, Kassab's unit was ready to go, and he was in the second tank behind the commanding officer's tank. The first tank pulled off into what was supposed to be shallow water and immediately sank out of site.

The C.O. appeared lost and Kassab, who had not been fully briefed on battle plans found himself in command of the tanks when they reached a proper depth and pulled off. This time, Kassab's tank was first.

Later he talked about it and said, "I wondered how many men gave their lives so I could drive on the beach. Here we were driving over their bodies." He had to make the hellish decision to order the tank driver to drive over the bodies if necessary.

Kassab and his unit were using recon tanks that were fast and they would go ahead to gather information to report back for the following larger forces. They gathered for a night in a circle after the beachhead was established.

One of the biggest problems Allied forces faced was getting through farming regions of Normandy crossing farmers' hedgerows. A particular problem for tanks was that when they went over a hedgerow, the thin bottom part of the tank was exposed to enemy fire. It was the most vulnerable part of the tank.

He said a sergeant in his outfit solved that problem by attaching heavy weight to the nose of the tank so it would not rear up in the air when mounting a hedgerow.

One of Kassab's memorable experiences was in Normandy when one night he slept atop a tank. Strafing German planes passed and bullets hit the top of his tank, just missing him and setting his blanket afire.

Once in heavy action, he had a brief experience as a prisoner of war when he was captured and questioned by a German officer who tried to insult him and finally spit in his face. Kassab hit the officer and for that got a terrific beating with rifle butts. The Germans left him unconscious, either believing he was dead or sure to die. He recovered and returned to duty.

It was in France that the commanding officer sent for Kassab who wondered if he was in some kind of trouble. Upon reporting, he learned he was receiving a battlefield commission as second lieutenant. The recruit of the 1940s who had done such duties as KP and tending horses at Ft. Jackson now was an officer. He wound up the war a first lieutenant.

His was one of the units that crossed the famed bridge over the Rhine at Remagen that the Germans had tried but failed to destroy. Many troops and equipment got across before the bridge finally collapsed, and finding that bridge intact is credited with shortening the war by allowing the Allies to get across the Rhine, a formidable obstacle.

Later Kassab's unit's tanks lined up with Soviet tanks after the armies met in Germany, but Kassab feared that the Soviets would be our next enemy.

His unit freed the Buchenwald concentration camp where mostly Jewish prisoners were worked and killed as part of Hitler's "Final Solution" Kassab was there when Eisenhower first saw the camp. Kassab once described cremation ovens, stacks of bodies and piles of teeth that were found there. He said that Ike turned red with anger and threw up.

It was enough to make the strongest of us weep in shame and pity, Kassab later said, "shame that any human being could allow his fellow man to fall into such a state of existence."

On the other side of the experience coin, at a celebration at the end of the war, celebrities and dignitaries were on hand, and Kassab was assigned to escort Ingrid Bergman.

He brought home a Silver Star, two Bronze Stars, two Purple Hearts, and numerous combat ribbons and campaign stars.

Settled in Florence after the war and married to the former Adele Baroody, Kassab became involved in community projects and is known as one of the founders of Francis

Marion University. They were community leaders that worked economically and politically to get the college established. He was chairman of the building committee that built Stokes Hall, the first campus building, now FMU administration building.

DALLAS WILLIE KEEFE

After finishing Florence High School in 1940, Dallas Willie Keefe became one of the Florence County men who went into the Army Air Corps before Pearl Harbor. He joined in July 1940.

He was at Hickam Field in Hawaii when the Japanese attacked that base and Pearl Harbor, then was based in Australia.

A gunner on a B25, Keefe was one of five aboard the plane when it crashed on April 21, 1942. The plane was en route from Port Moresby to Garbott Field, Australia, and was believed to have been shot down by the Japanese. He was lost when the plane went down and was one of the first, possibly first, Florence County man who died in World War II. Bodies of the crew were not found, but in 1991, a memorial marker for him was placed at the Florence National Cemetery during a memorial service.

WILLIE JAMES KELLY

Willie James Kelly of Timmonsville was a staff sergeant in the Army. He was in from Jan. 22, 1945 until Nov. 23, 1946. He served in the Philippines and the occupation of Japan.

★★★★

GEORGE KERETSES

George Keretses of Florence served from 1943 to 1945 in the Navy and became a petty officer, 1st class. He served on an LST as cook and gunner.

His units landed the first tank on the Phillipines' Leyte Island, Dulag Beach as the U.S. forces returned there on the way across the Pacific to Japan.

He also took part in the invasions of Mindoro, Mindanao, Borneo, Cebu and New Guinea.

EVERETTE V. LANGSTON

Everette V. Langston, a sergeant with the Army Air Corps, was killed in action while flying in a B17 over Germany on March 6, 1944.

Langston had served with the Army Air Corps from Sept. 22, 1944. He was awarded the Purple Heart posthumously.

★★★★

JAMES LEE

★★★★

WARNER L. LEE JR.

Warner L. Lee Jr. of Evergreen went into the army on Oct. 17, 1944.

He was shipped to Europe and was a technician fourth grade in Germany when the war ended.

Lee received the Bronze Star, European-African-Middle Eastern campaign medal, Good

Conduct Medal, World War II Victory Badge, Army of Occupation Medal, Combat Infantry Badge.

He received his honorable discharge on Aug. 7, 1946.

★★★★

RAY G. LEGETTE

Ray G. LeGette remembered being with James Grimsley, Harold Leach and Warner Lee after they all were drafted. They went through training, which was cut short, together but were separated after reaching Europe. He recalls two submarine scares during their voyage to England aboard a Liberty ship.

They went in on Oct. 17, 1944 and LeGette said when he reached combat duty as a machine gunner, Germans were surrendering in large numbers. He recalls one young prisoner identifying himself as a Russian and being separated from the others.

They made their way through Germany until "The Russians came and met us. It was a joyous occasion for all of us."

He then was training to go into the war against Japan, but after they surrendered, he was reassigned as a military policeman, a job he had to learn through "on-the-job" training.

★★★★

THEODORE LESTER

Theodore Lester thought he was overage when he was drafted, but wound up a corporal and with four Bronze Stars when he returned home. He served in Normandy, Northern France, the Rhineland and Central Europe.

A black enlisted man and a little older than most of his colleagues, Lester collected donations for the NAACP from other black soldiers before they spent it playing, his wife said.

Lester's most unusual experience came after the war ended. There was a point system which qualified soldiers for an early return home, and Lester had the required number but was not sent home while he felt that similarly placed white troops were getting a ticket home.

He wrote to S.C. Sen. Burnet Maybank to complain, and Maybank replied that he had no control over that and suggested he take it up with his commanding officer. He did. In fact, he wrote directly to Gen. Dwight Eisenhower, commanding general in Europe.

Ike replied that such a thing should not be happening, and Lester was quickly returned home. He had gone into the service on May 17, 1943 and was released at Ft. Bragg on Nov. 20, 1945.

Lester was active in community affairs after the war, and he became the first black member of the Florence School District 1 board. Theodore Lester Elementary School on East Palmetto Street was named in his honor.

★★★★

HERMAN R. LUHRS

Herman R. Luhrs of Florence served in the Navy. He was aboard LST 38 in the South Pacific.

JIM LYONS

Jim Lyons served as a PFC with the Army Air Force in England from 1942 until 1945.

★★★★

MAURICE MANLEY

Maurice Manley of Florence was a third class Navy Seabee who served on Iwo Jima. In 2006 he viewed a movie about the fighting on that island and said it "brought back a lot of memories."

The main reason U.S. forces wanted the island was to build a base for the Army Air Corps bombers. Manley recalled having Japanese shoot at them while working on the runway. "There was fighting all around us while we were working on the runway," he said.

★★★★

HORACE ZINGLE MATTHEWS JR.

Horace Zingle Matthews Jr. joined the Army at Ft Jackson on March 18, 1942, and trained at Camp Chaffee, Ark.

He became a sergeant and laid telephone lines and drove half-tracks. He received the Bronze Star, EAMET Service Medal and Good Conduct Medal and was discharged July 24, 1945.

★★★★

RIVERS MAXWELL & WILLIAM J. "RED" MAXWELL

Rivers Maxwell and William J. "Red" Maxwell both served in the Army Air Force, but took different routes.

Red went in on Dec. 9, 1942 and was discharged on Feb. 24, 1946, after having served with Headquarters 8th Air Force ground forces in the Rhineland and Central Europe campaigns.

Rivers served from July 1943 until December 1945 with the Army Air Force and put in time on Saipan.

★★★★

ROBERT SIDNEY "BUB" McCLAM

HAROLD "PAT" McELVEEN

Harold "Pat" McElveen of Lake City served as a PFC with the 86th Mountain Infantry-10th Mtn. Division in Italy. He entered the Army on April 20, 1944 and was discharged November 5, 1945.

✯✯✯✯

JAMES DAVIS "JIM" McELVEEN

James Davis "Jim" McElveen of Lake City served as a Staff Sergeant in the Army, HQ Company, 389th Infantry in the Pacific Theatre. His tour of duty lasted 3 years and 3 months.

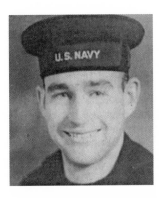

A. LAVERN McKNIGHT

A. Lavern McKnight was an Electrician 3rd Class in the Navy from 1942 until 1945 and was stationed at Pearl Harbor, Hawaii.

✯✯✯✯

JOSEPH M. McKNIGHT

Joseph M. McKnight was a medic with the 922 F.F. Bn., 97th Infantry Division and served in Europe and the Pacific. He remained in the USAR and retired.

✯✯✯✯

W.A. McLELLAN

William Archie McLellan went fromFlorence High School into the army. He served in the Army Air Corps during World War II.

JAMES R. MacMILLAN

James R. MacMillan was a buck sergeant and squad leader in the 87th Infantry Division, 347th Regiment Anti-Tank Company. He served in the Saar, Battle of the Bulge, Rhine River Crossing and crossed Germany to the border with Czechoslovakia. He had 34 months in the service and five in combat.

SAM McWHITE

Sam McWhite of Pamplico went into the Army on Dec. 31, 1942, and served until Dec. 20, 1945.

He served in the Western Pacific before returning to the U.S. and being discharged at Camp Gordon, Ga.

McWhite received the APT Service Medal, American Theater Service Medal and World War II Victory Medal.

CHARLES R. MEDLIN

One of the servicemen who lost his life in World War II was Charles Raymond Medlin who enlisted in early 1941 and was sent to the Philippines early in 1942.

When the Philippines were overrun by the Japanese, he became a prisoner of war and was held at No. 4 Camp Bilibid until October 1944.

Then Medlin was one of about 1,775 Allied prisoners who were being transferred to Japan to work in factories. On Oct. 24, 1944, the prison ship was torpedoed by an American submarine and sank in the South China Sea. The U.S. submarine crew, when they realized the ship carried prisoners of war, attempted to rescue all they could, but the job was too big. Medlin was among those lost.

★★★★

A. LARUE MILES

A. Larue Miles served as a Corporal in the Army in Germany from 1943 until 1946.

LEE MILES

Lee Miles served as a Corporal in the Marines from 1944 until 1946 and was stationed in China and Okinawa.

★★★★

HOWARD E. MOODY

Howard E. Moody was a gunner on a B17 crew that had flown together from Nebraska to Kimbolton, England with stops in Newfoundland and Scotland, arriving at the post in England on April 24, 1943.

They flew missions over the continent until Sept. 16, 1943 when they were headed for Nantes, France. They were hit by flak and the plane was badly damaged. Moody was hit by shrapnel that broke his right shoulder, then they were ordered to bail out.

Moody said he realized his right arm was useless and he would have to pull the ripcord with his left hand, which he did. The chute opened, and he landed in a field. Briefly unconscious, he awoke to see elderly people and children coming.

They took him to a farm house where he had trouble communicating, so when he asked for water, he got cider, wine and cognac. Two French teenagers who knew some English arrived and told him the French had looked for a doctor and also had notified the Germans, who soon arrived.

The Germans took him to a small hospital for POWs which had no pain killers, and they removed the shrapnel from his right side and

sewed him back up without anesthesia.

After a couple of weeks, he was shipped to Frankfurt by train and held in solitary confinement in a hospital. He was pressed for information but gave only name, rank and serial number.

Then he was shipped to a hospital that was run by British POWs and got better treatment for his arm and shoulder. In February, he was shipped to Stalag VI in East Prussia. By July 1944 he could see flashes and hear the rumble of guns. The Russians were approaching.

They were herded into the hold of a freighter with no food, water or toilet facilities. "I have been through some torture in my day but at the time I thought this was the worst thing that could happen to me," he said. The ship took them to a port where they were put onto a crowded boxcar which had no facilities and they still were not fed.

After the train trip Moody said two POWs were handcuffed together and were forced to walk through a long row of German marines with fierce-looking dogs and bayonets. The exhausted men were marched at a fast pace for two miles to Stalag Luft IV, a new camp with about 1,500 POWs. In 1945 at liberation there were about 10,000.

Early in 1945, the Russians were closing in again, and the prisoners were marched to another camp. This time the march was for 85 days and they slept in barns, sheds and in the open. He said they were told they had walked 600 miles during that march.

One morning during the march, the guards did not start them again, and there was a confused day when POWs walked around a village and farmhouses mostly unsupervised. Then the guards disappeared, and shortly after that, British troops arrived. Moody went through England before returning to the U.S. on a liberty ship.

He then married, was discharged and returned to Wofford College from which he graduated and went into public education, becoming a principal and superintendent. He died in February 2007 and is buried in the Florence National Cemetery.

ROBERT H. MOORE

Robert H. Moore was a sergeant in the Air Force and served with the 20th Air Force, 9th Bomber Group in the Tihian Islands from 1943 until 1946.

CHARLES DEWEY MUNN JR.

Charles Dewey Munn Jr. of Pamplico went into the Navy on May 10, 1944 and served until June 6, 1946. His career was highlighted by service in the campaign to liberate The Philippines.

MAXWELL H. MYERS

Maxwell H. Myers was a Staff Sergeant with the Army in Europe from 1943 until 1945.

RICHARD A. MYERS

Richard A. Myers went into the Army on May 27, 1944 and was discharged Feb. 8, 1946. He served in the infantry in the Pacific Theater, including occupation duty in Japan.

★★★★

WALTER B. NORMAN

As Marine Platoon Sgt. Walter B. Norman walked the USS West Virginia deck on a pleasant Sunday morning, he saw airplanes approaching and assumed they were Americans on a weekend training mission. He soon realized he had guessed wrong.

"I could make out the 'rising sun' on the

wings as the planes passed over," he said. The aircraft were part of a Japanese strike force that attacked Pearl Harbor on Dec. 7, 1941, and Norman possibly was the first Florence County serviceman to hear the sounds of American involvement in World War II.

The West Virginia, hit by a Japanese torpedo, sank. It was one of the battleships lost to the U.S. fleet that morning, but it was repaired and was in Tokyo Bay for the Sept. 2, 1945, surrender signing.

"We were tied up on Battleship Row and the USS Arizona was just aft. When the Arizona was hit and blown apart, the flash started fires on planes on the West Virginia," he said. The Oklahoma just beside Norman's ship was damaged, took on water and rolled over.

Norman came through the battle and the rest of the war, but his family had anxious moments at the start. The West Virginia first was reported lost at sea with all hands, and it was several days before his family realized the ship was at Pearl Harbor "but that I was all right."

Norman told the Morning News about his experience long after the war, and the paper in the few weeks after the attack reported other county men who had been at Pearl Harbor or a neighboring installation.

Among them were Fred Dudley, Robert Burrows, Jack Duffell, Carter Byrd, James Houle, Joe Golombek, Charlie Bensinger, Edwin D. Shuler, Cecil Davis, Joseph Harllee Powell, Fred Ward, Clemmie Nelson, Leon F. McCrary, William P. Stroud Jr., Gene Merrill Moore, W.C. "Skeet" Clark, Henry M. Parrish, Jack Walker, John Flowers, Walter Parker, J.W. Lawhon, James M. McPherson, Kenneth Hodge, John Henry Floyd, Walter Outz, John W. Anderson Jr., Willard R. Elmore, James Eugene Anderson, Tommie W. Turner, Ernest Yarborough, Griffin Cooper and James Graham.

FRANK C. NORRIS JR.

Early in 1942, Frank Norris went into the Army Air Corps and graduated as a lieutenant at Ft. Sumner, N.M., in November 1943.

He flew B17s from a base in England to targets in Germany.

On his 31st mission, his plane was shot down but he made it back. He returned to Florence and practiced as a CPA.

★★★★

BOBBY O'HARRA

Robert L. O'Harra would be the first person to tell you that he didn't see any combat in WWII, and he'd also be the first to tell you that was fine by him.

A quarterback at the University of South Carolina, O'Harra interrupted his education in 1942 to enlist in the Army Air Corps. He became a pilot, and it didn't take him long to start flying the most advanced planes of the time. He was such a good pilot that he was selected to be an instructor.

"I was checked out to fly both the B-17 Flying Fortress and the B-29 Super Fortress," O'Harra recalled during an interview at his home. "But by the time I had all of that training, we had already taken Okinawa, Japan."

The Japanese island south of that country's mainland was key to winning the war. It gave the pilots of American long-range bombers a base from which to operate. O'Harra would find himself there, at Kadena Air Base after the Island had been secured following a bitter ground battle. But O'Harra, who loved to fly, would end up in operations, planning bombing missions, which would ultimately force the Japanese to surrender.

Though O'Harra, who was qualified as a flight instructor for both of America's main long range bombers, didn't fly combat missions over Japan, he did get the chance to fly while stationed at Okinawa.

"We had a terrible problem with mosquitoes on Okinawa, and malaria was a real threat," O'Harra explained. "So we had regular spraying missions over the island. We had a crop duster which we used, and I had to fly those missions sometimes."

O'Harra laughed as he told the tale of the "Mission that almost got me killed."

"I was flying one of those spraying missions one day, and I started having engine trouble. I lost my engine and had to crash land the plane on the beach," O'Harra said. "I was trying to make to the air strip, but I just didn't have the altitude to make it. I ended up crashing pretty hard, and it almost killed me."

O'Harra broke his leg badly in that crash, which turned out to be because of some water in his fuel lines.

After the war, O'Harra went back to U.S.C. to complete his bachelor's degree in education. During the Korean Conflict, he was recalled by the United States Air Force as a B-29 pilot and served in the Far East. Mr. O'Harra retired from the United States Air Force as a Major.

A lifelong resident of Florence, Mr. O'Harra owned an insurance agency for 16 years, and was appointed Postmaster by President Lyndon Johnson. He retired from the Postal Service in 1997 after 30 years of service.

Sadly, O'Harra never had the opportunity to see this book in print. He died shortly after this interview, on Sept. 29, 2006.

CHARLIE CLARENCE OSBORNE

Charlie Clarence Osborne served in the Coast Guard aboard the USS Leonard Wood from 1942-45.

JAMES C. OWEN

Called to active duty in the Naval ROTC at the University of South Carolina in 1942, James C. Owen in February 1945 was commissioned as a Navy ensign.

He served in the Pacific aboard the LST 552, which transported Seabees and supplies in the Pacific Theater.

He was released from duty in Hawaii in 1946 and remained in the Naval Reserve until 1952.

★★★★

THOMAS MARVIN OWEN

Thomas Marvin Owen posthumously was awarded the Navy Cross for service aboard the USS Butler in the Pacific. He died in May 1945 of wounds received when a Japanese kamikaze pilot crashed his plane into Owen's ship.

The Navy Cross citation says that he "with resolute fortitude and complete disregard for his critical condition, secured the main steam line and then, proceeding upward through a head of scalding steam, threw open the hatch, enabling the trapped men to escape to the main deck."

During the June 6, 1944 Normandy invasion, Owen was aboard the Butler which supported the landings on Normandy on D-Day.

★★★★

ARTHUR M. PARKER JR.

Arthur M. Parker Jr. of Lake City was described in a Marine history, "Peleliu: Tragic Triumph" by Bill D. Ross. One of Parker's men called him "the most heroic Marine I have ever encountered."

He said that when Marines landed on the island, an invasion Admiral Bull Halsey had opposed, most of the Marines in his unit were pinned down by Japanese fire.

They had been trained to get off the beach, because it was sure eventual death if they remained there. They seemed too stunned to continue, but Parker, then a major, had had his tank stall. He got out and ran around threatening to shoot the Marines himself if they didn't get moving. They did, and he was credited with having saved many of that unit. One believed him to be the only man on his feet on that beach that day.

GENE PARROTT

Gene Parrott was one of the young men from Florence whose education was interrupted by World War II. He was in the Presbyterian College ROTC earlier but went on active duty in the Army on Aug. 9, 1943.

He crossed the English Channel with Co. E, 2nd Battalion, 301st Regiment, 94th Infantry Division about three months after D-Day and fought across Europe, including the Battle of the Bulge, winding up the war in Germany.

Along the way, he picked up a Purple Heart, a Bronze Star with Oak Leaf Cluster, American Campaign Medal, European-African-Middle Eastern Campaign Medal, World War II Victory Medal, Combat Infantryman Badge, Honorable Service Lapel Button and Marksman Rifle Medal.

"He was proudest of the Combat Infantryman's Badge," said his son, Chip Parrott, who said his father did not talk a lot about his experiences but would tell him a little from time to time.

One unusual thing he did, though, was mark passages and add his own personal comments in the margins of a book on the history of the 94th Infantry in World War II. Those offer his own thoughts and evaluations for those who care to dig into them.

At one point in the book margins, he wrote, "What bothered me most during the war was how long will it last and when will I get home, one year or 10 years? During the race to the Rhine, I realized that the war was coming to an end."

It was tough duty. At one time, his company of 180 men had been reduced to 38. It was near Sing, Germany, that he won the Bronze Star. Army records say that Parrott, then a tech sergeant, "led a squad... With two men, he crept around a house while the assistant squad leader with three men set up a base of fire."

They threw grenades into a house occupied by German troops and burst in, finding three killed and taking 12 prisoners. "Because of the courage, initiative and resourceful leadership of Sgt. Parrott, the attack mission was accomplished without further loss," the report said.

During his brief stay in England before crossing to the continent, Parrott told of having seen V-1 buzz bombs hit the London area. He also told of having run into John Albert Howell of Florence while on leave in London.

The 94th after landing on Utah Beach shortly after D-Day was assigned to confine German forces to the Brittany peninsula, isolating them from the main German forces. Then the division moved out to fight across France, whizzing through Paris a little too quickly to do much sightseeing. They finally crossed the Rhine on pontoon bridges and reached Germany.

One thing he told of near the end of the war was the large number of German troops who were rushing from the East to try to surrender to American or British forces and stay out of the hands of the Russians.

He was also much touched by the word in the closing weeks of the war that President Roosevelt had died. He called it a "tremendous burden" to lose the president and felt that he should have been able to see the end of the war. The troops held a commemorative ceremony for FDR in the field.

A strange experience he described was when his unit was fighting through the famous hedgerows of Normandy. He told of hiding behind a wall during a fire fight and sticking his head up to try to see what was going on, only to find himself staring eye to eye with a German solider who was doing the same thing. Both ducked, and neither fired on the other.

Parrott spent several months in Europe after the fighting stopped, then came home as a first sergeant and was discharged on Feb. 3, 1946.

★★★★

REUBEN PATE

Reuben Pate served as a PFC in the Army from 1941-45 in Belgium and Germany.

★★★★

NED WALLACE PATILLO

Ned Wallace Patillo served in the Army Air Corps from 1942 to 1945.

RUDOLPH C. PIERCE

Rudolph Pierce of Timmonsville went into the Army in 1936 and remained through World War II.

He served in South America, France, Belgium, England, Holland and Germany and received the Combat Infantryman's Badge with five battle stars and the Purple Heart.

Pierce served in the Panama Canal Zone, then in the Battle of the Bulge where the enemy overran his outfit's position. He and another solider hid in a haystack for several days behind enemy lines before the Underground helped them link back up with Patton's Army. Most of the rest of their unit had been killed or captured.

★★★★

LYN R. PHILLIPS

Lyn R. Phillips left the Atlantic Coast Line Railroad in Florence in 1942 to join the 757th Railroad Shop Division. He served in France and Germany before returning to the ACL but reentered the service in 1950 and served until 1953 in the Korean War, during which he received a Bronze Star and Purple Heart.

ARCHIE ALLEN PORTER

Archie Allen Porter was a PFC in the Army from 1944-46 in Germany.

LAWRENCE JAMES PORTER

Lawrence James Porter was a Corporal in the Air Force from 1944 until 1945. He served in the States.

OLIN HENDERSON POWELL

Olin Henderson Powell of Hanna served from June 25, 1941 until July 7, 1945 as a TSgt. in the Army Air Force. He was an aerial gunner on B-17's flying out of Bassingbourn and Nuthamstead England.

★★★★

CARLTON PRIDGEN

After going into the Marines in 1943, Carlton Pridgen went to the Pacific in January 1944 with the 18th AAA outfit.

He was with the 1st Marines on Okinawa and then was among the troops who were being prepared to land in Japan and end the war. Fortunately, he said, the atomic bombs convinced the Japanese to call it quits, and the invasion was unnecessary. It saved many lives, maybe a million or more, on both sides, he said, when the war ended without an invasion of Japan.

After V-J Day, he served in China and finally came home in April 1946, and got out, but that did not end his service. He went back in and went to Korea in mid-1951 and in June 1952 was wounded, again with the 1st Marines. He returned to the States and to several naval hospitals, including the one in Charleston. He then served at the weapons depot there and at Camp Lejeune.

He also served in Vietnam starting in August 1970 with the 1st Marine Air Wing and retired from the Corps in December 1973. Along the way, he picked up two Purple Hearts and retired as sergeant major.

Pridgen has been active in veterans' organizations, and was one of the first in the new local organization of Purple Hearts recipients. It is the James Elliott Williams Chapter 1890 of the Military Order of the Purple Heart. It is named for Williams, of Darlington, who received the Medal of Honor for his service in Vietnam.

There are 34 members now, he said, and among them are World War II vets John E. Floyd, Darrell W. Garner, Cuyler L. Jordan, Pridgen, Daniel Rogerson, William Stanton and Major Summerford.

★★★★

ROBERT EUGENE QUARLES

Robert Eugene Quarles served from 1944 to 1946 and was a radar man in the Navy. His ship carried Marines to Iwo Jima, then became a hospital ship and carried wounded from there to Guam. He also served on a geodetic survey ship, plotting ocean depths and making maps.

CHARLES E. RAINES

Charles E. Raines served from 1946 to 1948 and was in occupation forces in Okinawa and Japan. He was from Olanta.

★★★★

JOHN RAINEY

John Rainey was just 15 years old when he walked into an Army recruiter's office and said he wanted to join the war effort. There weren't a lot of opportunities for a young black man in South Carolina at that time, and like most young men of all races, he wanted to serve his country.

He didn't know that he was too young to join, and when the recruiter told him that he had to be at least 17, and had to have his parents' permission to join if he was younger than 18, he asked for the proper paper work to get his parents permission.

"I led him to believe that I'd come back when I was 17, and have my mother's permission," Rainey said.

But that's not what he did. He took the paper to his mother, told her that he'd gone to the recruiter and they needed her to sign the papers for him to join. Then he went to the Navy recruiter, knowing that the Army recruiter would recognize him, and he joined the Navy.

"I had that paper signed by my mother, and they were eager to take me," Rainey recalls. "So at 15, I was in the Navy."

This was the beginning of a long and storied military career for Rainey, but being a black, Rainey's duty were limited to being a steward on the ship. In those days, the highly segregated U.S. military relegated black men to mostly menial tasks, but Rainey still saw the opportunity to serve his country, and better his own life.

"I went to Norfolk, Va. for basic, then we were sent to Pennsylvania, to a ship yard where my ship was being built," Rainey said. "We were there training until the ship was finished."

That ship was the LST 264. A Landing Ship, Tank, LSTs were designed to carry tanks, equipment and soldiers directly to the beach in amphibious landings. They had a very shallow draft, and the bow of the ship opened like a set of doors to allow the quick off-loading of men and the machines of war.

The LST 264 was on its way to history, to participate in the June 6, 1944 D-Day invasion. It would ferry men and equipment from England to the beaches of Normandy, France.

"The noise was unbelievable," Rainey recalls. "Even down below, you could hear the shells coming in as we hit the beach that first day."

Rainey, as a steward, was also assigned the duties of manning a .50 caliber machine gun on the decks of LST 26. When the ship began making its initial run for the beach, loaded to the brim with infantry, tanks and other equipment, he was on the deck, ready to fire on any German aircraft that flew overhead. There weren't many to shoot at.

"No, we had a lot of our own planes in the air," Rainey said.

The noise of the landing, with thousands of Allied ships hitting the beaches simultaneously, shelling from German artillery, and the shelling from Allied ships returning fire, was deafening. So deafening that Rainey and many other men on his ship didn't even notice when the LST 26 hit an anti-ship mine floating in the water.

"There were so many explosions all around you, that the ship hit a mine and no one noticed, except the guys near where it hit," Rainey said. "I was down below, when someone came in and said, 'We hit a mine, we have a big hole in the side.'"

Fortunately, the hole was not big enough to sink the ship. It was a floating mine that the ship hit, and most of the damage to the LST 26 was above the waterline.

"We went back to England, or maybe it was Scotland, and they fixed the ship really quick, and we went back to work," Rainey said. "We shuttled troops and equipment from England to France for about a year after that."

But when the Germans surrendered and the European war was over, the U.S. was still battling the Japanese in the Pacific. Rainey was sent back to Norfolk, Va., where he boarded a destroyer headed to the Pacific.

"We went south to the Panama Canal, then across the Pacific to Hawaii, where we stopped for supplies and to refuel," Rainey said. "While we were there, the war ended."

With the war over, most of the men on Rainey's ship weren't needed anymore, and he was shipped back home, and discharged, but that wasn't the end of Rainey's career in the military.

"I got home and went to school on the G.I. Bill for a while, but I missed the military," Rainey said. "So in 1946, I joined the Army, like I originally planned."

When Rainey joined the Navy, there weren't a lot of jobs black men were allowed to do in the military, but he saw drastic changes over his career. He ended up serving in the infantry in Korea. Later, he became a member of one of the most elite fighting forces in the world when he was selected for the Special Forces, the infamous Green Berets.

"I ended up going to jump school, and then I went to Vietnam, where I served two tours with the Special Forces," Rainey said. "The military was a good career for me, and I enjoyed it very much."

HAROLD P. REEL

Harold P. Reel served as a Petty Officer with the Navy from 1944 until 1948 and was stationed in the South Pacific.

★★★★

DR. GEORGE RICHARDSON

Dr. George Richardson had just finished dental school when he found himself in uniform during the war. With a hospital unit he was shipped to Europe aboard the Queen Elizabeth. "When we went to the dock, the Queen Mary and Queen Elizabeth both were there, and we were waiting to see which one we would go on," he said.

Perhaps his most memorable experience of the war was on the trip over on the Elizabeth. British Prime Minister Winston Churchill was aboard the same ship with a party returning from talks in Washington. Richardson said at meals, Churchill's party sat at a table next to his, but they never visited.

However, "when we reached England, Churchill spoke to the troops. It was striking. We were ready to go fight."

He worked in hospitals in France, and as the war wound down, found himself treating more German POWs than anything else. "They were good patients," Richardson said of the Germans.

IRVIN J. ROGERS

Irvin J. Rogers died of wounds on Christmas Day 1944. It was during the Battle of the Bulge, and in that action, he posthumously was awarded the Silver Star as well as a Purple Heart.

Rogers, who was with the 84th Infantry Division, was buried in the Henri-Chapell U.S. Cemetery in Belgium.

★★★★

JESSE CLIFTON ROGERS JR.

Jesse Clifton Rogers Jr. went into the Navy on Jan. 22, 1944 and was discharged as a machinist mate on May 19, 1946.

He served with a repair unit on Tiburon and at Subic Bay Naval Yard in the Philippines. He was among Navy personnel being moved into place for an invasion of Japan, but the surrender came three days after his departure from the Philippines, and he returned there.

WILLIAM GLAZE ROLLINS

William Glaze Rollins was a Staff Sergeant with the Army Air Force from 1944-46. He was stationed in Italy and flew fifty missions in B24's.

★★★★

JACK RONEY

Jack Roney went to England with the U.S. Army Air Corps early in the war, and he brought back more than memories. He brought back a wife.

He apparently knew it right away. Olwen, his wife, was an English girl who lived near the famous Stonehenge.

As she explained, "I regularly met a girl friend on Wednesdays at a horse farm and went riding. If the weather was bad, we met at a pavilion on the beach at Bournemouth. One Wednesday, it was raining on my side of town but not on hers, so I went to the pavilion and did not find her there."

Three American servicemen were at a table she was accustomed to using, and she accused them of taking her table. They wound up asking her to dance, and she did.

Jack Roney happened to be watching, she said, and told a friend, "That's the girl I'm going to marry."

He asked her to dinner that night, but she declined because she had a Frank Sinatra program to listen to on the radio that night, but soon they became regular weekend companions.

Troops going over for D-Day left from the south coast of England near where she was, and she said the sky was nearly dark with aircraft going over to France on June 6, 1944. Travel was prohibited in the area for a week before the invasion.

They were married just after V-E Day. Roney returned to the U.S. in July, but she had to wait to be shipped over a little later.

"I had never seen the temperature over 80 in England," she said, and the heat here was an unpleasant surprise. There was nearly no air conditioning then, and it took time to get used to it.

★★★★

B.F. ROSE

B.F. Rose of Timmonsville served in the China-Burma-India Theater in World War II. He trained troops in that area to drive Army tanks.

ASBURY SALLENGER

Asbury Sallenger received a Silver Star and a Navy Cross for his actions in the Battle of the Atlantic.

He was a pilot who specialized in anti-submarine warfare and took part in kills of two German submarines. His plane was shot down during action, and his radioman was lost, something his nephew said was "the hardest blow of the war for him."

He also expressed sorrow at having to take enemy lives, according to Walter Wallace Sallenger, a nephew.

Sallenger retired from the Navy as a captain and in 2006 was living in Florida.

★★★★

NICHOLAS SAMRA

On Sept. 19, 1944, Lt. Nicholas Samra was bombardier on a four-engine bomber flying from England to targets at Madgeburg, Germany.

In his detailed, well-written diary of his war experiences, Samra wrote that flak starting rising toward them in Belgium and the bomber beside them was hit and on fire. They dropped their bomb load and turned toward Holland and safety, but soon their plane was hit three times. The pilot shut down one engine.

They left the formation but thought they could make it home. However, the plane soon was hit again and lost another engine. They jettisoned all they could, but steadily were losing altitude.

Soon it was apparent they could not make it to friendly territory. When they bailed out, they were at about 3,000 feet. His diary says that "with a sweet-sounding pop, my chute opened and I floated gently toward Mother Earth."

By chance he came down on an airport, surrounded by angry enemy civilians, but three German NCOs appeared and took him prisoner. He wrote that probably was good because the civilians might have used the picks and shovels they were threatening him with.

Samra had been a kid in Brooklyn but came to Florence as a youth when his mother moved south for her health. She later returned to Brooklyn, but he liked Florence and stayed. He enlisted in the Army Air Corps in June 1942 as an aviation cadet and went on active duty in February 1943.

His wife, Virginia Baroody Samra, joined him during part of his service in the U.S. Then he was shipped to England to serve with the 93rd Group, 409th Squadron.

His diary gives details of his first mission when as they passed Wilhelmshaven, they saw flak for the first time. It did no damage. "It was pretty," he wrote, while far away.

They dropped their bombs on their target, Waggum Airdrome, as the ship lurched through a field of flak. They headed back toward the coast, flew away from the antiaircraft guns, and then had the protection of U.S. fighters who kept the Luftwaffe at bay.

As they approached their base, they realized they had not lost a plane on the mission, and he wrote, "We know now that a man isn't human if he isn't at least a little afraid up there."

Several missions later, he had to bail out and became a POW.

One of the German officers by whom Samra was interrogated after his capture looked strangely familiar to him. After it became clear he was going to give only name, rank and serial number as specified by the Geneva Convention,

they had a conversation. Samra learned the officer once had lived in the U.S. and ran a deli where Samra's mother had shopped in his old Brooklyn neighborhood.

His diary gives a detailed account of life in the prison camp in which he was held near Barth, Germany. All of his bomber crew wound up in the camp, meaning all had survived, which was good news.

The accommodations were not good, and the food was not good, but it was enough to survive. The "wonderful Red Cross" sent packages that occasionally improved their diets and clothing.

Mostly, he showed a positive attitude, but at times bitterness crept into his writings. Once was when Max Schmeling, German boxer who once was world heavyweight champion, visited the camp. Samra was "disgusted at officers asking for his autograph." Schmeling, he wrote, was a Nazi and unworthy of American praise.

Samra had been a prisoner for a little more than three months when the year 1945 arrived, and he said a feature of that New Year's holiday was a drink they concocted with prunes and raisins they had hoarded from recent meals. The fruit was allowed to ferment, and they made a drink they named "Four Raisins." They set up a faux saloon and entertained many of the prisoners. Some wound up drunk.

Life in the camp was not pleasant, but most survived and kept up with news through the BBC. There was much anticipation as the war neared its end and they knew Russian troops were getting close.

The morning of May 1, 1945, the prisoners awakened to find that the German guards had disappeared. The senior officer among the prisoners took command, and they waited for the Russians allies to appear. At 10:15 p.m. they heard vehicles. Russian troops had arrived, and about 15 minutes later, they learned that Hitler was dead. "Never have I seem wilder and more heartfelt rejoicing," Samra wrote.

As part of the organization under which the

prisoners took control, Samra became part of the camp security and had a jolt awaiting him.

They went to a neighboring concentration camp he called filthy where the nearly starved prisoners were mostly German and Polish Jews. The Allies required German civilians from Barth to clean up the place and gave food and medical attention to the inmates who included women and children. They had suffered terrible abuse.

They helped those who were too weak to walk, and Samra wrote, "My manliness left me when a 7-year-old shaver, all skin and bone, gave his dying gasp when I was about to move him."

Meanwhile, the Russians were a little too freely sharing vodka with the Allied prisoners and some drunken former POWs celebrated too vigorously.

On May 12, the first B17 was seen over the camp, and others came to a nearby airfield. The bombers were used as transport planes, and on May 13, Samra flew on a B17 to Rheims, France. Then he genuinely felt his POW days were over.

Mrs. Samra donated his diary to the Eisenhower Center in Kansas, and she had correspondence about it with noted historian Stephen Ambrose, among others.

⭐⭐⭐⭐

Charles Schofield at right.

CHARLES SCHOFIELD

Charles Stikeleather Schofield was stationed in California in the Army before continuing to

New Guinea for service in the Pacific Theater.

He served as a supply sergeant because of the experience he had with the family business.

Besides the experience and decorations for service, he got a case of malaria as did many other Americans in that area and recuperated at home after the war. He was one of many WWII vets who talked very little about his experiences.

⭐⭐⭐⭐

CLAUDE "BO" SCRUGGS

⭐⭐⭐⭐

JAMES ALFRED SELF

James Alfred Self of Florence went into the Army on Aug. 20, 1941, and served with the 157th Infantry, 45th Division. He was in Italy, southern France and Germany.

He received five Bronze Stars with one arrowhead and was discharged on Sept. 28, 1945.

RAY B. SIMS

Ray B. Sims of Olanta was in the largest amphibious landing in the Pacific when the Marines attacked the Japanese island strongholds.

He was in the 6th Marine Division had basic training at Parris Island and combat training at Cherry Point. He served in California and the Philippines before Okinawa.

It was on Sugar Loaf Hill on that island that he was hit by metal from a bomb or hand grenade and received wounds on the right knee and ankles. There were 12,500 Marines killed on Okinawa. He received a Purple Heart.

Sims was taken from there to Guam for treatment. Later he was in China where he sent a 1945 Christmas card to his sister.

THE SMITHS

Dr. George Covington Smith volunteered for Army service in February 1941. He received a commission as first lieutenant and went to Camp Peay, Tenn., which later was renamed Camp Forrest for Confederate Gen. Nathan Bedford Forrest.

Smith helped set up the hospital at his post and was named medical officer for the facility. Then he volunteered for overseas duty and was sent to Puerto Rico to serve was a medical officer with the Army Air Corps.

He served there for two years, three months and was promoted to captain in December 1941 and then to major in April 1942.

At the end of the war, he was serving at Hammer Air Field in California and left active service from there in September 1945. He became a lieutenant colonel in the Reserve.

Probably the main event of his service, though, was in Puerto Rico where he met Lt. June Bockstanz who had volunteered in 1940 for a year's service with the Army. Doctors and nurses had been asked to do a year of service with the armed forces as the troop numbers were built through the first peacetime draft.

On Dec. 10, 1940, she was assigned to Selfridge Field in Mt Clemens, Mich., and "my year was up three days after Pearl Harbor- so I was in," she said.

She volunteered in August 1942 for overseas duty and was sent to an airfield in Puerto Rico. There she met Capt. George Smith. She worked in his ward at the beginning of her duty, and they were married on April 24, 1943. She was discharged in December 1943, more than two years before her new husband.

BOBBY SNIPES

Benjamin R. "Bobby" Snipes joined the Marines early in World War II.

He served in Okinawa and Japan during the war. Then he remained in the National Guard as a sergeant and served more than 30 years total.

★★★★

MILTON AND JOE HARRY SNIPES SR.

Joe Harry Snipes Sr. went into the Army in World War II and had service in three wars.

He served in World War II, was called back for the Korean War and served in Vietnam. Along the way, he received the Purple Heart and Bronze and Silver Stars.

After active and National Guard services in peacetime and three wars, Snipes retired from the service.

WILLIAM CLAYTON SNOW

Torpedoman's Mate, 3rd Class

★★★★

ALEXANDER McTAGGERT SPROTT

★★★★

LAWRENCE B. STANTON

Lawrence B. Stanton served in the Army, starting early in the war. Part of his service was in Europe and he became a Tech 5.

OLSEN RUDOLPH STEELE

Olsen Rudolph Steele served as a Chief Warrant Officer with the Navy from 1943 until his retirement in 1964. During the War, he was involved with both the Atlantic and Pacific Fleets as well as the European-African Campaign.

★★★★

DWIGHT L. STEWART SR.

Stewart (middle) stands in front of headquarters in Nara, Japan

Dwight L. Stewart served from 1941 to 1946. He became a sergeant in the 923rd Field Artillery, 98th Division.

JOSEPH FRANK STOKES JR.

Joseph Franklin Stokes won Aerial Gunnery Wings in Laredo, Texas, then was promoted to sergeant and joined a B24 bomber crew.

He went to Foggia, Italy in March 1944 with the 15th Air Force, 451st Bomb Group, 725th Squadron. As tail gunner, he flew 50 missions, hitting targets in the Balkans, northern Italy and southern France. He received the Air Medal with four Oak Leaf Clusters, European Theater Ribbon with Five Battle Stars, Presidential Unit Citation and Good Conduct Medal.

Stokes returned to the U.S. in August 1944 and served as an instructor in Laredo and at Ft. Myers, Fla.

★★★★

W.H. STOKES

W.H. Stokes served as a Major with the Army Air Corps from 1941 until 1945. He was stationed in England and Libya.

HENRY GRADY STONE

★★★★

CHARLES STRANGE

Charles Strange was a Sergeant with the Army from 1941 until 1945 in France and Germany.

★★★★

CHARLES WELDON STREETT

Charles W. Streett served with the U.S. Navy Seabees. He was in the service from Sept. 8, 1942 to Nov. 11, 1945, and served in the Pacific Theater.

ERNEST STREETT

Ernest H. Streett was a Navy communication officer and served at Pearl Harbor and the Asiatic Pacific Theater. He went in on June 27, 1944 and was discharged on Dec. 16, 1945.

★★★★

JIM STREETT

When Jim Streett finished Florence High School in 1943, young men knew they were headed for the service, and he enlisted and qualified for Navy flight school.

He did his flight training at Pensacola and was stationed at several other places briefly before being shipped to England. From the air, Streett looked for German submarines that, when spotted, were then attacked by the Navy.

"I was not in England long," Streett said. "I went briefly to North Africa and then the South Pacific. That was where I spent most of my time." One thing he remembers about the German U-boats was that sometimes when under attack, they shot clothing and other debris through the torpedo tubes. "They hoped that we would see that and think they had been sunk while they hid way down hoping we would go away," he said.

WILLIAM L. "BILL" STREETT

William L. Streett went into the Army in 1941 and made it a career, retiring in October 1966.He was in the Signal Corps and served in Germany, Okinawa, Korea, Canada and the U.S.

ARTHUR M. STRICKLAND II

When the nation began to mobilize for World War II, Arthur M. Strickland II was a lieutenant in the Florence National Guard unit. The unit was activated and went to Fort Moultrie in Charleston Harbor where coastal artillery defense was set up.

Later he was transferred to an engineering unit, and died of wounds on D-Day during the Normandy landing.

★★★★

KENNETH SUMMERFORD

Kenneth Summerford of Florence was one of the early ones who volunteered and served aboard a destroyer in the Pacific during the war.

A harrowing experience for him was when a Japanese kamikaze crashed into his ship during a battle. He was wounded when that happened, but not badly. He was moved to a hospital ship and treated after the battle, and he remembered being housed with another man who had

very bad wounds. He helped the medical personnel watch out for the man who he thought probably did not survive.

Summerford had been lucky because the kamikaze crashed into a gun emplacement where he had been serving. He had just been reassigned to another gun station before the crash occurred and probably would not have made it if he had been at his previous station.

After the war, he went to the University of South Carolina and its law school. He later served as solicitor for the 12th Judicial Circuit.

MAJOR SUMMERFORD

Major Summerford had an unfortunate name for a young Marine recruit at Parris Island.

"They did give me a hard time about it," Summerford said of his name, not his rank. "But it wasn't too bad. I guess it was just kind of funny to hear 'Private Major Summerford.'"

Summerford doesn't like to talk too much about his experiences during WWII, and he's quick to change the subject from his experiences to those of other people he calls heroes. An infantryman, Summerford carried a BAR, a Browning Automatic Rifle, at Okinawa during one of the bloodiest battles of the war.

Okinawa was one of the last Japanese controlled islands taken near the end of the war. The Japanese Army, defeated at one island after another, dug in deep at Okinawa, and they fought to the death. Summerford and his buddies had to clear out areas where those Japanese soldiers had dug themselves in, and it was tough fighting.

"They were tough," Summerford said. "They fought to the death, which made it hard, because you had to kill them, you couldn't just force them to surrender, because they wouldn't." Summerford ended up getting shot in the leg at Okinawa, but again, when he talks about his injuries he ends up talking about other heroes he met in Okinawa, some of whom he knew before the war began.

Summerford grew up with the Snipes boys, Bobby, Milton and Joe. When he signed up for the Marine Corps, he did with his buddy Bobby Snipes, and the two went off to Parris Island together for boot camp. They also ended up in the same place, Okinawa. Milton also joined the Marines, and he also ended up in Okinawa. Summerford would occasionally see the two brothers, particularly Bobby, because their units were near each other often during the battle for Okinawa.

Joe Snipes was a Sergeant in the Army, and ended up serving in Europe, earning several decorations.

★★★★

WILLIAM D. TALLEVAST JR.

1st Lt. William D. Tallevast Jr. of Florence flew over "The Hump," as a flight over the Himalayas was called, 26 times during the war. Their missions were to supply Chiang Kai-Shek and his Chinese Nationalists in their fight against Japanese invaders. All told, Tallevast had 310 combat hours and 26 missions over Japan.

According to 1945 news reports, he was flying as bombardier aboard a B26 that was hit by gunfire during a mission over Japan. He was forced to bail out, fortunately over Free China, where he broke a rib on landing but was in friendly territory.

In February 1945, Tallevast was home on leave, bringing along a Distinguished Flying Cross and Air Medal with Oak Leaf Cluster.

★★★★

WILLIAM P. TALLON JR.

After going into the Army in the early 1940s, Col. William P. Tallon Jr. served in World War II, Korean War and the Vietnam War.

Among his assignments during a career that ended in 1972, Tallon at one time served as commander of the 101st Airborne Division Artillery. He also was chief of staff of the 101st during the Vietnam War.

He received bachelors and masters degrees from George Washington University and later came to Florence as registrar at Francis Marion University after retirement. He helped make expansion of the National Cemetery in Florence a reality.

During his Army career, Col. Tallon was deputy commander of the John F. Kennedy Center for Assistance and Special Forces. He was an instructor at the Command and General Staff College and the War College.

He died in January 2007.

★★★★

KENNETH M. THOMAS

Kenneth M. Thomas was a Boatswain's Mate with the Navy C.B.'s from 1943 until 1946. He served in Guadalcanal and Tulaqi in the Southwest Pacific.

CARL A. THOMPSON

Carl A. Thompson was drafted and trained in Bakersfield, Calif., where he met movie stars and a prominent fortuneteller who told him some things he said came true.

He was a Tech. 5 with Battery. A, 572nd AAA, 12th Armored Division and was in a half-track crew that shot at enemy aircraft. He said once they saw a column of German soldiers headed back to Germany and their commander ordered them not to fire at them. He considered the C.O. a compassionate man.

He was wounded near Worms, Germany and received the Purple Heart. He was discharged in October 1945.

JAMES "BUDDIE" TIMMONS

James "Buddie" Timmons was a TH Sergeant with the Army from 1942 until 1944 in the European Theater.

ROBERT "BOB" TIMMONS

Robert "Bob" Timmons served as a Sergeant with the Army in France from 1940 until his death in 1942.

✰✰✰✰

DON HOMER TOMLINSON

Don Homer Tomlinson of Olanta was in the Navy from Jan. 21, 1943 until Nov. 10, 1945. He served in North Africa and then in the Pacific, including time in Saipan, the Marshalls and the Gilberts.

✰✰✰✰

RODGERS TOMLINSON

Five young men from the Olanta area went into the service together shortly after Pearl Harbor. They were brothers Rodgers and Cotton Tomlinson, brothers Presley and

William Frick and Allison Cousar.

Rodgers Tomlinson was a Marine who served through the island hopping of the South Pacific and had lost touch with his brother, Cotton. Then during a firefight on one island, he leaped into a foxhole with a couple of other guys, only to look up after he got himself together to find his brother, Cotton.

He told later of how much letters form people back home had helped. In fact, he carried a small Bible that an Olanta friend sent him throughout the war. And he had the seasickness on long troopship voyages that many men reported.

Despite all of the hardships of Marine activity in the Pacific brought, one pleasant thing was the people in Australia, who he said, warmly welcomed the American troops.

★★★★

RYAN EUGENE TOMLINSON

Ryan Eugene Tomlinson went into the Army on June 10, 1942, and served in England, France, Belgium and Germany.

Tomlinson was wounded in action and also was a prisoner of war from December 19, 1944 until May 8, 1945. He left the service Feb. 1, 1947.

BILL TRULUCK

Bill Truluck came out of Clemson College as a second lieutenant early in World War II and wound up serving 40 months in the Pacific.

After training in Hawaii, he went to Australia, then to New Guinea where the Allies started turning Japanese forces back.

They fought up through the Philippines, and he was on the beach when Gen. Douglas MacArthur landed on his promised return to the Philippines.

"I was in a city near the beach when I learned I might meet MacArthur back at the beach," he said. He went back and was there when MacArthur stepped off his landing craft into knee-deep water. "I didn't even get wet when I landed," Truluck said.

Truluck got to meet the famous general and talked with him. The general made a little speech, he said, thanking the troops on hand for their efforts in the campaign.

A captain, Truluck had been a company commander and later became a battalion commander and was due for promotion when he returned home.

He said he had his orders with his boat number and location on the boat for a landing on the Japanese home islands. However, when the atomic bomb drop was planned, the top brass knew the end was near, and Truluck got a chance to come home. He thought he might have been the first officer from the area to return to the States.

He took the chance to return home and was in San Francisco on V-J Day.

FREDIS TRULUCK

Fredis Truluck of Olanta served in the Navy from December 1942 to April 1946. He served in China.

★★★★

LOUIS F. TRULUCK

Louis F. Truluck served in the Navy aboard the USS Fargo and USS Portsmouth. They were mostly in the eastern Mediterranean, and he said on two occasions a three-star admiral was aboard his ships.

He said the only actual action he saw was in Naples, but they were the first U.S. ship to call in a small Turkish port.

WILMONT M. TRULUCK

Wilmont M. Truluck of Olanta went into the Army Air Force on Sept. 5, 1942. He served in the Pacific with a fighter and light bomber squadron. He became a sergeant and was discharged on Feb. 5, 1946.

ERNEST LEE TUCKER

Ernest Lee Tucker served as a PFC in the Army from 1943-45 in the European Theatre.

JULIAN VARNELLE TURBEVILLE

Julian V. Turbeville of Olanta was with Company C, 319th Medical Bn., serving from 1943 to 1946. He was in France, Germany, Luxemburg and Belgium, including the Battle of the Bulge.

THOMAS EDGAR TURBEVILLE

Thomas Edgar Turbeville Jr. of Olanta went into the Army Aug. 9, 1941 and became a Tech 4. He served in England, France, Luxembourg and Germany. He was discharged Sept. 19, 1945.

BILL TYSON

William B. "Bill" Tyson of Florence was in the Davidson College Class of 1942. He enlisted in the Navy just after Pearl Harbor and went directly from Davidson to midshipmen school at Columbia University.

"There were some Florence people there," he said, "including Nick Zeigler and Ray Parrott. The most famous person in that class was Herman Wouk who later wrote 'The Caine Mutiny'." It was an interesting place to go to school and an interesting time to be in New York. After that, he went on to training in Chesapeake Bay with underwater demolition teams of the type that later became known as SEALS.

Tyson shipped out to the South Pacific and was among early arrivals there as the United States started the long haul across the Pacific toward the Japanese home islands.

He served on four ships, the Custer, the El Dorado, the LCI(G) 471 and the Chilula. Probably the action highlight of Tyson's time in the Pacific came when the LCI(G) 471 was involved in paving the way for Marines to land on Iwo Jima.

"We went in two days before the big landing and underwater demolition men went to the beach to eliminate obstacles as much as they could and make it easier for the landing force." In fact, he said, they left a "Welcome to Iwo Jima" sign for the Marines to find when they landed two days later.

The small boats made one sweep near the beach to drop off underwater demolition teams like today's SEALS and returned for another sweep to pick them up.

The small landing type craft were targets of a ferocious Japanese attack from shore. They received heavy fire, and on the second sweep artillery or mortars hit Tyson's ship. The craft had to come to the aid of each other and fight their way back into the open sea. Being hit, Tyson's ship suffered seven killed and 13 wounded of a crew of 66. The group received a Presidential Unit Citation, Tyson said, and one of the crewmen in the 10-boat group received the Medal of Honor.

Some Japanese mistook Tyson's group's softening up job for the planned invasion of Iwo, and when the underwater demolition team ships withdrew, some Japanese thought they had halted the invasion. Tokyo Rose, he said, reported that the American landings at Iwo Jima had been repelled.

On the actual invasion day his ship joined those that bombarded the beach just before the landing. The battleships and cruisers were farther out to sea, but the smaller ships like his were closest to shore and easier targets for artillery fire from shore.

A highlight of that engagement that must have had many highlights was when Tyson saw the famous flag on Mount Suribachi. "It was the second flag, the one they made the famous picture of," he said. "In fact, I met Joe Rosenthal, the photographer, later."

Thinking back on it, he said, "It was tragic what happened to those men who put the flag up in that picture. Some were killed, others wounded and others wound up back home as alcoholics."

Among his unusual experiences during the war, one that stands out was when he was assigned to carry officer messenger mail. "They gave me all of these sets of plans and orders to carry to various commanders. Two enlisted men went with me, and we traveled by air, PT boats and jeep around a big area.

"The material was so secret it had to be carried by hand to individual commanders, and they told me delivery of those orders was vital to the war plans. A delay of 12 hours would impede the war effort, they said."

When they set out to make the deliveries, they had the highest travel priority to get from place to place. After they were delivered, he had little travel priority to return. "I guess that material was more important than I was," he said.

After the war ended, Tyson was part of the occupation forces in Japan. One highlight of that, he said, was visiting the harbor from which much of the Japanese fleet started their trip to the Pearl Harbor attack in 1941. "The Japanese were cooperative. There was no trouble," Tyson said, and he credited letting the emperor remain and Gen. Douglas MacArthur's handling of the occupation for that success. Also while in Japan, he was assigned to go to China to take supplies to the nationalist army of Chiang kai-Shek "We took guns, and ammunition to Tsingtao," he said.

He served as executive officer of the Chilula from August 1945 to April 1946. Then he returned home, went to law school at the University of South Carolina and practiced law. He also stayed in the Naval Reserve. During the war he had started as an apprentice seaman, then midshipman, served as ensign, lieutenant (jg) and lieutenant and later in the Naval Reserve as lieutenant commander.

DUNCAN W. TYSON

Duncan W. Tyson of Florence trained in artillery after joining the Army on March 17, 1943. He served with several units before winding up in England and preparing for combat on the continent.

When his outfit shipped from England to France on Christmas Eve 1944, a ship carrying part of his 66th Infantry was torpedoed, and they lost 69 men from his company. All told, he learned 700 were lost when that ship sank. They shipped up near the front on 40 and 8 boxcars and replaced another division that was pulling back for a rest. It was a cold, snowy holiday period for his outfit with intermittent exchange of fire with Germans.

After the German surrender, Tyson was assigned to Special Services in Vienna.

JAMES ISSAC VAUSE

James Isaac Vause of Timmmonsville was in the first wave of troops landing on Normandy on D-Day. He had enlisted on Jan. 2, 1941 and was discharged Aug. 21, 1945.

Vause was a machine gunner with the 4th Infantry Division, and was wounded in France. He received the Bronze Star, Purple Heart and Combat Infantry Badge.

He died April 17, 2006, after 67 years of marriage to Frances Saverance Vause.

MARION L. "JACK" WEATHERFORD

Marion L. "Jack" Weatherford served as an Army Ambulance Driver in the Phillipine Islands and Japan in 1945 and 1946.

JOE WEBB

Joe Webb of Florence went into the Army at 18 in late 1944. He trained at Camp Blanding, Fla., and went through Ft. Ord, Calif., before shipping to New Guinea.

Sent to the Philippines, Webb became a company clerk on Cebu as his unit prepared to invade Japan. However, Japan surrendered, and Webb joined occupation forces in that country.

T.W. WEBB

T.W. Webb was in the Navy from Nov. 13, 1942 to Feb. 26, 1946. He served in both the Atlantic and Pacific.

EMMITTE WELLS

Emmitte G. Wells of Florence figured in early 1941 that military service was in his future, and he wanted to fly. World War II had started in Europe. The U.S. already had a draft, and it was looking increasingly likely that we would become involved.

His best chance to fly, he decided, was in Canada. He went there and was accepted July 12, 1941, into a program from which he emerged as a Royal Canadian Air Force fighter pilot. Later Wells switched to flying multi-engine bombers.

He became a flying officer with the RCAF and served in England with them. While there, Wells was transferred to the U.S. Army Air Corps, where he became a first lieutenant and finally a captain.

One of the reasons he had been in Canada was the Army Air Corps required a college degree to be a pilot, which he did not have. The Canadian services gave him the chance to get into flight school.

As a U.S. bomber pilot, with the 407th Squadron, 92nd Bomber Group, 8thAir Force, he flew raids over the continent until Aug. 12, 1943.

That day, according to his flight records, Wells' plane had dropped its bombs near Gelsenkirchen in the Rhur when it was hit by flak and attacked by German fighter planes. The numbers 1 and 3 engines were lost, he reported, and he was forced to crash land the plane at Anaus, Germany. Before the crew could make much headway in trying to make their way to friendly territory, they were captured and began nearly two years as prisoners of war.

His daughter, Ann Baldwin of Darlington, has a cup and a recipe book he brought back from the prison camp. The prisoners had much time on their hands and actually took up hobbies of one sort or another to pass time. He made the cup and a metal recipe book cover from discarded cans.

"He said they sat around exchanging recipes and dreaming of eating good food. He wrote dozens of those recipes down and put them in this booklet," she said.

During much of their time, the prisoners tried to figure out ways to escape. They went to work digging a tunnel starting from underneath the stove in one barracks and under a fence about 150 feet away. It was a little like in the movie Stalag 17.

The day before the escape attempt was planned, the Germans thwarted the plot. They might have known for some time it was underway, he believed.

Wells said later it might have been a good thing they were caught before escaping because he learned later the Germans had shot escapees about that time.

One memorable incident as a prisoner was when Wells and his comrades were moved from one camp to another, and they had to march a long distance in snow, nearly freezing.

They stopped for the night in a church where Wells and some others went into a bal-

133

cony behind the altar. He noticed an electric heater off at the side and decided to plug it into a socket and try it. It worked, and the men dried their socks and warmed themselves. It might have saved some from frostbite.

The American prisoners, who organized themselves enough to have reunions later in America, remembered and in 1978, they donated stain glass windows to the German church.

Life as prisoners of war was not easy, of course. The food was not good but was enough, and Red Cross packages helped from time to time. Wells said, however, their treatment was consistent with the terms of the Geneva Conventions. After the war, the prisoners had some of the German guards flown over to their reunions in the United States.

As the war neared its end, Patton's 3rd Army freed prisoners at Moosburg. Wells said he saw Patton ride by on a tank.

He was released from the service on Jan. 6, 1946, having served in two countries' armed forces, flying in combat and spending time as a prisoner of war.

JAMES DOUGLAS WELSH

James Douglas Welsh of Olanta went into the Navy in June 1943. Part of his service was in Charleston, but also in California and the Aleutian Islands.

HAROLD G. "NIG" WHITE

Harold G. "Nig" White was a one-time assistant football coach at Florence High School who became a naval aviator and served in the Pacific.

He also was immortalized in literature. Capt. Ted Lawson, one of the Army Air Corps flyers in the famous Doolittle raid on Tokyo early in the war, roomed with White aboard the aircraft carrier, USS Hornet. The book followed the Hornet as it steamed toward Japan carrying Doolittle's Army bombers for a surprise raid on the Japanese capital, staged to boost U.S. morale and to make the point to the Japanese that they were not invulnerable.

Lawson called White "a big, hearty fellow" in his famous book, "Thirty Seconds Over Tokyo," which also became a successful movie. When the Doolittle party took off from the carrier, White helped Lawson carry his personal things up to the plane. The book says that after the crews got into the planes, White came up to shake hands and wish Lawson and his crew well.

White died in a plane crash near the end of the war.

★★★★

JAMES H. WHITEHURST

James H. Whitehurst Jr. went to radio school in Madison, Wis., and then served in Calcutta, India. A staff sergeant, he was in charge of his unit until the job was taken over by the British government.

WILLIAM HARRY WHITLOCK

William Harry Whitlock was a Staff Sergeant in the Air Force from 1944-46 in England.

★★★★

THE WILHOITS

There were 11 children in the Wilhoit family in Florence, six daughters and five sons.

They had the distinction, the American Legion said, of being the South Carolina family that had the most members in the armed forces during World War II. All of the sons and one of the daughters were in uniform.

The American Legion gave them an award in 1947 for that service. There is a picture at the old American Legion Hut in Florence of the five who were at home. One was still in the service in Germany.

L to R, Clarence Richmond, Clarence E. Jr., Monty, Charleton, and Cecil T. Wilhoit.

A couple of them worked with Wilhoit Steel Erectors in Florence, and they had contracts to build aircraft hangars at bases in the Southeast. By 1943, steel was scarce, and the Wilhoits had built their last hangar, which happened to have been at the old Florence Army Air Field, now Gilbert Field, the city's commercial airport. Clarence Richmond Wilhoit had worked on the hangar in Florence, and then went into the Army as a lieutenant. That was early in 1943, and he was the last of the siblings to put on a uniform.

He went into the combat engineers and was assigned to the Air Transport Command. Then he went to the 3rd Air Force Command England. He trained for and became a bombardier navigator and was prepared for European combat in an A26.

However, Germany surrendered, and he then trained for combat against the Japanese in the Pacific, but the Japanese soon surrendered. He was in from April 1943 to November 1945. Cecil T. Wilhoit had worked with Richmond until early in 1943 and then preceded him into service, joining the Navy.

He became a chief petty officer and served aboard repair ships that worked in the Pacific Theater, repairing damaged ships and returning them to battle. The Wilhoits put their construction and engineering background to good use in the military. He served from Jan. 28, 1943, until June 24, 1946.

Clarence E. Wilhoit Jr. enlisted in the Navy. He served aboard minesweepers in the Pacific and North Atlantic. He became a first class petty officer and was in uniform from April 27, 1942, to October 14, 1946.

PFC Monty Rae Wilhoit served in the Marines during their march across the Pacific toward Japan. One of his battles was in the invasion and occupation of Iwo Jima. He served from February 21, 1942, to Sept. 30, 1946.

Their sister, Charleton Wilhoit, enlisted in the Navy WAVES. She became an aviation machinist mate second class and trained in Atlanta and Cedar Rapids, Iowa, before being stationed at Barbers Point Naval Station in Hawaii.

She became active in local politics in Virginia after the war and served as mayor of Newsome, Va., where she settled after the war. Her military service was from May 9, 1942, to September 1947.

Ezekiel Quintus Wilhoit saw combat in Germany and rose to the rank of master sergeant. He stayed there to serve in the occupation and rebuilding of that nation after the war. He was in the Army from Feb. 28, 1942, to Dec. 12, 1948.

While his first siblings were at a dinner in their honor at the Florence American Legion Hut in 1947, he was still serving in Germany.

★★★★

JOHN WALTER "JACK" WILKINSON

Lt. John Walter "Jack" Wilkinson led a rifle platoon at Ft. McLellan, Ala., for nine months, teaching infantry tactics and weapons use. Then he served for 11 months in the Asiatic Pacific Theater in the Philippines. For a time he was a superintendent in Manila.

Wilkinson went on active duty in February 1944 and served until Aug. 24, 1946. He was called back in for Korean War duty between December 1950 and June 1952, when he was released from active duty as a captain.

TOMMY AND BOBBY WOLFE

There were a number of Florence brother combinations who served in the U.S. armed forces during World War II. Among them were Tommy and Bobby Wolfe, who were in the Navy.

Tommy, the older, came out of Florence High School in 1943 and joined up. He served aboard the USS Marquette and came home with the American Area Medal, Euro-African Mideast Medal, Asiatic Pacific Medal and Victory Medal.

Bobby went in later and was in when the war ended. He must have had a good time because his sister, Ann Ayres, has a picture of him clowning in the Pacific.

Tommy brought back a picture of himself made at the Parthenon in Athens during the war. Years later on a visit to Athens, he had a picture made in the same place -- by the same photographer.

The brothers were released from the Navy as seamen first class.

FREDERICK E. WOOD

Frederick E. Wood was a Tech. Sergeant in the Marines from 1942-46 in the Pacific Theatre and was involved in the Battle at Iwo Jima.

RENTZ WOODRUFF

On Dec. 14, 1942, Rentz Woodruff went into the Marines, and he was involved in some of the heaviest fighting of the war.

The Americans landed on Jan. 31, 1944, and it was the easiest of Woodruff's campaigns. Nine days were required, and the Japanese had 3,561 killed, compared to 312 Marines killed and 502 wounded.

Saipan was much harder, and Woodruff said the Japanese counterattacked the day after the landing to try to drive them into the sea. There were 50,000 Marines against 30,000 defenders.

It was on Saipan that he said he jumped into a foxhole with a buddy who lost a leg in an explosion. They also learned that a picture of missing flyer Amelia Earhart was found on the island, and they speculated that she had been taken to Japan before the war.

Then he was in the landing on Tinian where the 4th Marine Division faked a landing on one side of the island before the 2nd Division landed on two small beaches on the other side. Japanese resistance was broken that night when they launched an unsuccessful counterattack.

On Iwo Jima, he said planners expected a three-day operation and it took 26 bloody days. He called it "the bloodiest Pacific battle of the war."

The Japanese had about 22,000 men on the island, and only about 200 surrendered. He said some troops and civilians jumped off a cliff on the island to avoid capture because they so feared the American cruelty they had been warned about.

★★★★

ED YOUNG

Edward L. Young was brought up on a farm between Florence and Timmonsville. He graduated from Florence High School and from Clemson College in 1941.

War clouds were rising during his years of schooling, and soon after Young finished Clemson, he found himself in the U.S. Army Air Corps. There would be no separate Air Force until after World War II. He went through flight training, and early in the war he found himself headed for the South Pacific.

He had trained to and became a fighter pilot. First he flew P39s, a sleek, one-engine plane with a pointed nose that had the engine behind the pilot. If the engine quit, the pilot needed to get out in a hurry, he said. Then he flew P38s, a twin engine, twin-fuselage fighter-bomber that was one of the glamour planes of World War II.

"It carried 1,000 pound bombs in addition to its capability as a fighter plane," Young said. They often carried wing tanks that lengthened the planes' range. But if they found themselves in combat with Japanese fighters, they needed to get rid of the wing tanks to increase their maneuverability. "They were fine planes."

There was a sea lane called "The Slot," which Japanese ships went down to bring and supply troops as they threatened Australia. U.S. forces wanted to go the other way to start their march across Pacific islands toward Japan. When Young arrived in the South Pacific early in 1942, everything had gone Japan's way in the war. They had attacked Pearl Harbor, captured islands and moved down through the East Indies.

When they reached New Guinea, they were only one island away from Australia. It was believed, probably correctly, that if the Japanese could establish a presence in Australia, it might take years to get them out of there, let alone make progress toward the Japanese home islands.

Young was brought into the American effort to stop the Japanese short of Australia and turn them back toward home. He was with the 67th Fighter Squadron, 13th Air Force.

Young flew 196 missions and was credited with one sure kill of a Japanese airplane. If they had lost New Guinea, Australia would have been open to Japanese invasion, and much of Young's career in the Army Air Force was devoted to seeing that the Japanese did not enjoy that success. Then his time was largely involved in the Allied effort to drive the enemy from Guadalcanal and New Guinea.

Once the Japanese were turned back from Australia and New Zealand, he said, the U.S. started out taking islands for strategic purposes. Some were bypassed. "They could cut them off from supplies" and just leave enemy troops to either be irrelevant or surrender.

Young was not assigned there but saw Australia during R&R periods and said, "It was beautiful country."

As he headed home near the end of the war, Young said he flew over a U.S. invasion fleet headed toward the Marianas. "It was the most ships I ever saw," he said.

The whole World War II experience was a difficult one with lots of death and destruction, but "it was a great experience. I made good friends and have a lot of memories."

Flying has stayed with him. Now in his mid-80s, Young is still flying. "I have a Cessna 182 that I still fly, and I love it," he said.

He has been active since the war, too. He took over the family farming interests between Florence and Timmonsville, largely as a dairy farmer, and served for a time as president of Coble Dairies, a cooperative that processed and furnished milk for consumers in the Southeast. He also became interested in politics and in the late 1950s was elected to the S.C. House of Representatives. Later he served in Congress from the 6th Congressional District when it still was a Pee Dee district.

★★★★

GIVENS YOUNG

On Aug. 3, 1944, Army 2nd Lt. J. Givens Young, spent his 23rd birthday landing on Utah Beach on the coast of France. Young,

commanding a platoon of 40 soldiers in the 80th Infantry Division, would go on to fight through the German lines. Within a year he was commanding a company, more than 200 people, all the while keeping in his mind that his first job was to keep as many of his men alive as he could.

"I always tried to get the mission accomplished without getting my men killed," Young said, reflecting on the 60th anniversary of the end of World War II. "Sometimes it didn't happen that way, and people got killed."

The weight of responsibility carried by Young was tremendous and he knew it, even at such a young age.

"I was responsible for the lives of 200 people," Givens said. "That was more responsibility than I ever had for the rest of my life."

The sense of responsibility carried over into Young's civilian life after the war, when he came home to run his father's small pecan business. Young quickly transformed the small family business into the world's largest pecan shelling company, which eventually garnered over 70 percent of the world's pecan market.

"When I came back, I brought some of that experience with me," Young said. "Opened the plant at 6 a.m. and closed it at midnight every night. I worked like that for about three years, and at the end of that time I had a fully mechanized plant."

Years after the war, Young was convinced by his family to record his WWII experiences for future generations.

"My grandfather was in the Confederate Army, but we never knew where he was, or what he did," Young said. "My children and grandchildren thought it would be a good idea to put it all down, so I hired a ghost writer to help me write a book about my experiences."

Young ended up self publishing a hard back book for his family, so that they would have a history of his experiences, from the day he decided to turn down an offer to attend medical school to fight in Europe, to the day he got home. In between those events he got married, started a family and lived through the most horrifying moments of his life.

"We were in Patton's Army, so we were always on the attack, and when you're on the attack, you're out in the open getting shot at," Young said. "We lost a lot of people. I was seeing people killed all the time, young boys with their heads blown off, their legs blown off."

"Experience like that builds a bond between men that is always there," Young said. "It's a bond you can't break."

Of the 200 soldiers in Young's company during the war, only 25 returned home. Young said only about five of the veterans in his unit are still alive. He said the reunions are joyous occasions; where men who survived the worst that mankind has to offer get together to celebrate the good in their lives.

"We never tell any horror stories," Young said. "We tell stories that now, 60 years later, have a lot of humor to them. They might not have been so humorous when they happened, but with time you tend to find the humor in things."

★★★★

NICK ZEIGLER

E.N. "Nick" Zeigler of Florence came out of the University of the South in 1942 and went into the Navy. He served through World War II as a naval officer and was released in 1946 and went to Harvard Law School.

He served on four aircraft carriers, the USS Ranger, Cabot, Cape Gloucester and Siboney in the Atlantic and Pacific during his active duty and remained in the reserve in which he became a Navy captain.

Zeigler later practiced law and served in both houses of the Legislature before being Democratic candidate for the U.S. Senate in 1970.

★★★★

Florence County members of what Tom Brokaw called "The Greatest Generation" came back from the war and directed their talents to civilian life.

One unexpected veteran to turn up in Florence after World War II was Sad Sack. The cartoon character that had boosted soldiers' morale during the war while also giving voice to their frustrations with the military bureaucracy, wound up a Florentine, sort of.

Fred Rhoads, a veteran and cartoonist who was a principal creator of the Sad Sack cartoon strips after the war, lived in Florence for years afterwards and did his cartoon work from here. Sad Sack even enlisted in things like the Florence United Way drive, boosting the local effort in special cartoons, before Rhoads moved on to Arizona in the 1960s.

Our part of The Greatest Generation raised families, built, created and served. They made the world better than they found it, and they won't be forgotten.

THEY LIVE WITH US IN GRATEFUL MEMORY
OF THEIR SACRIFICE
WORLD WAR II

JOHN HENRY ISENHOWER
WILLIAM JAMES MAXWELL, Sr.
HENRY GRADY STONE, Jr.
ARTHUR MORRISON STRICKLAND
DALLAS KEEFE
KIRKLAND STEWART
ERNEST HUTCHINSON
ROBERT BURROWS, Jr.
BENJAMIN R. EASTERLING, Jr.
HERBERT GREGG EASTERLING
JAMES M. FIELDS
HARRY B. GOODSON, Jr.
CHARLETON HOLLADAY
CHURCHILL A. MARVIN
HERMAN J. GERDES, Jr.
GEORGE EDWIN FURMAN

WILLIAM M. McLEOD
THEODORE L. McLENDON
GEORGE R. MIMS, Sr.
A. RAYMOND SELLERS, Jr.
HAROLD (NIG) WHITE
C. JACKSON GASQUE, Jr.
DAVID E. LAWSON, Jr.
C. RAYMOND MEDLIN, Jr.
FRANCIS M. RAIN
WILLIAM WALKER GARDINER
TRACY HOWARD JACKSON
MASON BACOT ROGERS
WILLIAM MILLING ROYALL
W. E. (SONNY) STAFFORD
M. F. (JACK) SCHNIBBEN, Jr.

ERECTED BY WOODLAND GARDEN CLUB

Woodland Garden Club Memorial at Mount Hope Cemetery

★ ★ ★ ★

CHAPTER TEN:

Lest We Forget

I have given a lot of thought in recent years to the importance of World War II and how well younger people understand what it was all about.

On a trip for Slovakia several years ago, we visited a former concentration camp that the Nazi Germans had used to try to "cleanse" Europe of those they considered undesirable. They included lots of people, for instance gypsys and homosexuals, but mostly Jews. The brutality and lack of empathy for other humans is frightening.

It was part of what led me to produce this book. "Lest We Forget," we want to remind later generations of the importance of that war and also of the parts that people from Florence played.

Following are some of the photos I brought back from that concentration camp, hoping that they will help younger people with a connection to Florence understand how big the WWII stakes were and why it was essential for us to have won that war.

In these camps, people were imprisoned, starved, sometimes worked to death and other times just put to death with such chilling efficiency. America must always stand against such tyranny. We must never forget what we fought against.

Photos taken by Hal Campbell in Slovakia.

Billy Campbell

**Birkineau
Train Track**

Auschwitz Gallows

"MUSIMY UWOLNIĆ NIEMIECKI NARÓD
OD POLAKÓW, ROSJAN, ŻYDÓW I CYGANÓW"
OTTO THIERACK
/MINISTER SPRAWIEDLIWOŚCI III RZESZY/

"WE MUST FREE THE GERMAN NATION
OF POLES, RUSSIANS, JEWS AND GYPSIES"
OTTO THIERACK
/MINISTER OF JUSTICE OF THE THIRD REICH/

**Auschwitz
Crematory**

Auschwitz Crutches

**Auschwitz
Torture Room**

Auschwitz
Execution Wall

AUSCHWITZ 1940-1945

- NAJWIEKSZY HITLEROWSKI OBÓZ
  KONCENTRACYJNY DLA WIĘŹNIÓW
  RÓŻNEJ NARODOWOŚCI
- OD 1942 R BYŁ RÓWNIEŻ CENTRUM
  ZAGŁADY EUROPEJSKICH ŻYDÓW

- THE BIGGEST NAZI CONCENTRATION
  CAMP FOR PRISONERS OF VARIOUS
  NATIONALITIES
- SINCE 1942 IT WAS A CENTER FOR
  EXTERMINATION OF EUROPEAN JEWS

Auschwitz
Shoes

Birkineau
Inside
Barracks

★ ★ ★ ★

AFTERWORD

When World War II ended, Florence County looked forward to the ending of war shortages. Stores quickly were flooded with once-scarce goods, and new automobiles soon came out for the first time in years.

Rationing ended. Wartime taxes lingered longer.

Anticipated most eagerly, of course, was welcoming the "boys" -- as the newspapers usually had called them during the war -- back home. They didn't come back "boys," but nobody much raised that point. We were just glad they were coming back.

But there were those who did not return. Everybody remembered someone who was lost in the war, sometimes someone so close that the pain would never go away.

Some who came back literally left parts of themselves overseas, results of amputations and other emergency battlefield treatment. Others left a part of their hearts and souls over there, which was why many of them were reluctant to talk about it for years afterwards.

Some of the stories in this book were told for the first time because the pain had been too great for veterans to discuss their experiences, and they talked now because they needed finally to break their silence.

This book does not come close to telling all of the stories of all Florence County men and women who served in World War II and the occupations that followed. We have not attempted to do that. It would have been impossible.

It is not even possible, apparently, to obtain a complete list of all Florence County people who served in the war, let alone learn all of their stories.

We didn't try to describe the military history of the war. That has been done many times. But this book is a sampling of the experiences of Florence County people who were in that greatest of all wars. We hope it also will be understood as a salute to those we were unable to mention.

Still a railroad town when the war ended, Florence's importance as a rail center has nearly disappeared, as have many of the industrial jobs that came here in the 1960s and 1970s. However, medicine has become Florence's main economic engine as the 21st Century develops.

When the "boys" came back from war, they plunged into completing their educations, and into careers and marriages. Many moved to other places. Many remained here to build and serve the community. Over the years we welcomed many veterans from other parts of the country who came here and contributed to what Florence County has become.

Among them were people who were business leaders, some who literally built things, and others who went into in professions or became members of a productive labor force. Some led community efforts.

Most WWII veterans have died in the 60-plus years since the war, but they left behind children and grandchildren, many of whom are unaware of the roles these people played in subduing totalitarianism and protecting and advancing our country.

Some fought again in Korea and Vietnam and their grandchildren fight now in Afghanistan and Iraq.

Veterans from all over the country overcame the Great Depression, won World War II, then moved our country to the top of the world economically while winning the Cold War.

Tom Brokaw had it right about "The Greatest Generation". This book is an effort to tell stories of some of those from Florence County who fought in the Greatest Generation's greatest war.

Sponsors

On these pages, we recognize and thank our sponsors.

Putting together this type of volume is not cheap, and the businesses and individuals represented here have helped to pay the cost of producing and printing this book. They participated because they believed we were doing something important. They shared our belief that Florence County people should remember what their friends and neighbors did in the greatest war and what it was all about.

Without their help, it might not have happened, and we hope that the community will share the appreciation we have for their sense of history and of community.

★ ★ ★ ★
SPONSORS

★ ★ ★ ★
SPONSORS

★ ★ ★ ★
SPONSORS

★ ★ ★ ★

SPONSORS

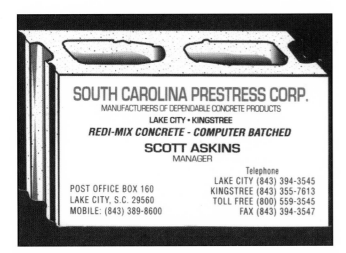

★ ★ ★ ★
SPONSORS

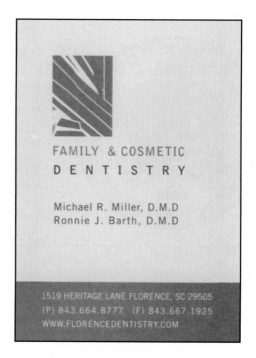

★ ★ ★ ★
VETERANS LISTINGS

This information was compiled by the Three Rivers Historical Society from records of the job placement service under the Selective Service and Training Act of 1940. The cities listed are the addresses of the next of kin.

NAME	CITY	ENTRY DATE	DISCHARGE
Abdelnor, Albert S	Florence SC	10/26/1942	2/15/1944
Abraham, General Washington	Florence SC		1/15/1946
Abraham, Rufus A	Florence SC	2/17/1942	10/9/1945
Abraham, Scipio	Claussens SC	12/6/1944	
Abraham, William N	Effingham SC	7/18/1943	2/15/1946
Abramek, Edward T	Woonsocket RI		
Abrams, Joseph W	Florence SC	1/17/1941	8/16/1945
Abrams, Robert Thomas, Jr	Florence SC	2/9/1943	2/14/1946
Adams, Edward	Timmonsville SC	12/7/1945	12/7/1946
Adams, Glenn	Pamplico SC	11/26/1945	6/7/1946
Adams, Thomas Lee	Florence SC	4/26/1944	1/7/1946
Adams, Victor John, Jr	Stroudsburg PA	5/30/1944	6/15/1946
Adams, Vincent Darrel	Florence SC		6/9/1946
Addison, Lee C	Florence SC	6/15/1944	11/12/1946
Addison, Samuel David	Florence SC	1/21/1943	3/16/1946
Adkins, James Wilbur	Florence SC	1/17/1941	
Aiken, John Davis	Florence SC	8/4/1944	5/14/1946
Alexander, Cillford Randolph	Florence SC	1/6/1943	11/3/1945
Alexander, Ernest	Florence SC	12/11/1941	12/17/1946
Alexander, Leroy	Florence SC	12/29/1944	12/10/1946
Alexander, Ossie	Florence SC	2/5/1945	3/13/1946
Alexander, Willie	Florence SC	11/19/1943	3/3/1946
Allen, Basil Ernest, Jr	Savannah GA	12/22/1944	3/23/1946
Allen, Edward E	Florence SC	12/15/1944	3/20/1946
Allen, Joe Luther, Jr	Florence SC	7/31/1942	8/1/1946
Allen, Marcus Henderson	Maxton NC	4/1/1943	
Allen, Norman	Effingham SC	11/4/1942	12/20/1945
Allen, Pleasant G	Florence SC	1/13/1941	12/20/1945
Allen, Robert Deal	Florence SC	1/27/1943	10/7/1945
Allen, Robert Russell	Effingham SC	10/2/1943	3/28/1946
Alston, Allen F	Florence SC	3/8/1943	1/12/1946
Alston, Julius	Florence SC		10/17/1945
Alston, McKenley	Florence SC	7/20/1943	2/19/1946
Alston, Nathaniel R		12/15/1943	1/30/1946
Alston, Toli	Florence SC	9/15/1944	
Alston, Walter, Jr	Florence SC	9/4/1943	1/12/1946
Altman, Daniel	Johnsonville SC	1/17/1943	9/1/1945
Altman, James Olen	Andrews SC	6/25/1941	11/23/1945
Altman, William David	Florence SC	2/23/1942	1/5/1946
Anderson Samuel Miles	Florence SC	7/29/1942	2/16/1946
Anderson, Bert Lloyd	Timmonsville SC	8/22/1944	10/19/1946
Anderson, James	Florence SC	8/13/1945	5/31/1946
Anderson, James	Florence SC	8/3/1943	3/9/1946
Anderson, Marvin Edgar	Florence SC	8/3/1943	

NAME	CITY	ENTRY DATE	DISCHARGE
Anderson, McKinley	Florence SC	3/12/1943	12/17/1945
Anderson, Oscar	Florence SC	2/25/1943	2/7/1946
Anderson, Richard Arnett	Florence SC		10/23/1944
Andrew, Charles	Pamplico SC	7/7/1944	7/6/1946
Andrews, Carlysle James	Florence SC	8/21/1945	10/6/1945
Andrews, Luther H	Florence SC	4/26/1945	11/10/1946
Armentrout, Richard D	Florence SC	7/6/1942	9/26/1945
Arris, John B	Florence SC	4/20/1943	12/20/1945
Arrowsmith, Mitchell H	Florence SC	5/23/1941	11/30/1945
Arthur, Henry	Lynchburg SC	10/14/1942	2/17/1946
Ashby, Peyre E	Florence SC	10/29/1943	4/25/1946
Ashley, Curtis Boyd	Florence SC	7/21/1943	12/13/1945
Ashley, Theodore	Florence SC	3/6/1944	
Askins, Allen Dewitte	Florence SC	10/12/1943	5/16/1946
Askins, Giles C	Florence SC	1/27/1941	7/13/1945
Askins, Isaac S	Florence SC	8/8/1943	4/2/1946
Askins, Lawrence Carl	Florence SC	8/5/1941	11/8/1945
Askins, Willie	Florence SC	5/12/1944	5/18/1946
Ateyeh, Mitchell	Florence SC		10/13/1944
Atkinson, Ivory T	Timmonsville SC	6/23/1945	1/27/1947
Atkinson, James R	Timmonsville SC	9/30/1942	12/4/1945
Atkinson, John Roberson, Jr	Florence SC	2/10/1943	3/19/1946
Atkinson, William Tracy	Florence SC	4/3/1944	2/3/1946
Atwill, Joseph Harvey	Florence SC	2/10/1943	
Austin, Benjamin, Jr	Lake City SC		
Austin, Benjamin, Jr	Lake City SC	10/25/1943	1/6/1947
Avant, George Thomas	Florence SC	1/7/1944	10/30/1945
Ayres, Everette E	Florence SC	11/30/1942	11/21/1945
Backus, Alphonso	Florence SC		7/8/1944
Backus, Vandroth	Florence SC	8/28/1943	3/2/1946
Bacote, James	Florence SC	11/15/1945	3/28/1946
Bacote, Johnnie	Florence SC	8/26/1943	1/21/1946
Badder, Eli Shady	Florence SC	2/5/1943	1/28/1946
Badgett, Cecil Dewitt	Savannah GA	2/25/1940	
Baggett, Julius Herbert	Florence SC	6/18/1943	12/19/1945
Bailey, Andrew L	Florence SC		1/14/1945
Bailey, Charlie Alison	Florence SC	4/15/1945	1/2/1947
Bailey, Curtis I	Florence SC	3/26/1942	12/15/1945
Bailey, James E	Florence SC	6/11/1943	11/5/1945
Bailey, John A	Florence SC	1/13/1941	8/12/1945
Bailey, Joseph	Florence SC	12/1/1945	12/28/1946
Bailey, Larry Gilmore	Florence SC	9/21/1945	8/31/1946
Bailey, Lawrence Yancy	Florence SC	11/11/1941	11/28/1945
Bailey, Ralph Elliott	Florence SC	12/15/1942	11/1/1945
Bailey, Robert Manjay	Florence SC	9/22/1944	10/29/1946
Bailey, Wilson H	Florence SC	11/17/1942	12/17/1945
Bair, Robert Lide	Florence SC	1/10/1944	5/13/1946
Baitzer, Eugene K	Florence SC	4/1/1942	11/26/1945
Baker, David Everette	Florence SC	1/28/1943	1/4/1946
Baker, Ezekial Boot	Florence SC	4/28/1943	10/24/1945
Baker, Marion McLauren	Florence SC	2/2/1943	11/2/1945
Baker, Rayo Byfield	Effingham SC	2/23/1946	7/19/1946
Baker, Vergil Ivan	Florence SC	11/4/1942	2/11/1946
Baker, William Revell	Florence SC	8/9/1943	
Baker, Willie	Florence SC	10/28/1942	10/17/1945

★ ★ ★ ★

NAME	CITY	ENTRY DATE	DISCHARGE
Baker, Willie Mayo	Florence SC	11/17/1942	11/16/1945
Baldwin, John Kenneth	Florence SC	6/28/1944	2/7/1946
Ballentine, James Carl, Jr	Florence SC	9/25/1940	11/25/1945
Banks, James	Florence SC	7/30/1942	10/20/1945
Bankston, Douglas D	Florence SC	3/19/1943	2/12/1946
Barber, Gene Tunney	Florence SC	12/11/1940	11/8/1945
Barbour, Bobby	Timmonsville SC	7/24/1940	11/5/1945
Barefood, Clarence H	Florence SC		8/12/1943
Barfield, Legrand D	Florence SC	7/1/1944	9/30/1945
Barfield, Thomas Jefferson	Florence SC	6/28/1944	2/3/1945
Barnes, Cecil R	Florence SC	2/22/1942	9/1/1945
Barnes, Hally Reese	Florence SC		10/20/1945
Barnes, Randolph	Coward SC	12/15/1944	11/4/1946
Barnes, Willis R	Cowards SC	7/10/1941	1/9/1946
Barnhill, Harry Franklin	Florence SC	3/6/1944	8/3/1946
Barnhill, Richard William	Hyman SC	9/19/1940	9/24/1945
Barnhill, Thomas Eugene	Newport News VA	1/5/1945	3/20/1946
Barns, Clyde	Florence SC	2/18/1944	1/3/1946
Barns, Wallace P	Florence SC		
Baroody, Murray Arthur	Florence SC	1/7/1944	2/2/1946
Baroody, Naseeb Bshara, Jr	Florence SC	6/12/1943	3/28/1946
Baroody, Theodore Alexander	Florence SC	4/7/1943	10/27/1945
Barr, Alonzo	Florence SC	10/6/1943	12/20/1945
Barr, James Wesley	Florence SC	12/15/1944	9/21/1945
Barr, John Wesley	Florence SC	12/3/1943	4/20/1946
Barr, Rufus Walter	Effingham SC	1/31/1945	4/16/1946
Barr, William	Florence SC		1/19/1946
Barrett, Jack Littlefield	Florence SC	5/10/1944	8/8/1946
Barrett, Thomas Lanier	Florence SC	7/6/1945	12/30/1946
Barrett, William Robert	Florence SC		
Barringer, John Laurence, III	Florence SC	12/15/1942	1/17/1946
Barringer, Thad Jones	Florence SC	6/25/1945	7/7/1946
Bartell, David Lawrence, Jr	Florence SC	12/29/1943	12/22/1945
Bartell, Louis	Florence SC	3/9/1945	12/28/1945
Bartelle, Talmadge Lewis	Florence SC	6/25/1942	12/15/1945
Bartlett, Richard S	Bishopville SC	3/8/1943	12/28/1945
Barton, George Alexander	Florence SC	12/14/1942	12/8/1945
Barwick, Lide Ryan	Florence SC		7/3/1945
Barwick, Robert Sinclair, Jr	Ashville NC	5/27/1944	10/21/1945
Baskins, Richard Murphy	Florence SC	1/13/1941	11/19/1945
Bass, Jerome, E	Florence SC	4/7/1943	1/26/1946
Bass, Joseph F	Florence SC	8/16/1940	9/20/1945
Bass, Julian Hemeric Peter	Florence SC	1/25/1945	5/20/1946
Bass, Ruby F	Florence SC	9/1/1943	8/17/1945
Bateman, James M	Florence SC	8/10/1940	7/22/1945
Bateman, John Ray	Florence SC	7/25/1944	6/5/1946
Bauknight, William Emory, Jr	Florence SC	9/13/1943	4/1/1946
Baxley, Dewey K	Lake City SC	10/30/1945	1/9/1947
Bazen, Hilton Pleasant	Pamplico SC	2/13/1943	12/8/1945
Bazen, John Wesley	Darlington SC	7/19/1945	12/24/1946
Beaty, Joseph Kershaw	Florence SC		5/11/1944
Beaty, Thomas L	Florence SC	9/11/1940	4/18/1945
Beck, Waldo McRee, Jr	Florence SC	8/6/1943	3/7/1946
Bee, James	Baltimore MD	4/22/1941	1/19/1946
Bee, Woodrow	Florence SC	1/20/1943	12/14/1945

★ ★ ★ ★

NAME	CITY	ENTRY DATE	DISCHARGE
Belin, Coleman	Florence SC	9/26/1942	12/29/1945
Belin, David S	Pamplico SC	7/17/1942	11/19/1945
Bell, Bishop Alton	Florence SC	10/1/1942	11/15/1945
Bell, Floyd Earnest	Hartsville SC	1/5/1945	3/10/1946
Bell, Richard Wallace	Florence SC	5/20/1942	11/23/1945
Bell, Vernon Hasell	Florence SC	4/9/1946	5/10/1946
Bell, Willard Louis	Florence SC	4/26/1944	10/31/1945
Bell, Williams Adams	Florence SC	6/3/1942	12/11/1945
Bellamy, David	Conway SC	2/17/1942	11/5/1945
Bellamy, Lawyer Judge	Florence SC	3/30/1944	2/24/1946
Bellamy, Oscar Heyward, Jr	Florence SC	5/29/1943	3/7/1946
Belvin, James Murrice	Florence SC	2/18/1943	2/19/1946
Benenhaley, Albert M	Florence SC		
Benjamin, Albert	Florence SC	8/28/1943	1/7/1946
Benjamin, Arlington	Washington DC	4/10/1943	12/29/1945
Benjamin, Ivory	Florence SC	11/9/1942	10/27/1945
Benjamin, Leroy	Florence SC	12/1/1945	12/9/1946
Bennett, Abe	Florence SC		1/1/1943
Bennett, Allen Coope	Raleigh NC	3/3/1942	1/15/1946
Bennett, John L	Florence SC	1/27/1944	1/8/1946
Bennett, Max Wilson	Pamplico SC		1/26/1946
Bennett, Norfal, Jr	Florence SC		1/24/1945
Bennett, William Webster	Lanes SC	2/16/1942	7/26/1945
Benton, George Adolph	Florence SC	6/2/1943	12/13/1945
Benton, Oscar Thedwood	Florence SC	6/2/1943	10/20/1945
Berger, Jacob William, Jr	Florence SC	2/26/1944	4/6/1946
Berry, James Dlyn Q	Florence SC		4/6/1945
Berryhill, Calvin M	Charlotte NC	9/17/1942	8/10/1945
Billingley, Benjamin F	Florence SC		
Billups, Andrew Jackson	Florence SC	9/9/1944	10/13/1945
Bishop, Woodrow W	Cowards SC	3/1/1943	11/15/1945
Black, Sammie	Timmonsville SC	1/21/1943	3/12/1946
Black, Walter Earl	Florence SC	12/2/1944	4/20/1946
Blackmon, Arnis McKinley	Cowards SC	3/27/1944	10/21/1945
Blackmon, Cyril Wells	Timmonsville SC	12/27/1941	10/17/1945
Blackmon, Gene Horace	Florence SC	12/14/1945	11/4/1946
Blackmon, Julius Vernon	Florence SC	2/9/1943	4/14/1946
Blackwell, James Wilmot	Florence SC	4/26/1941	1/17/1946
Blackwell, Robert B	Newport News VA	10/24/1945	1/13/1947
Blackwell, William Hayden	Florence SC	10/27/1942	5/5/1946
Blankship, Charles Guy	Florence SC	2/1/1944	6/26/1946
Blick, Elijah H, Jr	Timmonsville SC	6/5/1940	3/9/1947
Blunk, Elmer C	Florence SC	5/4/1942	10/24/1945
Boatwright, Governor	Marion SC	12/10/1945	1/5/1947
Boatwright, Hoyt Barwick	Marion SC	9/21/1943	11/21/1945
Boatwright, Moses	Johnsonville SC	12/6/1945	12/19/1946
Boatwright, Thomas	Florence SC	8/12/1944	10/10/1945
Bochette, John Marion	Hyman SC	9/29/1943	11/11/1945
Bodtain, Edwin P	Tarboro NC	3/3/1945	9/4/1945
Boggs, Darrell C	Timmonsville SC	11/6/1945	11/29/1946
Bogus, Roscoe B	Florence SC	7/31/1942	10/22/1945
Bohan, Robert J	Florence SC	7/31/1942	2/13/1946
Bolden, Walter Lee	Honea Path SC		1/29/1943
Bolen, George Emanuel	Florence SC	5/27/1944	6/2/1946
Bollinger, Robert N	Florence SC	2/24/1942	2/26/1946

★ ★ ★ ★

NAME	CITY	ENTRY DATE	DISCHARGE
Bolon, Benjamin Lee	Black Eagle MT	4/8/1943	11/4/1945
Bonoparte, Curtis NMN, Jr.	Florence SC		
Boomershine, Paul E	Florence SC	5/22/1941	8/30/1945
Bostic, Jacob, Jr	Florence SC	7/17/1946	12/14/1946
Bostick, Robert Roland	Florence SC	1/7/1942	11/11/1945
Boswell, David Benjamin	Florence SC	4/20/1945	7/18/1946
Boswell, Frank Cornelius	Florence SC	5/13/1944	11/29/1945
Boswell, Gleen Cleon	Florence SC	8/5/1943	1/6/1946
Boswell, Jack Lowery	Scranton SC	11/20/1944	2/1/1946
Boswell, Joseph Evander	Pamplico SC	7/11/1940	9/22/1945
Bovette, William E	Florence SC	4/18/1942	9/10/1945
Bowers, Edward Berry	Florence SC	10/12/1939	1/26/1946
Brackett, William David	Florence SC	6/30/1943	2/8/1946
Bradford, Clarence E	Lincolnton GA	1/17/1942	12/5/1945
Bradford, James	Florence SC	7/16/1943	2/27/1946
Bradford, James Marion	Florence SC	4/7/1943	3/15/1946
Bradford, Willie jG	Florence SC		
Bradham, Preston Earl	Florence SC	7/24/1942	2/11/1946
Bradham, Stobo W	Florence SC	9/1/1943	9/11/1945
Bradley, Charles Edward	Florence SC	2/26/1943	11/18/1945
Bradley, Ira	Florence SC		
Bragdon, Elwood Clifton	Lake City SC	12/19/1945	2/24/1947
Bragdon, James Allen	Florence SC		12/29/1944
Branch, Willie Harris	Tampa FL		6/2/1945
Branstiter, George Wesley	Florence SC	1/2/1942	10/25/1945
Bregman, Irwin	Norfolk VA	5/29/1944	4/18/1946
Brendel, Paul Herman	Florence SC	6/25/1941	12/13/1945
Briggs, Boston	Florence SC	9/11/1943	1/3/1946
Briggs, Nthan	Florence SC		8/17/1944
Brigham, Paul G	Florence SC		5/28/1945
Brigham, Raymond	Florence SC		10/23/1944
Bright, Arthur N	Florence SC		7/20/1945
Brigman, Raymond	Florence SC		6/19/1943
Briskin, Sam	Florence SC	10/11/1941	10/27/1945
Bristow, James Robert	Florence SC	7/21/1945	10/4/1945
Broach, Carl Lavaughan	Florence SC	4/7/1943	4/5/1946
Broach, Charlie McMaster, Jr	Effingham SC	4/23/1945	2/28/1947
Broach, Edward McIntyre	Florence SC	6/13/1945	3/2/1947
Broach, Lee Hubert	Florence SC	6/2/1943	11/24/1945
Broad, James Clayton	Lake City SC		
Broadway, Murray Allen	Florence SC		3/25/1946
Brockington, Douglas	Florence SC	11/10/1944	6/16/1943
Brockington, James, Jr	New York NY	3/6/1943	11/24/1945
Brockington, Jason Junius	Florence SC		
Brockington, John	Newport News VA	5/19/1944	2/19/1946
Brockington, Oque	Florence SC	1/20/1943	3/14/1946
Brockington, Philip	Florence SC	10/31/1945	11/23/1946
Brockington, Span	Florence SC	10/9/1943	4/6/1946
Brockington, Wilbert	Florence SC	1/13/1943	1/17/1946
Brooks, Alton Franke	Florence SC	2/5/1946	1/1/1947
Brooks, Coboy	Florence SC	4/27/1945	7/23/1946
Brooks, Elijah	Florence SC	1/3/1944	6/2/1946
Brooks, Frank	Florence SC		10/1/1943
Brooks, Garfield	Florence SC		1/26/1946
Brooks, Hugh Wilson	Florence SC	12/11/1944	7/19/1946

★ ★ ★ ★

NAME	CITY	ENTRY DATE	DISCHARGE
Brooks, Prince	Wilmington NC	7/31/1943	3/5/1946
Brooks, Rowland, Jr	Florence SC	8/13/1945	9/27/1945
Brooks, Thomas Frederick	Timmonsville SC	11/14/1945	11/22/1946
Brown, Albert Joseph	Dillon SC	4/1/1946	5/5/1947
Brown, Colie Bill	Timmonsville SC	5/5/1945	11/22/1946
Brown, Cooper	Bronx NY	10/29/1943	1/17/1946
Brown, David Grodon	Timmonsville SC	4/10/1945	11/2/1946
Brown, Edward	Florence SC	3/7/1944	1/17/1946
Brown, Eugene	Florence SC		7/18/1944
Brown, Frederick Dewling	Florence SC	4/18/1942	11/23/1945
Brown, Gus	Florence SC		
Brown, Haywood S	Florence SC		4/23/1945
Brown, Herbert R, Jr	Harris TX	3/24/1943	2/19/1946
Brown, Hubert Marion	Florence SC	12/1/1945	11/26/1945
Brown, James Edward	Florence SC	2/4/1942	12/8/1945
Brown, Jimmie	Florence SC	3/15/1943	12/1/1945
Brown, Jimmie	Baltimore MD	3/6/1943	12/1/1945
Brown, Joe Eugene	Florence SC		12/15/1944
Brown, Joseph	Florence SC	3/14/1944	
Brown, Joseph Righten	Florence SC	1/3/1942	11/1/1945
Brown, Kenneth Jackson	Florence SC	3/29/1944	12/15/1944
Brown, Leroy	Baltimore MD	7/27/1943	4/3/1946
Brown, Leroy	Florence SC	4/23/1944	12/15/1944
Brown, Mable V	Florence SC	11/10/1942	2/6/1946
Brown, Otis	Florence SC	12/31/1942	2/20/1946
Brown, Robert	Florence SC	3/3/1945	5/1/1946
Brown, Robert J	Cowards SC	12/31/1942	12/15/1944
Brown, Roscoe Boyd	Florence SC	9/10/1943	12/31/1945
Brown, Vernie Bacter	Sumter SC	11/13/1944	12/15/1944
Brown, Wilbur Edward	Florence SC	12/31/1942	2/11/1946
Brown, William Clyburn	Kingstree SC	2/2/1943	3/31/1946
Brown, William L	Florence SC	9/28/1942	1/10/1946
Brown, William Nelson	Florence SC	9/8/1944	10/3/1945
Brown, Willie	Pamplico SC	2/3/1944	7/4/1946
Browne, Charles Halbert	Florence SC	4/27/1944	4/28/1943
Bruce, Jeff Williad	Effingham SC	6/26/1940	6/11/1945
Bruce, William Clifford	Florence SC	1/5/1945	5/17/1946
Brunson, James F, Jr	Florence SC	4/12/1943	12/15/1945
Brunson, Jerome	Florence SC	5/5/1943	12/27/1945
Brunson, Mason Chandler, Jr	Florence SC	6/19/1942	10/24/1945
Bruorton, James Atkinson, Jr	Hemmingway SC	2/10/1943	12/15/1944
Bruton, Franklin Richard	Florence SC	12/14/1942	10/5/1945
Bruton, William Donald	Florence SC	1/14/1942	1/24/1946
Bryant, Dewey Jerome	Florence SC	1/21/1943	1/11/1946
Bryant, James O	Florence SC	10/20/1942	4/15/1946
Bryant, Monroe Lucas	Florence SC	5/25/1944	
Bryant, Richard Hartwell	Florence SC	1/24/1942	2/17/1945
Bryant, Robert Lee	Florence SC	3/8/1945	8/22/1945
Bryce, George Wilson	Florence SC		4/21/1945
Buck, John S	Florence SC	4/26/1943	1/7/1946
Buff, Andrew Manning	Florence SC	5/6/1942	9/20/1945
Buffkin, Bruce E	Florence SC	9/25/1943	12/20/1945
Buffkin, Buren F	Augusta GA		7/14/1945
Buffkin, Joseph	Darlington SC	9/19/1945	12/14/1945
Bull, Leroy	Darlington SC		

★ ★ ★ ★

NAME	CITY	ENTRY DATE	DISCHARGE
Bulls, Kedrick J	Florence SC	9/27/1943	2/19/1946
Bulter, Clarence, Jr	Florence SC	12/14/1939	8/12/1945
Bulter, TC	Latta SC	3/28/1946	3/5/1946
Bulter, Willis	Florence SC		4/17/1944
Bultman, John P	Florence SC	11/15/1943	3/29/1946
Burch, Cleveland	Florence SC	10/28/1942	11/15/1945
Burch, Henry	Florence SC	11/10/1943	4/29/1946
Burch, Laneaue Jr	Florence SC	4/29/1943	3/7/1946
Burch, Maxie Byrd	Florence SC	11/5/1942	12/8/1945
Burgess, Leon Handy	Newport News VA		
Burgess, Nelson	Florence SC	1/1/1942	11/13/1945
Burgess, Rudolph	Florence SC	5/11/1944	8/7/1946
Burgess, William D	Coward SC	3/21/1943	12/15/1944
Burgh, John Oliver	Alemedia CA	3/31/1943	11/26/1945
Burleson, John Martin	Florence SC	6/1/1943	3/17/1946
Burnett, Amos J, Jr	Florence SC	12/7/1942	12/15/1944
Burnett, Edward Leon	Florence SC	3/3/1945	7/12/1946
Burns, Phillip L	Florence SC	2/4/1946	5/5/1947
Burrell, Victor Gregory, Jr.	Florence SC	5/10/1943	
Burris, Boyd J	Effingham SC	12/17/1936	11/24/1945
Burris, J G	Effingham SC		11/2/1944
Burroghs, Charlie Bolden	Florence SC	8/5/1943	11/23/1945
Burroughs, William H, Jr.	Florence SC	7/16/1943	1/1/1946
Burrows, Edwards	Scranton SC	11/11/1944	1/23/1946
Bussey, William Royal	Florence SC	4/13/1944	7/9/1946
Butka, John E	Glen Lyon PA	2/22/1943	4/4/1946
Byerly, Armitt B	Thoamsville NC		10/23/1945
Bynum, Sylvester	Timmonsville SC	11/14/1945	12/20/1946
Byrd, C Carter	Florence SC		
Byrd, Edward NMN	Florence SC	12/31/1942	8/8/1945
Byrd, George Talmadge	Darlington SC	2/26/1944	5/13/1946
Byrd, Gilbert G	Florence SC	2/28/1945	12/14/1945
Byrd, Henry Pinkney	Florence SC	7/17/1943	10/20/1945
Byrd, Leroy	Florence SC		8/1/1943
Byrd, Leroy	Florence SC		
Byrd, Robert Junius	Darlington SC		
Byrd, Willie D	Florence SC	1/19/1943	3/12/1946
Cade, Charlie Junior	Florence SC	4/29/1944	3/11/1946
Cain, Arthur C	Claussens SC	10/4/1945	12/3/1946
Cain, Edward	Claussens SC	2/19/1942	
Cain, LaBruce	Florence SC	4/20/1941	10/24/1945
Cain, Louis	Florence SC	5/11/1944	3/15/1946
Calcutt, Dannie	Pamplico SC	10/18/1945	9/10/1945
Calcutt, Harry McInnis	Florence SC	4/7/1943	12/15/1945
Calcutt, Julian I	Florence SC	9/30/1942	12/24/1945
Calcutt, Thadis	Florence SC	12/8/1939	8/4/1945
Calhoun, Lester N	Florence SC	9/8/1939	7/7/1945
Camlin, William Benjamin	Georgetown SC		12/20/1945
Cammander, Augustine Cates	Baltimore MD		
Campbell, Dudley Howard	Florence SC	2/24/1942	10/9/1945
Campbell, Edward R	Florence SC		1/14/1944
Campbell, Furnie Monroe, Jr	Florence SC		12/15/1944
Campbell, James, Jr	Florence SC		5/6/1943
Campbell, John Tyson	Florence SC	10/12/1942	11/20/1945
Campbell, Marion DeBose	Claussens SC		

★ ★ ★ ★

NAME	CITY	ENTRY DATE	DISCHARGE
Campbell, Martimer Reese	Claussens SC	2/9/1943	2/2/1946
Campbell, Robert L	Florence SC	1/9/1943	1/20/1946
Campbell, Southern F, Jr.	Florence SC		'10/14/1945
Campbell, Walter Clifton, Jr.	Columbia SC	8/23/1943	12/21/1945
Campbell, William Myers	Florence SC	6/14/1943	2/15/1946
Cannon, John Lyles	Florence SC	6/2/1943	2/21/1946
Cannon, Leroy, Sr.	Florence SC	3/10/1944	2/27/1946
Cannon, Oscar Draughon	Florence SC	9/14/1942	2/8/1946
Cannon, Samuel	Washington DC	3/15/1943	11/16/1945
Capps, John William	Conway SC	7/28/1943	5/25/1946
Carlisle, Arlie Carl, Jr.	Florence SC	10/26/1946	11/10/1945
Carnell, John Henry	Florence SC	1/17/1940	2/15/1946
Carpenter, John Robert	Florence SC		5/20/1946
Carr, Cal Junior	Florence SC	12/31/1942	1/13/1946
Carr, James Hamilton	Florence SC	12/14/1942	1/1/1946
Carr, Orien	Timmonsville SC	7/27/1943	1/18/1946
Carraway, Larvin Laverne	Effingham SC	11/14/1942	12/15/1944
Carraway, Lowell	Cowards SC	10/1/1943	
Carrington, John Otis		3/18/1943	12/6/1945
Carter, Charles Golson	Florence SC	7/24/1943	5/18/1946
Carter, Charles Rivers	Florence SC	7/28/1942	12/29/1945
Carter, David H		5/24/1943	2/17/1946
Carter, Earle Gore	Loris SC	4/17/1944	12/8/1945
Carter, Henry Fred, Jr.	Florence SC		4/4/1945
Carter, Herbert Leroy	Florence SC	2/9/1943	10/29/1945
Carter, Jack Carel	San Antonio TX	5/11/1942	10/9/1945
Carter, Joe T	Florence SC	2/18/1939	9/4/1945
Carter, John D	Florence SC	5/6/1942	12/19/1945
Carter, Lawrence E	Florence SC	10/15/1943	12/25/1945
Carter, Ruben Givan	Florence SC	3/30/1945	3/17/1946
Carter, Thomas J, Jr.		1/30/1944	3/23/1946
Cary, John W	Greensboro NC	10/15/1941	10/9/1945
Case, C G	Cowards SC		4/10/1946
Casley, Eugene A	Florence SC	3/20/1942	
Casley, James	Florence SC	2/25/1944	1/30/1946
Casper, Orson Taylor			12/21/1945
Caston, James Pinckney, Jr.	Florence SC	2/28/1944	
Caston, Mell	Florence SC	4/21/1943	12/11/1945
Cato, George	Florence SC	11/3/1942	1/23/1946
Cato, Herman Leroy	Patterson NC	1/28/1944	4/2/1946
Cato, John Burell	Florence SC	11/20/1943	2/4/1946
Cato, Samuel Lee	Florence SC	11/22/1943	10/5/1945
Chambless, John	Florence SC	3/23/1943	10/17/1945
Chambless, Roy Harrison	Pelham GA	4/25/1945	12/12/1945
Champey, John Weldon	Columbia SC	3/31/1945	8/19/1945
Chandler, Sam Frierson	Florence SC	1/14/1941	9/11/1945
Chandler, Walter Oglesby	Florence SC	8/28/1942	12/15/1944
Chapman, Elting Lagare, Jr.	Florence SC	4/20/1943	2/20/1946
Chapman, Jay F	Highlands NC	2/20/1945	7/18/1946
Charles, Alonza	Florence SC	1/12/1946	1/14/1947
Charles, Comaders	Florence SC		1/18/1945
Charles, Harry G, Jr.	Florence SC	5/24/1943	8/26/1945
Charles, Harry G, Jr.	Florence SC	12/31/1942	3/28/1946
Charles, Harvey Man, Jr.	Florence SC	1/14/1943	11/17/1946
Charles, Irvin	Florence SC	11/11/1942	1/15/1946

★ ★ ★ ★

NAME	CITY	ENTRY DATE	DISCHARGE
Charles, James Preston	Greenville SC	4/26/1941	11/19/1945
Charles, John Murrell	Florence SC	3/29/1944	6/2/1946
Charles, Lindberg Lester	Florence SC	7/10/2026	7/23/1946
Charles, Marion	Florence SC	6/16/1944	2/6/1946
Charles, Samuel	Florence SC		2/15/1945
Chase, Maitlan Sutter, Jr.	Florence SC		5/7/1942
Chasteen, Elmer Ellis	Florence SC	1/20/1943	4/22/1946
Chavis, Fred Dee	Bennettsville SC		
Chavis, Gary	Marion SC	6/2/1943	11/25/1945
Cheek, Frank A	Atlanta GA		4/8/1946
Cheek, Gerald R	Florence SC		12/15/1945
Cheeseborough, Ruby			6/6/1944
Cherry, Sam	Effingham SC	5/11/1944	3/22/1946
Chewning, Gene M	Greenville SC	7/30/1942	10/17/1945
Childers, Herman C	Summerton SC	2/10/1943	3/16/1946
Childs, David Augustus	Columbia SC	12/10/1942	12/4/1945
Chosta, Frank		6/11/1943	5/4/1946
Christopher, James Elmore	Florence SC	1/13/1941	1/21/1945
Christopher, James Pringle	Florence SC	1/5/1945	4/20/1946
Christopher, William Elbert, Jr.	Daytona Beach FL	2/23/1944	3/24/1946
Clam, Ashton C	Timmonsville SC	4/7/1943	1/26/1947
Clarke, James Anderson	Florence SC	1/19/1942	10/13/1945
Clarke, James Henry, Jr.	Florence SC	7/10/1943	1/10/1946
Clarke, Percy Odell	Florence SC	2/9/1943	10/25/1945
Clarkson, Marion C, Jr.	Florence SC	2/22/1943	
Clements, James Harold	Florence SC	8/19/1944	7/7/1946
Clifford, William P, Jr	Florence SC	10/13/1942	11/13/1945
Coachman, John E	Florence SC	7/22/1943	3/24/1946
Cobb, Leroy, Jr.	Florence SC	1/6/1944	2/19/1946
Cochran, Harold J	Florence SC	11/12/1943	11/5/1945
Cockfield, Bennie Tillman	Florence SC	8/21/1945	12/24/1946
Cockfield, Robert Colman	Florence SC		11/26/1946
Cockfield, Robert Lee	Florence SC	7/13/1943	10/24/1945
Cockroy, Claude Milton	Florence SC	2/20/1941	7/16/1945
Cody, James B	Florence SC		7/19/1945
Coe, Jasper	Florence SC	12/31/1942	1/13/1946
Coker, Alfred Richard	Cowards SC	1/23/1940	10/11/1945
Coker, George H	Philadelphia PA	8/25/1943	2/14/1946
Coker, Leon Harkless	Florence SC	5/24/1943	
Coker, Sam	Florence SC	5/19/1943	
Coker, Thomas Marion Leo	Turbeville SC	11/3/1945	1/27/1946
Colburn, Richard David	Easton PA	6/18/1943	1/10/1946
Cole, Alfred hamer	Florence SC	10/1/1941	11/20/1945
Cole, Howard Preston, Jr.	Florence SC	7/17/1939	11/2/1945
Cole, Jake C	Turbeville SC	12/10/1942	2/2/1946
Coleman, Arthur Benjamin	Pamplico SC	1/19/1942	11/10/1945
Coleman, Edward Luther	Scranton SC	4/13/1943	1/7/1946
Coleman, James Wallace		1/12/1943	1/25/1946
Coleman, Jimmie Perris	Hopinsville KY		8/31/1943
Coleman, Ludie M, Jr.	Pamplico SC	12/14/1942	10/26/1945
Collins, Charles Q	Florence SC	11/5/1941	9/21/1945
Collins, Earl Lamar	Florence SC	1/15/1943	4/19/1946
Collins, Earnest Allen	Effingham SC	11/8/1945	11/18/1946
Collins, Edward C	Florence SC	12/21/1943	1/1/1946
Collins, Emory L	Cowards SC	3/5/1946	2/2/1947

★ ★ ★ ★

NAME	CITY	ENTRY DATE	DISCHARGE
Collins, Herbert Millard	Florence SC	10/13/1945	3/26/1946
Collins, Jesse Herman	Marlboro SC		3/22/1945
Collins, Louis Samuel	Rome GA	7/3/1943	12/15/1944
Collins, Millage Birl	Florence SC	12/30/1944	4/4/1946
Collins, Otis Patric	Olanta SC	6/2/1943	10/8/1945
Collins, Wesley Ledell	Florence SC	11/18/1942	2/4/1946
Collins, Willard E	Florence SC	4/10/1945	11/30/1945
Collins, William Preston, Jr.	Florence SC	2/9/1943	10/22/1945
Commander, James Allen	Florence SC	10/28/1942	2/27/1946
Commander, Vernon Walters	Florence SC	2/1/1941	5/14/1946
Connell, John Ray	Augusta GA	6/28/1944	10/30/1945
Conner, Albert R	Florence SC	7/8/1942	1/18/1946
Conner, Edward B	Hemmingway SC	3/30/1945	7/24/1946
Conner, Delmer Eugene	Effingham SC	8/15/1944	10/27/1945
Convington, William Adrian	Florence SC	4/8/1943	1/28/1946
Conyers, Grady Leroy	Florence SC		
Conyers, John Robert	Effingham SC	10/9/1943	1/15/1946
Conyers, John W	Florence SC	12/31/1941	10/28/1945
Coogler, James Collins	Florence SC	3/25/1944	11/12/1945
Cook, John A	Aynor NC		
Cook, Leslie S	Florence SC	12/15/1941	10/26/1945
Cook, Sam	Florence SC	5/6/1942	1/11/1946
Cook, Wilbur Edward	Florence SC	9/21/1944	11/26/1946
Cooper, Andrew		1/21/1943	2/23/1946
Cooper, Archie Lee	Florence SC	1/19/1942	11/12/1945
Cooper, Burnie Ralph	Timmonsville SC	11/6/1945	1/7/1947
Cooper, Charles D	Memphis TN	10/26/1942	2/21/1946
Cooper, Dudley	Florence SC		12/2/1944
Cooper, Granison, Jr.	Florence SC	1/20/1943	2/14/1946
Cooper, James	Effingham SC	7/18/1942	1/9/1946
Cooper, James, Jr.	Florence SC	1/20/1943	12/15/1944
Cooper, John		9/8/1942	11/30/1945
Cooper, Johnnie	New York NY	1/25/1946	11/30/1946
Cooper, Lester	Florence SC	4/27/1945	12/4/1946
Cooper, Mack	Florence SC		11/1/1946
Cooper, Nathaniel	Florence SC	7/3/1943	2/13/1946
Cooper, Robert Eliga	Florence SC	12/27/1943	5/2/1946
Cooper, Will B	Florence SC	11/6/1945	4/7/1947
Cooper, William Alfred	Effingham SC	6/1/1943	1/9/1946
Cooper, William H	Florence SC	10/22/1943	12/4/1945
Copeland, Howard Milton	Florence SC	10/20/1943	2/2/1946
Copeland, James Claude, Jr.	Florence SC	5/27/1943	3/1/1946
Copeland, John Henry		12/24/1942	12/14/1945
Copeland, Warren	Florence SC	11/24/1942	
Corbin, Henry Jefferson	Florence SC		4/7/1945
Corder, Andrew M	Florence SC	10/12/1942	10/6/1945
Corder, Lewis E	Florence SC	1/26/1942	10/17/1945
Cordrey, Alfred Edward	Florence SC	4/1/1944	9/10/1945
Cornwell, James Ely	Florence SC	4/7/1943	12/15/1944
Coultrain, Robert	Cowards SC	2/26/1944	1/17/1946
Courtney, Dudley Hall	Florence SC	10/15/1945	3/12/1946
Covington, Dixon G	Cheraw SC	4/12/1942	9/20/1945
Covington, Leroy Duncan	Florence SC		6/21/1945
Covington, Tracy P	Florence SC	1/10/1943	10/10/1945
Coward, Ernest Edward	Florence SC	1/30/1940	9/27/1945

★ ★ ★ ★

NAME	CITY	ENTRY DATE	DISCHARGE
Coward, Joseph Warren	Timmonsville SC	10/2/1943	2/9/1946
Cox, Arthur Zeno	Effingham SC	10/8/1943	3/22/1946
Cox, E Lee	Florence SC		
Cox, Edward Ardell	Florence SC	11/5/1941	10/15/1945
Cox, Edwin Lewis	Florence SC	4/7/1943	2/15/1946
Cox, Ernest Evander	Florence SC	1/20/1943	10/20/1945
Cox, Ezra Isiah, Jr.	Florence SC	2/8/1943	4/24/1946
Cox, Franklin Garner	Florence SC		3/16/1945
Cox, George Wesley	Florence SC	1/13/1941	12/11/1945
Cox, Huge Lesesne	Florence SC	11/16/1942	10/27/1945
Cox, Joe Boswell	Florence SC		9/28/1945
Cox, Maxie Harrison	Florence SC	8/29/1943	12/15/1944
Cox, Porter Lee	Florence SC	8/12/1942	9/13/1945
Cox, Preston Lee	Florence SC	12/24/1945	1/26/1947
Cox, Raleigh Lee	Florence SC	9/16/1942	9/26/1945
Cox, Ralph Clifton	Florence SC	10/28/1942	2/1/1946
Cox, Selmon Lee, Jr.	Florence SC	9/30/1943	2/22/1946
Cox, Uyless Byrd, Jr.	Florence SC	8/21/1942	
Cox, Wade H	Florence SC		7/18/1945
Cox, William Evander	Florence SC	2/2/1943	12/18/1945
Cox, Willis DeLeon	Florence SC	1/5/1945	3/31/1946
Coxe, Kenneth Eugene	Florence SC	4/7/1943	
Craig, Frederick G		4/18/1942	8/21/1945
Craven, James T	Florence SC	7/29/1942	5/14/1946
Craven, Johanna I		6/22/1944	7/12/1945
Craven, William Archie	Florence SC	2/10/1945	12/6/1946
Craver, James Thomas	Florence SC	10/8/1941	
Crawford, Eathern Lester	Florence SC	1/8/1942	11/13/1945
Crawford, Heyward, Jr.	Florence SC	8/4/1941	10/27/1945
Crawford, James Squash	Florence SC	7/24/1943	5/3/1946
Crawford, James William	Florence SC	8/2/1943	3/2/1946
Crawford, Johnnie Lide	Florence SC	1/23/1943	1/10/1946
Crawford, Lourea	Cowards SC		2/25/1946
Crawford, Thomas Asger	Cowards SC	11/11/1944	5/3/1946
Creech, James Alex	Florence SC	5/27/1942	2/23/1946
Creel, Europe J	Florence SC	1/13/1941	8/12/1945
Creel, Harold Jennings	Poston SC		10/27/1945
Creel, Robert E	Claussens SC	8/22/1944	3/9/1946
Creel, Willie	Florence SC	3/29/1940	6/24/1945
Cribb, Remo Emerson	Florence SC	1/9/1943	1/9/1946
Cribb, Zane	Florence SC	2/9/1943	12/7/1945
Cromer, Thomas Suber	Florence SC	5/28/1943	6/13/1946
Crosby, James Fred, Jr.	Florence SC	4/29/1946	4/13/1947
Crosby, William LeRoy	Charleston SC		9/16/1944
Crosswell, John Thomas	Atlanta GA	11/4/1942	11/27/1945
Crouch, John Bunyan	Florence SC	7/1/1943	
Crowley, Edward Laverne	Florence SC	7/4/1942	10/4/1945
Crowley, William Clyde	Florence SC	11/18/1940	11/22/1946
Culbertson, Robert Lee	Greenville SC	2/6/1943	12/11/1945
Cummings, Foster	Effingham SC	1/22/1943	
Cunningham, Rufus	Florence SC		
Curry, James	Johnsonville SC	2/25/1943	1/30/1946
Curry, John	Johnsonville SC	2/16/1943	1/14/1946
Cusaac, Roland Wainwright	Bennettsville SC		
Cusack, Kedirc Leroy	Pamplico SC	12/10/1943	12/6/1945

★ ★ ★ ★

NAME	CITY	ENTRY DATE	DISCHARGE
Cutler, Earl Clyde, Jr.	Florence SC	4/8/1943	4/22/1946
Cutler, Howard Kenneth	Florence SC	10/30/1946	11/27/1946
Cutter, Cecil Norman	Florence SC	10/15/1943	1/5/1946
Cutter, Clyde I	Florence SC	4/17/1944	4/13/1946
Cutter, John F	Florence SC	4/8/1943	1/15/1946
Cyrus, Eddie	Florence SC		
Dabiels, Patrick LeRoy, Jr.	Effingham SC	8/5/1944	10/30/1946
Dallaire, Pierre W	Florence SC		
Daniels, George, Jr.	Florence SC		1/16/1946
Daniels, George, Jr.	Florence SC		1/16/1946
Daniels, James G	Florence SC	12/15/1943	2/12/1946
Daniels, Osie		10/28/1942	2/5/1946
Daniels, Richard L	Hyman SC		6/19/1945
Dargan, Henry Flinn	Florence SC	7/3/1942	3/4/1946
Dargan, James	Florence SC	10/23/1942	1/8/1946
Darity, Leon Ivy	Florence SC	1/13/1941	12/9/1945
David, Clyde Roland	Florence SC	6/1/1943	12/15/1944
Davidson, Ward G			3/10/1945
Davis, Aaron	Effingham SC	4/2/2025	
Davis, Adam	Florence SC	2/20/1943	3/29/1946
Davis, Arthur, Jr.	Florence SC		
Davis, Barnwell	Florence SC		9/25/1943
Davis, Ben	Pamplico SC	10/4/1943	2/1/1946
Davis, Bill Thomas	Florence SC	6/30/1944	5/15/1946
Davis, Charles Minitre	Florence SC	6/25/1941	10/9/1945
Davis, Charlie	Florence SC	7/10/1941	11/19/1945
Davis, Charlie W	Effingham SC	4/19/1944	5/22/1946
Davis, Clarence C	Florence SC	5/27/1940	5/28/1945
Davis, Clarence, Sr.	Florence SC		
Davis, Clifton	Florence SC	10/28/1942	11/29/1945
Davis, David Jerome	Wilmington NC	1/19/1944	11/11/1946
Davis, Don	New York NY		
Davis, Edward Richard	Florence SC	3/29/1944	11/22/1945
Davis, Edwin D	Marion SC		
Davis, Ernest	Florence SC	5/23/1944	
Davis, Ernest	Florence SC	3/1/1943	12/15/1944
Davis, Evander, Jr.	Florence SC	1/19/1944	11/9/1945
Davis, Frank M	Florence SC	4/11/1941	7/3/1945
Davis, Freddie	Florence SC	7/12/1944	6/25/1946
Davis, Glasco	Florence SC	7/4/1942	12/15/1944
Davis, Isaac	Pamplico SC	3/8/1944	12/18/1946
Davis, James Alton	Camden SC	9/2/1943	11/19/1945
Davis, James C	Washington DC	7/28/1943	1/10/1946
Davis, James Keet	Darlington SC	1/18/1944	12/15/1944
Davis, James Webb	Florence SC	11/1/1945	11/29/1946
Davis, Jessie	Florence SC	12/31/1942	9/15/1944
Davis, Jeva Franklin	Lakeworth FL	2/15/1944	
Davis, John Tillman, Jr	Florence SC	6/3/1944	2/3/1946
Davis, Joseph	Florence SC	6/7/1946	2/2/1947
Davis, Joseph Huge	Florence SC	6/6/1940	11/2/1945
Davis, Kenneth	Florence SC	3/2/1944	2/15/1947
Davis, Leila M	Florence SC		1/29/1945
Davis, Liston	Florence SC	5/11/1945	
Davis, Marvin Clyde, Jr.	Johnsonville SC	6/7/1945	11/6/1945
Davis, Melvin	Florence SC	10/12/1942	11/13/1945

★ ★ ★ ★

NAME	CITY	ENTRY DATE	DISCHARGE
Davis, Mitchell	Pamplico SC	8/4/1944	3/21/1946
Davis, Mose	Florence SC		1/21/1944
Davis, Otis	Florence SC	5/6/1941	11/17/1945
Davis, Roscoe	Florence SC	12/11/1945	12/14/1946
Davis, Sammie, Jr.			
Davis, Samuel Milbert	Florence SC	1/14/1943	1/6/1946
Davis, Shellie	Poston SC	11/13/1945	12/3/1946
Davis, Walter King	Florence SC	3/20/1944	12/22/1945
Davis, Wilbur Osma	Florence SC	2/23/1942	12/15/1944
Davis, Wile Joe	Florence SC	2/17/1942	11/2/1945
Davis, William B	Florence SC		
Davis, William Wood	Florence SC	11/15/1946	12/15/1944
Davis, Willie	Florence SC	10/2/1942	1/30/1947
Davis, Woodrow	Pamplico SC	5/10/1943	2/7/1946
Dawkins, John William	Florence SC		
Deas, Gregg W	Florence SC	1/13/1941	9/20/1945
Deas, Ronald Ashley	Florence SC	7/27/1945	8/23/1946
Deas, Ruben	Florence SC		12/28/1943
Deas, Wilson Edwards, Jr.	Florence SC	3/31/1943	4/1/1946
Deas, Woodrow Carlie	Florence SC	8/5/1944	7/31/1946
DeBar, Eugene	Florence SC	8/6/1942	11/5/1945
DeBerry, Frederick H	Florence SC	2/12/1942	11/19/1945
DeBerry, Harry Stevens, Jr.	Florence SC	7/15/1943	7/1/1946
DeFee, Alvie Carol	Florence SC	4/7/1943	2/10/1946
DeFee, Arnold Eugene	Timmonsville SC	10/17/1945	2/1/1947
DeFee, Austin	Florence SC		6/19/1945
DeFee, Curtis Samuel	Florence SC		
DeFee, David E	Florence SC	8/21/1943	11/2/1945
DeFee, John Alex	Florence SC	9/7/1940	12/3/1946
DeFee, Samuel E	Florence SC	4/17/1944	10/13/1945
Delain, William, Jr.	Washington DC		
Delay, Leonard	Florence SC		2/24/1944
DeMartini, Salvatore	Savannah GA	3/3/1943	10/8/1945
Denham, Julius Edward	Timmonsville SC	6/28/1944	7/23/1946
Denmark, Buster	Florence SC		1/10/1945
Dennis, James A	Florence SC		
Dennis, John Alvin	Lake City SC	10/20/1937	1/28/1946
Dennis, Julian Allston	Lake City SC	0720/42	3/7/1946
DesChamps, Johnnie H	Florence SC	2/26/1943	12/17/1945
DeWitt, Aubrye Larue	Florence SC	1/24/1944	10/10/1945
DeWitt, Charlie Bird	Florence SC	12/16/1941	10/24/1945
DeWitt, William G	Florence SC	5/10/1943	11/6/1945
Dickerson, Walter	Columbia SC		7/20/1944
Dickson, Sam		8/28/1943	10/22/1945
Dillingham, Jesse Prince, Jr.	Florence SC	10/1/1942	11/3/1945
Dillingham, Stanley Dale	Florence SC	10/30/1945	12/15/1946
Dingle, Willie Arthur	Florence SC	10/13/1942	2/27/1946
Dinkins, Joseph, Jr.	Florence SC	5/18/1943	12/15/1944
Dixon, Clarence Blease	Florence SC	9/16/1940	12/2/1945
Dixon, Dandy	Florence SC	10/28/1942	2/18/1946
Dixon, George	Timmonsville SC	8/24/1943	1/17/1946
Dixon, George Alphonso	Florence SC	10/28/1942	1/18/1946
Dixon, Marion	Florence SC	4/23/1944	5/17/1946
Dixon, Samuel Newton	Florence SC		
Dixon, William H		7/1/1944	2/4/1946

★ ★ ★ ★

NAME	CITY	ENTRY DATE	DISCHARGE
Donalds, John Henry	Florence SC	1/14/1943	12/5/1945
Dorsey, Rubin Owems	Cromwell CT		9/20/1944
Doughty, John Harold	Florence SC	10/21/1942	11/16/1945
Douglas, Frederick Earl	Florence SC		10/25/1944
Douglas, John Davis	Brooklyn NY	7/30/1943	1/16/1946
Dowdy, Major Junior	Florence SC	2/25/1944	6/19/1946
Dower, Haynie Lee	Florence SC	9/21/1943	5/2/1946
Dowling, Edward Sylvester	Florence SC		5/14/1945
Downs, Herman	Florence SC	8/20/1943	3/25/1946
Dozier, Ben, Jr.	Florence SC	8/27/1943	1/5/1946
Dozier, Jesse Ludy	Claussens SC	10/9/1943	12/19/1945
Drew, John Wheeler	Florence SC	10/2/1946	1/10/1947
Driggers, Alexander Vender	Florence SC		6/18/1945
Driggers, Ralph C	Florence SC	11/28/1942	11/21/1945
Dubose, Fred	Florence SC	4/23/1944	4/18/1946
Dubose, Fred Sidney	Florence SC	4/6/1944	1/20/1946
Dubose, James, Jr.	Florence SC	8/24/1942	11/24/1945
Dubose, Robert Newsome	Florence SC		9/22/1944
Dudley, George Fred		11/29/1939	12/6/1945
Dudley, John Richard	Florence SC	6/3/1943	11/10/1945
Duffell, Jack	Florence SC	1/4/1940	8/29/1945
Dukes, Clarence E	Florence SC		12/15/1944
Dunnaway, James D	Florence SC	12/15/1941	9/9/1945
Dupree, David	Florence SC		
Dupree, srather Beel	Florence SC	4/19/1944	2/21/1946
Dupree, Wilbur	Philadelphia PA	10/28/1943	4/6/1946
Durant, Clarence, Sr.	Florence SC	4/23/1944	1/7/1946
Durant, Jerry	Florence SC	2/17/1942	10/16/1945
Durant, Samuel	Florence SC		10/3/1944
Durant, Samuel	Florence SC		
Eaddy, Archie	Cowards SC	11/3/1942	11/19/1945
Eaddy, Benjamin J	Florence SC	12/2/1942	12/8/1945
Eaddy, Caleb Lee	Florence SC	10/16/1945	2/15/1947
Eaddy, David T	Florence SC	4/1/1943	12/15/1944
Eaddy, Henry Benjamin	New York NY	4/27/1943	3/7/1946
Eaddy, James	Florence SC	2/7/1944	11/8/1945
Eaddy, James	New York NY	6/21/1944	7/2/1946
Eaddy, John Wesley		12/5/1944	5/6/1946
Eaddy, Leonard	Effingham SC	11/13/1945	11/8/1946
Eaddy, London J	Florence SC	1/11/1943	1/18/1946
Eaddy, Nathaniel J	Florence SC		
Eaddy, Robert Ernest	Pamplico SC	11/16/1945	2/6/1946
Eaddy, Samuel Washington	Baltimore MD		
Eaddy, Solomon	New York NY		
Eaddy, Thomas Luke	Effingham SC	11/13/1945	11/8/1946
Eaddy, Thomas Spence	Florence SC	1/8/1943	1/8/1946
Eagerton, John David, Sr.	Florence SC	1/9/1945	1/30/1946
Eagleton, Berah Lee	Florence SC	1/17/1942	11/21/1945
Eagleton, Maxie	Baltimore MD	6/1/1945	5/5/1946
Eagleton, Rennon	Effingham SC	6/12/1944	5/18/1946
Eagleton, V Randolph	Florence SC	5/6/1941	10/21/1945
Early, Charles Nolen, Jr.	Asheville NC		
Early, Thomas Patrick, Jr.	Florence SC	6/28/1944	2/9/1946
Easterling, Fred	New York NY	6/26/1941	12/28/1945
Easterling, James Douglas, Jr.	Florence SC	10/6/1943	3/24/1946

★ ★ ★ ★

NAME	CITY	ENTRY DATE	DISCHARGE
Easterling, Lucius	Florence SC		9/27/1945
Easterling, Samuel Rogers	Florence SC	6/17/1942	4/30/1946
Eaton, William Kenneth	Florence SC	1/31/1944	1/9/1946
Echols, Fred	Florence SC	9/17/1943	12/15/1944
Echols, Leroy	Portmouth VA		3/29/1945
Echols, Thomas Waddell	Florence SC	8/5/1941	11/1/1945
Edens, Robert Earl	Florence SC	9/11/1944	8/23/1946
Edgerton, Edward Joseph	Florence SC	4/12/1945	11/29/1946
Edgerton, James Warren	Florence SC	6/22/1940	8/11/1945
Edmonds, William M, Jr.	Florence SC	10/31/1944	10/23/1944
Edwards, Arthur Rufus, Jr.	Florence SC	11/19/1945	1/13/1947
Edwards, C H, Jr.	Florence SC	3/5/1943	5/5/1946
Edwards, Dan	Florence SC	1/20/1943	1/13/1946
Edwards, Frank	Florence SC	7/6/1942	11/23/1945
Edwards, Henry		12/31/1942	1/19/1946
Edwards, Improvement, Jr.	Florence SC	6/14/1945	11/23/1946
Edwards, James Arthur	Florence SC	10/19/2004	5/15/1946
Edwards, Jessie	Florence SC	1/16/1946	4/15/1947
Edwards, Stephen, Jr.	Florence SC	5/10/1944	1/10/1946
Eggers, William Joseph	Florence SC	10/14/1943	2/5/1946
Eggleton, Johnny	Florence SC	1/29/1941	11/12/1945
Ellerbe, James Edwin	Florence SC	8/7/1943	2/19/1946
Ellerbe, Theodore R		5/27/1943	3/27/1946
Elliott, Archie Lewis	Florence SC	1/21/1943	2/9/1946
Ellison, John Sr.	Johnsonville SC	1/7/1943	1/8/1946
Ellison, Leroy	Florence SC	1/20/1943	1/23/1946
Elmore, John H	Florence SC	8/8/1943	
Ennie, Arthur F	Florence SC	5/17/1943	11/27/1945
Ergle, John Terrell	Ridge Springs SC	2/9/1943	2/20/1946
Ervin, Edwin D	Florence SC	5/14/1943	10/15/1945
Ethridge, Benjamin Grover	Charleston SC	9/2/1942	1/19/1946
Evans, Charles Stuart, Jr.	Florence SC	1/23/1942	12/23/1945
Evans, Edward LeRoy, Jr.	Pamplico SC	9/15/1942	2/18/1946
Evans, Elbert Winford	Florence SC	8/8/1942	9/12/1945
Evans, James Lamar	Florence SC	11/14/1942	2/6/1946
Evans, Johnnie J	Cowards SC	7/14/1942	7/3/1946
Ezell, Ella M	Florence SC	7/12/1944	12/15/1944
Faircloth, Jesse J	Horry SC	8/30/1946	1/9/1947
Fanters, Laverne Harold	Heningway SC	10/30/1941	2/1/1946
Farley, Victor V	Florence SC	8/10/1944	2/16/1946
Farmer, Elias	Florence SC	7/5/1944	10/31/1946
Farmer, Johnnie W	Florence SC	4/14/1944	1/16/1946
Fate, Hazel	Florence SC	3/4/1943	1/18/1946
Fickett, Charles James	Boise ID	8/15/1941	10/19/1945
Fields, Clifton (Son)	Florence SC		11/4/1945
Fields, Julian M	Florence SC	5/11/1942	11/26/1945
Fields, Norman	Timmonsville SC	1/22/1944	2/28/1946
Fields, Richard Soule	Florence SC	10/16/1946	3/10/1947
Fields, Willboy Westfel	Florence SC	4/14/1943	10/9/1945
Fields, William Herbert	Florence SC	3/10/1941	12/11/1945
Finklea, Ace Godbolt	Pamplico SC	1/16/1944	1/22/1946
Finklea, Lewis C, Jr.	Pamplico SC	4/14/1942	11/15/1945
Fitzgerald, James Benjamin	Florence SC	12/15/1942	10/26/1945
Fitzharris, John Donald	Florence SC	5/6/1942	10/27/1945
Fladger, Conwell Christopher	Lakeview SC	11/17/1942	12/31/1945

★ ★ ★ ★

NAME	CITY	ENTRY DATE	DISCHARGE
Flake, William Clinard	Florence SC	4/21/1942	12/8/1945
Fleming, George A	New Britian CT	6/9/1942	12/14/1945
Fletcher, Franklin David	Spartanburg SC	7/17/1942	12/11/1945
Flowers, Fredric W	Florence SC		2/16/1944
Flowers, George Lelon	Cowards SC	10/10/1943	8/17/1946
Flowers, Herbert Elonder	Pamplico SC		
Flowers, James C	Florence SC	1/13/1941	10/29/1945
Flowers, Walter Monroe	Florence SC	1/13/1941	10/23/1945
Flowers, William G	Florence SC		6/21/1945
Floyd, Ernest R	Cowards SC	10/23/1943	1/9/1946
Floyd, Ira Maxie, Jr.	Effingham SC	9/22/1945	8/25/1946
Floyd, James Willard	Effingham SC	4/10/1945	8/27/1946
Floyd, Lloyd George	Florence SC	12/3/1945	3/12/1947
Floyd, Wiley Eugene	Florence SC	11/13/1945	2/14/1947
Floyd, William Harrison	Cowards SC	7/10/1942	1/10/1946
Fogla, Donald Barton	Orangeburg SC	3/30/1945	11/4/1945
Folsom, John Ray	Greenville SC	12/13/1943	3/15/1946
Ford, Junius		4/15/1944	3/5/1946
Ford, Norman C	Florence SC	2/16/1946	3/26/1947
Foster, Abner W	Florence SC	5/2/1939	8/7/1945
Fountain, Eddie Jasper	Florence SC	2/4/1942	12/15/1944
Fountain, John D	Florence SC	4/1/1943	10/27/1945
Fowler, Arthur Bartley	Florence SC	1/7/1944	12/9/1945
Fowler, Everett C, Jr.	Florence SC	1/8/1942	10/28/1945
Fowler, Frances Andrew	Cowards SC	6/3/1944	6/9/1946
Fowler, Joe William	Florence SC	8/23/1943	4/4/1946
Fowler, Luther, Jr.	Florence SC	10/21/1944	12/7/1946
Foxworth, Dudley Hall	Roanoke VA	12/26/1945	1/6/1946
Foxworth, Ernest Everett	Florence SC		10/29/1945
Foxworth, Harry T	Monck Corner SC		7/6/1945
Foxworth, Pierce G	Hyman SC	3/27/1941	9/29/1945
Foxworth, Raymond Anthony	Florence SC	7/29/1946	8/22/1946
Fraley, Furman Nelson	Florence SC	10/16/1942	11/7/1945
Fralix, Shuler W	Mullen SC	1/13/1941	10/3/1945
Framer, Epp	Florence SC	8/20/1941	10/19/1945
Franks, Eddie George	Florence SC	9/4/1943	11/15/1945
Frazier, Albert	Florence SC		6/29/1944
Frazier, Calvin C	Florence SC	3/10/1943	2/25/1946
Frazier, Ernest James	Florence SC	5/16/1944	1/26/1946
Frazier, Henry	Brooklyn NY	2/7/1943	12/13/1945
Fred, Edmond, Jr.	Florence SC	2/26/1943	4/5/1946
Fred, James	Florence SC	4/27/1945	12/31/1946
Frederick, Henry Lewis	Timmonsville SC	9/29/1944	11/1/1946
Freeman, Lawson Weslet	Florence SC	4/17/1944	1/19/1946
Freeman, Willie F	Florence SC	6/18/1942	12/8/1945
Frenchman, Sampson Jr.	Florence SC	10/13/1942	9/5/1945
Friar, Everett L	Cowards SC	4/8/1943	3/12/1946
Friar, Jerome C	Florence SC	1/27/1944	11/9/1945
Fulp, Kenneth E	Florence SC	8/31/1942	11/23/1945
Fulp, Spencer Marion	Florence SC	11/7/1940	7/16/1945
Fulton, Frank Dudkey	Florence SC	9/8/1944	8/30/1946
Fulton, Raymond R	Florence SC	8/21/1943	12/28/1945
Fulton, Ulysses S	Florence SC	1/20/1943	9/29/1945
Fulwood, Clifton James	Timmonsville SC	7/10/1945	11/17/1946
Funderburk, Jerry Carson	Florence SC	5/31/1943	12/15/1945

★ ★ ★ ★

NAME	CITY	ENTRY DATE	DISCHARGE
Furman, James Warren	Florence SC		
Gaddy, Johnnie M	New York NY	8/9/1944	10/14/1946
Gaddy, William Alexander	Florence SC	4/21/1943	10/24/1945
Gaile, Huerta	Pamplico SC	5/5/1945	7/30/1946
Gainey, Andrew	Florence SC		9/21/1945
Gainey, Cecil Harrison	Hartsville SC		
Gainey, Ernest	Florence SC		
Gainey, Freddie	Florence SC	9/22/1942	
Gainey, Harold	Florence SC	1/20/1943	12/15/1944
Gainey, I J		4/29/1944	
Gainey, Ray	Florence SC	4/10/1944	11/20/1946
Gainey, Robert Bultman	Florence SC	12/13/1943	11/3/1945
Gainey, Sammy Edwards	Florence SC	7/21/1945	8/24/1946
Galeassi, John A	Florence SC		12/18/1944
Gallishaw, John W	Florence SC	7/3/1943	12/28/1945
Galloway, Boyd Lupton	Springfield MA		
Galloway, Thomas Harold	Timmonsville SC	1/5/1945	12/2/1946
Gamble, Wesley Jacob	New York NY	5/17/1943	4/4/1946
Gamble, William E	Florence SC		
Game, Boyd Gilmore, Jr.	Florence SC	7/14/1942	10/6/1945
Gandy, Ernest Laverne	Florence SC	4/21/1943	4/5/1946
Gandy, James Willard	Florence SC	3/7/1942	12/10/1945
Gandy, Jaynes Irving	Baton Rouge LA	11/14/1941	12/6/1945
Gandy, Marion William	Florence SC	11/19/1946	12/15/1944
Gandy, Robert Manuel, Jr	Florence SC	11/3/1945	1/28/1947
Garcia, Tony J	Oelwein, IA		9/16/1945
Gardiner, Charles Seymore, Jr	Florence SC	5/6/1943	7/2/1946
Gardner, Don Hugh	Florence SC	11/11/1944	8/7/1946
Gardner, Paul Junius	Florence SC	4/23/1944	6/11/1946
Gardner, Richard Howard	Florence SC	3/25/1944	6/20/1946
Gardner, Thomas Archie	Florence SC	8/4/1943	3/25/1946
Gardner, William Haskell	Florence SC	4/1/1946	3/15/1946
Gardner, Willie Laurie, Jr.	Florence SC	8/12/1942	12/15/1944
Garland, James	Florence SC	9/16/1942	1/24/1946
Garrett, Frank O	Florence SC	12/6/1942	1/22/1946
Garrett, Hubert J	Florence SC	12/17/1944	1/7/1946
Garrison, Charles McCown	Florence SC	6/5/1942	11/10/1946
Garrison, James Edward	Florence SC	2/20/1941	10/4/1945
Garrison, Rogers Cooley	Florence SC	4/8/1943	2/10/1946
Garrison, Thomas Fred	Florence SC	10/30/1942	9/22/1945
Garvin, Willie	Florence SC	12/1/1945	3/18/1947
Gasque, Thomas Nelson	Ridgeway SC	7/8/1942	2/26/1946
Gause, Caldie Livingston	Hansford WA		8/26/1943
Gause, Henry Lee	Hyman SC	1/5/1944	6/5/1946
Gause, Larue D	Florence SC	9/11/1941	8/2/1945
Gay, Billy Joe	Florence SC	4/8/1943	2/12/1946
Gayle, Charlie	Florence SC		8/11/1945
Gearhart, Claude Lafayette	Florence SC	10/15/1942	9/20/1945
Gee, Chester	Timmonsville SC		
Gee, Leon	Florence SC	3/14/1944	1/1/1946
Gentry, Claude Dewey, Jr.	Orangeburg SC		12/24/1945
Gentry, William Brown	Orangeburg SC	7/4/1944	6/29/1946
George, Clifford Donald	Florence SC	4/21/1945	12/19/1945
George, King	Florence SC	1/20/1943	1/13/1946
Gettis, Emanuel Pete	Florence SC	1/29/1943	12/31/1945

★ ★ ★ ★

NAME	CITY	ENTRY DATE	DISCHARGE
Gettys, Donald R	Camden SC	8/11/1945	10/21/1945
Gibbs, Charles R	Florence SC		
Gibbs, Edward	Florence SC	8/31/1943	3/5/1946
Gibbs, James Vernon	Darlington SC	11/4/1943	5/7/1946
Gibbs, Liston Murrell	Florence SC	8/22/1945	11/5/1946
Gibbs, William Herbert	Florence SC	6/1/1943	12/29/1945
Gibson, Clarence	Florence SC	11/24/1943	4/25/1946
Gibson, Jack Evans	Florence SC	8/19/1942	11/6/1945
Gibson, James W	Florence SC		8/20/1945
Gibson, Leon Marion	Florence SC	3/4/1943	2/19/1943
Gibson, Nelson Benjamin, Jr.	Florence SC	10/9/1943	12/24/1945
Gibson, Richard Louis	Florence SC	4/21/1943	2/6/1946
Gibson, Wade	Florence SC	7/1/1943	12/17/1945
Gibson, William C	Florence SC	4/21/1944	2/22/1946
Gibson, Willie Pat	Florence SC	5/6/1944	12/23/1943
Gilbert, Claude Livingston	Florence SC	6/18/1943	11/10/1945
Gilbert, Herbert McTyeire	Florence SC		
Gilbert, Leroy	Florence SC	11/17/1945	1/19/1947
Gill, Wallace McNeil	Florence SC	6/5/1943	5/11/1946
Gilmore, James	Baltimore MD		3/12/1945
Gissendaner, Emory Woodrow	Columbia SC	1/13/1941	10/30/1945
Gissendanner, William R	Florence SC	2/23/1942	9/27/1945
Glass, Jake G	Raleigh NC	2/20/1941	8/18/1945
Godbolt, J C	Florence SC	3/18/1946	3/28/1947
Godfrey, James Benjamin, Jr.	Florence SC	7/1/1944	2/8/1946
Goff, Robert Lang	Florence SC	9/9/1942	12/8/1945
Goodman, Edward Earl	Florence SC	11/3/1942	4/3/1946
Goodman, Eugene	Washington DC	1/3/1945	10/22/1945
Goodman, Walter F	Florence SC		8/16/1944
Goodson, Sim J	Florence SC	3/13/1944	6/13/1946
Goodwin, Robert James	Philadelphia PA		4/12/1944
Gore, Julius Bennette	Nashville Tenn	2/27/1943	
Goss, Bennie Dorant	Florence SC		11/16/1944
Graham, Allston Kent	Florence SC	1/14/1941	10/11/1945
Graham, Charles Newell	Florence SC	12/19/1942	11/10/1945
Graham, Charlie Albert	Baltimore MD	7/15/1944	10/27/1946
Graham, Dozier	Effingham SC	1/7/1943	2/22/1946
Graham, John LeRoy	Florence SC		9/14/1944
Graham, Leroy	Florence SC	04/34/46	3/21/1947
Graham, Theodore	Lake City SC	1/21/1943	3/10/1946
Graham, Tommy Ralston	Olanta SC	11/25/1944	4/4/1946
Graham, Walter Alvin	Florence SC	8/21/1941	10/20/1945
Graham, William Thomas	Greensboro NC		
Grainger, Maynard Hoyt	Florence SC	3/20/1942	11/16/1945
Grainger, Samuel Willard	Florence SC	4/8/1943	2/20/1946
Granger, Robert	Florence SC	4/7/1944	12/15/1944
Grant, David Nathaniel	Florence SC	1/20/1943	12/2/1945
Grant, Luther B	Covington GA	3/29/1944	
Grant, Luther Benson, Jr.	Griffin GA	3/29/1944	12/16/1945
Grant, Mikel, Jr.	Pamplico SC	9/18/1942	1/4/1946
Grant, Samuel B	Florence SC	10/20/1942	2/11/1946
Grant, Stone W	Pamplico SC	9/26/1942	12/15/1944
Grant, William D	Florence SC		5/15/1944
Grantham, Kenneth Winfred	Florence SC	8/20/1945	11/25/1946
Green, David Son	Timmonsville SC		3/8/1946

★ ★ ★ ★

NAME	CITY	ENTRY DATE	DISCHARGE
Green, Edward C	Hyman SC	1/18/1943	2/3/1947
Green, Henry D, Sr.	Columbia SC	4/13/1944	1/12/1946
Green, Jesse	Florence SC	1/24/1942	10/15/1945
Green, Jethro H	Florence SC	11/25/1941	9/2/1945
Green, Richard, Jr.	Florence SC	2/1/1946	11/19/1946
Green, Wilbur	Mars Bluff SC	9/10/1945	8/18/1946
Green, William James	Florence SC		12/1/1944
Greenberg, Samuel	Florence SC		9/12/1944
Gregg, Arthur C	Florence SC	1/13/1941	10/22/1945
Gregg, Benjamin H	Florence SC	8/9/1943	6/17/1946
Gregg, Charles Eli	Florence SC	12/1/1942	10/24/1945
Gregg, Charlton	Florence SC	3/8/1943	12/15/1944
Gregg, Eddie	Washington DC	7/20/1942	12/6/1945
Gregg, Edward Thomas	Florence SC	10/2/1944	12/1/1946
Gregg, Ernest Stewart	Florence SC	12/30/1943	5/3/1946
Gregg, Herman Eddie	New York NY	12/31/1942	10/20/1945
Gregg, Howard Alvin	Florence SC	8/26/1941	12/27/1946
Gregg, James C	Florence SC		6/4/1946
Gregg, James Nathaniel	Florence SC	7/28/1943	4/14/1946
Gregg, Kedron T	Cleveland OH	11/4/1941	10/8/1945
Gregg, LeVerne	Florence SC	6/7/1946	12/20/1946
Gregg, Marshall	Florence SC	4/19/1944	5/27/1946
Gregg, McKinley	Florence SC	7/13/1944	12/15/1946
Gregg, Nathaniel		1/20/1943	1/31/1946
Gregg, Roland Charlie	Florence SC	12/31/1942	2/12/1946
Gregg, Thomas M	Florence SC	1/20/1942	10/22/1945
Gregg, Wayne B	Florence SC	1/5/1943	3/9/1946
Gregg, William E	Florence SC	7/16/1941	12/28/1945
Gregg, Wilson Elison	Florence SC		10/3/1945
Gregory, John Gary	Olanta SC	9/29/1941	10/1/1945
Gregory, Willis, Jr.	Florence SC	8/18/1944	6/9/1946
Grey, Ashby Ervin	Florence SC	2/26/1944	6/2/1946
Grey, Hoyt	Florence SC	4/13/1941	11/16/1945
Grier, Jimy Lide	Florence SC	6/19/1944	7/9/1946
Griffen, James E	Florence SC	3/30/1945	
Griffin, Robert Perrin	Florence SC	1/21/1943	5/5/1946
Griffin, Willard Henry, Jr.	Raleigh NC	4/20/1942	12/15/1945
Grimes, Thomas Edwin, Jr.	Columbia SC	12/5/1942	12/26/1945
Grimsely, Marion Keith	Florence SC	4/27/1943	12/15/1944
Grimsley, James Haulford	Florence SC	10/17/1944	8/7/1946
Grimsley, Joseph Benjamin	Florence SC	6/16/1941	10/1/1945
Griste, Leroy	Florence SC	11/5/1943	1/24/1946
Griste, Wiley Grimes, Jr.	Ocean Drive SC	6/16/1942	12/1/1945
Grooms, James Silas	Cowards SC	11/13/1944	8/21/1946
Gross, Howell Frederick	Florence SC	5/4/1942	10/11/1945
Guiles, Alexander L	Pamplico SC	7/17/1941	9/25/1945
Gunter, Walter P	Florence SC	11/9/1940	9/2/1945
Gunter, Walter P	Florence SC	11/9/1940	4/1/1945
Gurley, Elbert	Florence SC	5/4/1943	11/17/1945
Gurley, Emanuel	Florence SC	1/31/1944	4/26/1946
Gurley, James W	Newport News VA	12/26/1942	1/4/1946
Hacklin, David Ernest	Florence SC	7/29/1943	10/30/1945
Haines, Visen F	Pamplico SC	6/25/1941	10/10/1945
Halford, Joseph C	Macon GA	6/11/1940	7/1/1945
Hall, Gerald William	Florence SC	6/22/1943	6/15/1946

★ ★ ★ ★

NAME	CITY	ENTRY DATE	DISCHARGE
Hall, Joseph	Florence SC		10/22/1944
Hallmon, Harrell	Washington DC	8/11/1944	8/26/1946
Ham, Carl E	Effingham SC	3/27/1946	12/6/1946
Ham, Clarence Woodrow	Florence SC	11/26/1943	2/2/1946
Ham, Leory	Effingham SC		6/29/1944
Ham, Rollie	Effingham SC	4/26/1945	8/13/1946
Ham, Samuel S	Florence SC		
Hamlin, Thomas Crosby	Effingham SC	7/11/1945	2/18/1947
Hamly, Alexander Theodore	Wentworth GA		
Hancock, James H	Columbia SC	1/19/1942	9/2/1945
Hancock, Tracey W	Effingham SC	1/13/1941	
Hand, Robert B, Jr.	Florence SC	9/30/1942	8/21/1945
Hanna, Hosie	Lake City SC	1/20/1943	12/15/1944
Hanna, James Julius	Effingham SC		5/30/1945
Hanna, William Jennings, Jr.	Florence SC	6/28/1944	2/27/1946
Hanna, Wilson	Florence SC	10/21/1943	1/3/1946
Hanna, Wilson Columbus	Florence SC		1/3/1946
Hannah, David	Lake City SC	11/17/1942	11/11/1945
Hannah, James	Scranton SC		11/28/1946
Hannah, Wadell	Florence SC	7/5/1946	11/21/1946
Harbort, Hugh Valetine	Florence SC	2/16/1942	10/28/1946
Harkless, Paul George	Florence SC	9/12/1945	11/29/1945
Harless, Freeland	Florence SC		11/1/1944
Harley, Handy	Florence SC	11/3/1942	2/1/1946
Harley, Lawrence	Florence SC	3/3/1945	7/27/1946
Harper, Arthur Lyde	Florence SC		5/31/1946
Harper, Nathaniel	Florence SC		
Harrell, Benjamin Fulton	Lake City SC		7/4/1945
Harrell, Carey Randolph	Florence SC	4/4/1941	11/19/1945
Harrell, Charlie H	Florence SC	7/21/1945	7/9/1946
Harrell, David Cuttino	Florence SC	3/26/1942	2/28/1946
Harrell, David Leon	Florence SC	8/22/1944	5/18/1946
Harrell, Erma E	Florence SC		6/20/1945
Harrell, Ernest	Florence SC	5/27/1944	6/6/1946
Harrell, Fred F	Tuscaloom AL		5/3/1945
Harrell, George Hepburn	Pamplico SC	5/21/1945	12/15/1944
Harrell, James Alebert	Florence SC		
Harrell, Joseph	Florence SC	10/1/1945	12/30/1946
Harrell, Maxie Bryany	Florence SC	7/20/1945	12/10/1945
Harrell, Richard Randolph	Timmonsville SC	12/23/1944	8/18/1946
Harrell, Wade H	Florence SC	10/20/1943	12/30/1945
Harrell, Wilbur	Florence SC	3/12/1943	11/5/1945
Harrell, William M	Pamplico SC	2/14/1944	12/27/1946
Harris, (Mrs.) Carol J	Florence SC		11/4/1944
Harris, Barnwell B	Florence SC	4/7/1943	4/7/1946
Harris, James Laula	Florence SC	12/26/1944	6/26/1946
Harris, Jesse W	Florence SC	4/8/1942	9/9/1945
Harris, Jesse W	Florence SC	4/8/1943	9/9/1945
Harris, Robert Brown	Florence SC	1/15/1942	10/17/1945
Harris, Rufus Oglshy	Florence SC	4/3/1943	11/26/1945
Harrison, Charlie	Florence SC	12/31/1942	
Harrison, Henry E	Florence SC	2/4/1943	12/15/1944
Harrison, James Lee	New York NY	11/3/1942	12/15/1944
Harrison, Leroy	Florence SC	6/24/1944	4/14/1946
Harrison, Ned	Florence SC	9/22/1943	2/15/1946

★ ★ ★ ★

NAME	CITY	ENTRY DATE	DISCHARGE
Harrison, Thomas H	Florence SC	2/9/1943	10/22/1945
Hart, George Dyson	New York NY	7/13/1944	7/8/1946
Hart, William Judge	Newport News VA		
Harter, Marion A	Florence SC	10/22/1943	7/25/1945
Hartis, William Abernathey	Hickory NC	9/20/1943	4/12/1946
Haselden, Alton Courtney	Florence SC	5/16/1942	12/15/1944
Haselden, Daphne	Florence SC	11/14/1942	11/11/1945
Haselden, Evertt James	Florence SC	3/25/1944	11/12/1945
Haselden, Heyward Legrand	Florence SC	2/24/1944	3/3/1946
Haselden, Hobson W		9/28/1940	
Haselden, Hobson W	Florence SC	2/24/1944	3/3/1946
Haselden, Norman Lester	Florence SC	6/25/1943	5/11/1946
Haselden, Ray Molton	Johnsonville SC	1/9/1945	7/17/1946
Haselden, Stephen Young, Jr.	Florence SC		4/23/1945
Haskins, Henry Wilbur	Pearson GA	9/3/1942	6/5/1946
Hasty, Leonard J	Camden SC	8/20/1942	1/1/1946
Hatchell, Earl Rhodes	Florence SC	12/1/1942	10/9/1945
Hatchell, Emmett R	Florence SC	7/11/1941	12/15/1944
Hatchell, Fulton Edward	Florence SC	10/20/1943	12/15/1945
Hatchell, Leo Carl	Florence SC	2/9/1943	
Hatchell, Levi Hartwell	Columbia SC	4/7/1943	9/26/1945
Hatchell, Richard Woodrow	Florence SC	2/21/1943	12/5/1945
Hatchell, Talmadge Rudolph	Florence SC	10/30/1944	5/29/1946
Hatchell, Wallace Traxler	Florence SC	5/27/1944	1/30/1946
Hatfield, General Major	Florence SC	3/28/1946	2/11/1947
Hatfield, Walter D	Florence SC		7/9/1945
Hatfield, William E		10/29/1942	11/28/1945
Hawkins, Earl	Florence SC	5/11/1944	
Hawkins, Francis	Florence SC	10/24/1941	9/27/1945
Hawkins, Lawrence Allen	Effingham SC	11/13/1945	11/13/1946
Hawkins, Leo	Effingham SC	2/26/1944	1/27/1946
Hawley, Jack Edwin	Florence SC	3/29/1946	12/17/1947
Hawley, Matthew R	Florence SC	2/9/1943	12/29/1945
Hayes, Douglas	Florence SC	11/2/1941	8/8/1945
Hayes, Junius T	Hyman SC	4/14/1945	7/5/1946
Hayes, Walter Hall	Florence SC	7/1/1944	1/18/1946
Hayes, Woodrow	Florence SC	8/2/1943	2/27/1946
Haynes, Carl William	Darlington SC	8/6/1942	1/13/1947
Haynes, Dean Berry	Florence SC	10/9/1943	1/5/1946
Haynes, Ernest Earl	Effingham SC	1/26/1940	1/25/1946
Haynes, John Henry	Pamplico SC	4/21/1943	12/10/1945
Haynesworth, Hazel	Florence SC	3/12/1946	1/11/1947
Haynie, Francis McFarlain	Darlington SC		10/25/1944
Hayward, Willie Learn	Florence SC	2/26/1944	9/25/1946
Haywood, Thomas Owen	Florence SC	3/14/1942	11/27/1945
Head, Donald D	Florence SC	6/6/1943	12/24/1945
Head, John S, Jr.	Florence SC	12/1/1943	4/4/1946
Heard, Harry Howell	Florence SC	1/31/1944	9/27/1945
Hearne, Rodolphus T, Jr.	Pineville NC	6/5/1942	11/1/1945
Helms, James Theron, Jr.	Florence SC	10/1/1943	5/1/1946
Hemingway, Adam Levi	Florence SC	5/5/1943	12/15/1944
Hemingway, Hoyt	Aynor SC	3/21/1941	12/9/1945
Henderson, Alex K	Florence SC	12/31/1940	10/8/1945
Henderson, John	Florence SC	11/23/1945	2/4/1947
Henicke, James, Jr.	Knoxville TN		4/3/1942

★ ★ ★ ★

NAME	CITY	ENTRY DATE	DISCHARGE
Hennighen, Lamar	Florence SC	5/6/1944	3/8/1946
Hennix, Nathaniel	Philadelphia PA	1/28/1944	11/8/1945
Henry, Julius	Florence SC	8/25/1942	12/19/1945
Hepburn, Harry Brunson	Florence SC		
Hepburn, Kenneth C	Florence SC	2/11/1942	10/2/1945
Hepburn, Robert Stuart, Jr.	Timmonsville SC	4/26/1941	12/1/1945
Hepburn, Thomas Eugene	Florence SC	12/12/1945	6/22/1947
Herbert, Henry Williams		8/11/1942	
Herring, Benjamin P, Jr.	Florence SC	3/15/1944	5/5/1946
Hewett, Benjamin E	Florence SC		6/8/1945
Hewett, Charles B	Florence SC	5/9/1945	7/20/1946
Hewett, George	Florence SC	11/23/1940	8/23/1945
Hewett, Joseph Junior	Florence SC	7/22/1941	8/15/1945
Hewitt, James E	Florence SC		10/10/1945
Hewitt, John Pheonix	Florence SC		
Hewitt, Rufus Cogburn	Florence SC	7/28/1942	2/5/1946
Hewitt, Thurman Ashberton	Florence SC	6/11/1943	12/3/1945
Hicks, Ashton H	Cowards SC	1/13/1941	11/1/1945
Hicks, Chalmus Moses	Florence SC	12/13/1942	4/25/1946
Hicks, Charles Edward	Budford OH		1/31/1944
Hicks, Dessie LeRoy	Florence SC	6/2/1943	12/7/1945
Hicks, Elijah Logan	Florence SC	5/27/1944	2/9/1946
Hicks, Isaac	New York NY	6/20/1944	12/15/1944
Hicks, James Allen	Timmonsville SC	4/2/1945	1/26/1947
Hicks, James Ernest	Florence SC	2/19/1943	1/18/1946
Hicks, Jesse L	Florence SC	6/1/1943	12/31/1945
Hicks, John Wesley	Hyman SC	4/17/1944	11/19/1945
Hicks, William Leon	Florence SC	11/18/1944	7/7/1946
Hicks, William Stroud	Bishopville SC	12/27/1943	1/2/1946
Hickson, Evander C	Florence SC	2/12/1945	1/25/1946
Hickson, James	Tranton NJ	1/30/1945	1/5/1946
Hickson, Otis, W	Florence SC	4/2/1943	4/5/1946
Higgens, Randolph Connor	Florence SC	12/3/1942	4/8/1946
High, Hubert Worth, Jr.	Florence SC	8/2/1943	3/12/1946
Hill, Ernest I, Jr.		7/28/1942	1/23/1946
Hill, George Woodrow	Florence SC	7/1/1944	5/30/1946
Hill, James David	Timmonsville SC	2/2/1943	4/6/1946
Hill, Jesse Lee	Florence SC	9/4/1942	11/4/1945
Hill, John Micheal, Jr.	Florence SC	8/14/1943	3/6/1946
Hill, Robert B	Florence SC	10/12/1942	12/24/1945
Hill, Taz	Florence SC	10/31/1945	3/20/1947
Hill, Willaim Ray	Florence SC	1/7/1944	6/4/1946
Hinds, Edward J	Florence SC	8/23/1943	4/20/1946
Hinds, Grover Cleveland	Florence SC		3/14/1944
Hinds, Grover Cleveland, Jr.	Florence SC		
Hinds, Leon	Florence SC	7/20/1942	1/22/1946
Hinds, Maxie A	Pamplico SC	2/4/1943	12/24/1945
Hinds, Stanley W	Pamplico SC	8/20/1940	12/15/1944
Hines, Albert Brown, Jr.	Florence SC	1/31/1945	12/9/1946
Hines, Freddie	Claussen SC	8/5/1944	6/28/1946
Hines, Jake C	Florence SC	9/27/1944	1/12/1946
Hines, Moses	Florence SC	1/30/1945	7/23/1946
Hines, Thinel A	Florence SC	1/16/1942	10/27/1945
Hines, Thomas H	Florence SC	6/17/1943	1/28/1946
Hinsen, Frank Elias	Florence SC	5/25/1943	12/23/1945

★ ★ ★ ★

NAME	CITY	ENTRY DATE	DISCHARGE
Hoard, Edward Leslie	Florence SC	6/24/1944	3/12/1946
Hodge, George Washington	Florence SC	11/7/1942	1/7/1946
Hodge, Layton	Lake City SC	1/24/1944	3/28/1945
Hodge, Leonard NMN		1/5/1945	2/21/1946
Hodge, Loyd D	Timmonsville SC	8/19/1941	12/10/1945
Hodge, Thomas Allen	Florence SC	3/31/1941	3/7/1945
Hoffmeyer, Harmon Fredrick	Florence SC		3/13/1945
Hoffmeyer, William Johannas	Florence SC	1/28/1943	1/30/1946
Holland, Edwin Spence	Florence SC	10/10/1942	2/20/1946
Holland, Fred Dayton	Florence SC		
Holland, Jack Peter	Florence SC		11/17/1945
Holland, Robert C	Florence SC		9/27/1945
Holley, Charles Robert	Florence SC	7/3/1945	9/7/1945
Holley, Ernest Starhard, Jr.	Florence SC	1/24/1944	5/31/1946
Hollimon, Robert Lee	Brooklyn NY	11/19/1943	4/25/1946
Hollis, Charles Franklin, Jr.	Tampa FL	3/11/1944	1/18/1946
Hollis, Willard Franklin	Florence SC	7/30/1942	12/15/1944
Holloway, Joseph K	Florence SC	7/8/1944	6/19/1946
Holloway, Tom Baker	Florence SC		
Holmes, Archie Edward	Florence SC	12/31/1942	11/20/1945
Holmes, David	Florence SC	1/21/1944	4/18/1946
Holmes, James Allen	Florence SC	12/31/1942	2/23/1946
Holmes, Nathaniel	Florence SC		11/11/1943
Holmes, Theodore	Florence SC		
Holt, Milton Edward	Florence SC		7/5/1944
Hooke, Leslie Eugene	Florence SC	6/10/1943	1/22/1946
Horne, Edward James	Effingham SC	7/7/1944	7/18/1946
Houlles, Steve Demetrous	Toledo OH		1/30/1943
Houser, Thomas E	Florence SC	4/20/1943	12/15/1944
Howard, Charles L	Florence SC	10/25/1943	3/7/1945
Howard, Edward	Florence SC	1/20/1943	11/14/1945
Howard, James Earl	Florence SC	1/5/1944	12/29/1945
Howard, James Lenwood	Alexander Rapid LA	1/16/1942	11/11/1945
Howard, Keith	Florence SC	3/27/1941	9/1/1945
Howard, Leo Cooper	Florence SC	1/27/1941	1/5/1946
Howard, Ray A	Timmonsville SC	11/19/1945	4/19/1947
Howard, Sammie James	Florence SC	8/21/1945	6/22/1946
Howe, Edward G		4/19/1941	10/15/1945
Howell, John Albert	Florence SC	4/7/1943	1/30/1946
Howell, Robert McDuffie	Florence SC		4/12/1945
Howerton, John Layton	Florence SC	8/23/1943	3/3/1946
Howington, Thomas Gridle	Florence SC	7/17/1943	7/11/1945
Howle, Harry Clark	Florence SC	8/12/1944	3/24/1946
Howle, Thomas L, Jr.	Florence SC	5/19/1941	
Howle, William Sweday	Florence SC		6/25/1945
Hubater, Ernest Louis, Jr.	Florence SC		
Hubbard, Charles Rast	Conway SC	10/15/1941	10/12/1945
Hubbard, Mason H, Jr.	Pamplico SC	8/5/1944	
Hubbard, Samuel Grady, Jr.	Florence SC		10/4/1945
Hudson, Cleveland		9/9/1943	4/25/1946
Hudson, Henry T	Florence SC		9/21/1945
Hudson, James Elbert	Florence SC	8/16/1943	3/12/1946
Hudson, Jim	Florence SC	10/29/1942	2/1/1946
Hudson, John H	Florence SC	2/9/1945	11/26/1946
Hudson, Lenwood H	Timmonsville SC	11/10/1945	12/26/1946

NAME	CITY	ENTRY DATE	DISCHARGE
Hudson, William	Effingham SC	5/25/1944	4/20/1946
Huggins, Andrew Alonzo	Florence SC	1/5/1944	12/10/1945
Huggins, Elimore Bryant	Florence SC		1/10/1945
Huggins, Percy Powell, Jr.	Florence SC	4/7/1943	3/11/1946
Hughes, Ernest Elwood	Simons Island GA	5/12/1944	12/10/1945
Hughes, John William Jr.	Florence SC	6/30/1944	5/15/1946
Hughes, Woodrow Wilson	Darlington SC	2/6/1943	12/2/1945
Humphries, Gloria C	Florence SC		5/12/1944
Humphries, Hazel H	Florence SC		9/1/1944
Humphries, Herbert Synder	Florence SC	7/21/1941	
Humphries, James Henry	Florence SC		
Humphries, Robert Owen	Florence SC	7/30/1942	1/24/1947
Hunt, Claude McDonald	Chesterfield SC	4/18/1942	11/14/1945
Hunter, Frank Armfield	Effingham SC	2/5/1943	11/2/1945
Hunter, Randolph	Florence SC	1/13/1943	2/20/1946
Hunter, Raymond	Florence SC	1/15/1943	3/7/1946
Hurst, James	Charleston SC		
Hutchinson, Harold	Florence SC	1/28/1942	1/12/1946
Hutchinson, Harry Lee	Florence SC		9/22/1945
Hutchinson, Hubert Moultrie	Effingham SC	12/21/1945	
Hutchinson, Hubert O'Neil	Effingham SC	2/21/1942	5/21/1946
Hutchinson, Jallie Eugene	Florence SC	8/2/1942	8/8/1946
Hutchinson, James Charlton	Johnson SC	7/16/1940	10/19/1945
Hutchinson, James Lester	Marion SC	5/6/1942	10/19/1945
Hutchinson, Lenward Keels	Florence SC	1/13/1941	1/18/1946
Hutchinson, Leo Dudley	Florence SC		11/30/1944
Hutchinson, Lonnie R	Florence SC		9/29/1944
Hutchinson, Nathan Dwight	Florence SC	8/20/1940	10/8/1945
Hutchinson, Randall Holmes, Jr.	Tampa FL	1/5/1945	8/6/1946
Hutchinson, Thomas Elonza	Florence SC	2/8/1944	12/30/1945
Hutchinson, Willard J	Florence SC	6/21/1943	2/7/1946
Hutte, John B	Florence SC		7/13/1945
Hutte, John Emerson	Florence SC	10/16/1941	11/3/1945
Hyatt, Preston Allen	Florence SC	6/18/1940	6/20/1946
Hyman, Dallas William	Florence SC		
Hyman, Deck	Pamplico SC	4/2/1941	9/2/1945
Hyman, Ernest	Florence SC	3/3/1943	11/20/1945
Hyman, Francis Eugene	Florence SC	8/25/1942	3/5/1946
Hyman, Geffery Eugene	Dillon SC	8/13/1942	2/6/1946
Hyman, Jack Benjamin	Tabor City NC	4/17/1942	12/15/1945
Hyman, Jack NMN	Pamplico SC		12/15/1944
Hyman, James Thomas	Jacksonville FL		
Hyman, Myrl	Pamplico SC	11/28/1942	2/13/1946
Hyman, Peter Dewitt	Florence SC	6/25/1943	1/18/1946
Hyman, Robert I	Pamplico SC	10/30/1943	10/20/1945
Hyman, Russell	Pamplico SC	2/28/1942	10/11/1945
Hyman, Thadeus Elliot	Florence SC	5/13/1942	11/24/1945
Hyman, Walter Junior	Pamplico SC	9/9/1942	11/15/1945
Hyman, Will	Pamplico SC	1/19/1942	12/13/1945
Hyman, Willie Booth	Hyman SC	7/13/1943	2/11/1946
Inabinet, Wyman	Swansea SC	4/17/1944	12/18/1946
Ingram, Curtiss L	Florence SC	2/14/1942	9/29/1945
Ingram, Fred Dewey	Martinsville VA	10/7/1941	10/28/1945
Irby, Wilson C	Long Beach CA	10/2/1945	1/21/1947
Irby, Wilson Crawley	Florence SC	12/4/1944	

★ ★ ★ ★

NAME	CITY	ENTRY DATE	DISCHARGE
Irick, James Hammond	Florence SC	2/20/1941	7/18/1945
Irick, Louie Lee	Florence SC	5/7/1945	12/15/1944
Isaac, Eddie	Florence SC	5/6/1944	12/15/1944
Isaac, James Elliott	New York NY	12/31/1942	11/29/1945
Isaac, Rudolph	Norfolk VA		
Isaiah, Willie	Florence SC	5/17/1943	12/7/1945
Isenhower, Willie Joe	Florence SC		7/16/1945
Isgett, James W	Florence SC	6/18/1943	2/2/1946
Isgett, Monroe W	Florence SC	7/20/2006	10/12/1945
Isiah, Samuel	Florence SC	8/20/1943	
Isom, Olin G, Jr.	Florence SC		6/1/1945
Jackson, Clarence	Florence SC	11/17/1942	12/9/1945
Jackson, Edward	Florence SC	7/29/1943	2/27/1946
Jackson, Edward NMN	Florence SC	11/21/1945	11/12/1946
Jackson, Edwardf	Florence SC	7/29/1943	2/27/1946
Jackson, Frank	Timmonsville SC	11/26/1943	3/10/1946
Jackson, Frank	Timmonsville SC	11/26/1943	3/10/1946
Jackson, Hazekiah	Florence SC	8/10/1945	4/3/1947
Jackson, Hubert	Florence SC	12/31/1943	3/25/1946
Jackson, Hubert	Florence SC	12/31/1942	3/25/1946
Jackson, Larry Artope	Florence SC		11/16/1945
Jackson, Leroy	Oakleand CA	6/27/1944	6/16/1946
Jackson, Leroy	Oakleand CA	6/27/1944	6/16/1946
Jackson, Robert Lee	Timmonsville SC	1/16/1946	2/14/1947
Jackson, Sandy	Florence SC	4/19/1944	2/10/1946
Jackson, Thomas	Florence SC	3/18/1944	1/7/1946
Jackson, William, Jr.	Pamplico SC	8/14/1945	10/24/1946
Jacob, Donald R	Kingston NY	2/13/1942	11/26/1946
Jacob, George Washington	Norfolk VA		
Jacobs, Hoses	Florence SC	11/13/1945	1/19/1946
Jacobs, Mack	Florence SC	7/13/1943	2/15/1946
Jacobs, Willie	Florence SC	2/19/1943	1/5/1946
Jacobs, Wooster	Florence SC	1/21/1943	2/22/1946
Jaillette, Harold Prentiss	Florence SC	12/21/1943	4/11/1946
James, A Albert		5/10/1943	3/29/1946
James, Arthur, Jr.	Florence SC	12/31/1942	2/13/1946
James, Benjamin	Florence SC	3/4/1943	3/13/1946
James, Buster		10/28/1943	12/20/1945
James, Cecil	Florence SC	3/18/1946	1/5/1947
James, David	Florence SC	1/14/1943	2/7/1946
James, Douglas L	Florence SC	5/8/1944	1/21/1946
James, Douglas Lee	Florence SC	5/8/1944	1/21/1946
James, Earl Nathaniel	Florence SC	5/11/1943	11/14/1945
James, Edward, Jr.	Florence SC	3/3/1946	1/5/1946
James, Edward, Jr.	Wilmington NC		2/23/1946
James, Frank	Florence SC	2/26/1943	1/10/1946
James, Freddie	Florence SC		
James, George Baxter	Florence SC	5/28/1941	10/23/1945
James, George W	Claussen SC	5/11/1943	11/7/1945
James, Harding	Florence SC	5/26/1943	12/15/1945
James, Harry LaVerne	Florence SC	12/29/1943	6/21/1946
James, Henry	Claussen SC	11/17/1942	12/15/1944
James, Isaac	Baltimore MD		
James, John	Pamplico SC	11/17/1942	11/22/1945
James, Johnnie	Florence SC	3/17/1942	6/27/1945

★ ★ ★ ★

NAME	CITY	ENTRY DATE	DISCHARGE
James, Johnnie	Florence SC	7/17/1943	1/7/1946
James, Lee Ernest	Florence SC	5/11/1944	6/9/1946
James, Lee Mathheo	Florence SC		
James, Leroy	Florence SC	9/4/1943	
James, Louis	Florence SC	12/30/1944	7/23/1945
James, Major Chancelor	Florence SC	4/19/1944	12/28/1945
James, McKinley B	Florence SC	10/28/1942	3/28/1946
James, Melvin	Florence SC	2/23/1943	1/22/1946
James, Ravenell	Florence SC	7/17/1943	3/27/1946
James, Sidney E	Aynor SC	6/4/1942	7/12/1945
James, Sidney, Jr.	Florence SC		9/7/1945
James, Thasseus S	Florence SC	3/9/1944	1/3/1946
James, William Rutledge	Florence SC	8/11/1942	
James, Willie T	Florence SC		11/24/1944
James, Woodrow	Florence SC	3/3/1943	3/13/1946
Jameson, Charlie Lee	Florence SC		6/30/1945
Jasper, Thomas	Florence SC		5/29/1945
Jeffers, Joe Clyde, Jr.	Florence SC	8/14/1942	1/11/1946
Jeffers, John James	Florence SC	6/1/1943	3/16/1946
Jeffers, John Thomas	Florence SC		
Jefferson, Wesley	Rocky Mount NC	11/19/1943	9/16/1946
Jefford, John C	Columbia SC	10/23/1934	2/19/1946
Jeffords, Boyd E	Florence SC	12/12/1941	2/10/1946
Jeffords, Clarence James	Atkinson NC	10/31/1945	11/8/1946
Jeffords, Colin Quintillus	Florence SC	6/18/1943	2/19/1946
Jeffords, Hugh H	Florence SC	2/2/1943	10/26/1945
Jeffords, M C	Timmonsville SC	8/30/1943	4/4/1946
Jeffords, William Albert, Jr.	Florence SC	12/14/1942	3/23/1946
Jenerette, Giles Altman	Mullins SC		1/27/1946
Jenerette, Lucius Victor	Florence SC	9/4/1943	12/18/1945
Jenkins, Albert	Florence SC	11/3/1942	4/4/1946
Jenkins, Andrew Haile	Florence SC	11/19/1943	3/2/1946
Jenkins, Ernest	Florence SC		
Jenkins, James	Florence SC	4/28/1944	12/29/1945
Jenkins, Leo	Florence SC	3/9/1943	
Jenkins, Warren Edward	Timmonsville SC	11/13/1945	11/18/1946
Jensen, Albert F	Duluth MN	11/7/1941	12/15/1944
Jernigan, Garner Lee	Fayetteville NC	4/18/1942	3/4/1946
Jernigan, James Nelly	Florence SC		
Jernigan, Leroy Daveport	Florence SC	8/28/1943	3/22/1946
Jeter, Harold Hubert, Jr.	Florence SC	10/13/1943	4/25/1946
Johnson, Beler Joseph	Hartsville SC	6/3/1943	12/10/1945
Johnson, Bennie W	Florence SC	12/3/1942	10/6/1945
Johnson, Buster Bosster	Trenton NJ	11/30/1942	1/10/1946
Johnson, Charles Edward	McBee SC	1/28/1946	2/17/1947
Johnson, Charles Thomas	Timmonsville SC		
Johnson, Curtis	New York NY	11/5/1943	12/24/1945
Johnson, David	Florence SC	6/24/1943	1/15/1946
Johnson, David	Effingham SC		2/13/1947
Johnson, Delwyn Newton	Florence SC	4/6/1943	12/15/1944
Johnson, Dover	Florence SC		6/10/1945
Johnson, Eddie	New York NY		
Johnson, Edward	Florence SC		4/23/1945
Johnson, Eugene	Florence SC		
Johnson, Evander Jordan	Florence SC		8/26/1946

★ ★ ★ ★

NAME	CITY	ENTRY DATE	DISCHARGE
Johnson, Foster Leroy	Timmonsville SC	3/7/1946	1/6/1947
Johnson, Frank Sterling	Florence SC	7/1/1944	5/29/1946
Johnson, Frank, Jr.	Timmonsville SC	9/29/1944	2/23/1946
Johnson, Fred James	Florence SC		
Johnson, George	Florence SC		
Johnson, George	Florence SC	6/28/1941	12/15/1944
Johnson, Gus	Newark NJ	3/15/1943	10/10/2004
Johnson, Harry	Blackville SC	6/22/1944	
Johnson, Hezikiah B	Effingham SC	3/20/1944	12/20/1945
Johnson, Jack	Florence SC		5/5/1944
Johnson, Jack Willard	Conway SC	4/27/1945	2/8/1946
Johnson, James	Florence SC	8/6/1945	11/24/1945
Johnson, James	Florence SC	1/21/1943	1/28/1946
Johnson, James Floyd	Florence SC	8/21/1944	10/19/1946
Johnson, James Floyd	Timmonsville SC	9/30/1942	1/8/1946
Johnson, James Lester	Fair Bluff NC	1/28/1943	5/24/1946
Johnson, January B	Florence SC	11/26/1945	11/26/1946
Johnson, John	Florence SC	5/10/1944	7/27/1946
Johnson, John Samuel, Jr.	Columbia SC		
Johnson, John T	Hartsville SC	2/2/1944	4/30/1946
Johnson, Joseph Argo	Effingham SC		10/10/1945
Johnson, Kenneth Edward	Aiken SC	9/1/1942	10/12/1945
Johnson, Leo Clyde	Effingham SC		1/1/1947
Johnson, Leroy	Florence SC	3/13/1944	4/6/1946
Johnson, Leslie	Florence SC	1/19/1942	9/12/1945
Johnson, Lewis	Florence SC		3/22/1944
Johnson, Louis Edward	Florence SC	4/11/1944	
Johnson, McKenzie	Timmonsville SC	8/29/1944	12/15/1944
Johnson, Melvin A	Florence SC	12/14/1943	5/24/1946
Johnson, Murray Bee	Florence SC	6/10/1943	1/6/1946
Johnson, Sam	Florence SC		
Johnson, Sammie	Florence SC	4/13/1945	8/16/1945
Johnson, Samuel Louis	Baltimore MD	5/18/1943	1/23/1946
Johnson, Wallace McNeil	Florence SC	4/20/1943	1/13/1946
Johnson, Walter	Florence SC	7/20/1943	4/19/1946
Johnson, Wilbert	Florence SC	9/24/1943	12/20/1945
Johnson, Wilbur	Florence SC	6/22/1944	3/21/1946
Johnson, William David		6/30/1943	3/3/1946
Johnson, Willie	Florence SC	9/4/1943	11/11/1946
Johnston, James Rufus		4/17/1939	7/15/1945
Johnston, Reuben Cooper	Florence SC	6/1/1943	12/13/1945
Jones, Ashley Gibson	Sumter SC	2/10/1945	10/10/1946
Jones, Barry Webb	Florence SC	2/28/1944	9/27/1945
Jones, Charles Waymon	Florence SC	3/25/1944	5/23/1946
Jones, Clyde Cato	Florence SC	4/19/1944	1/19/1946
Jones, George Washington	Florence SC	5/2/1946	7/17/1946
Jones, Glenn Wilbur	Florence SC	8/16/1940	11/14/1945
Jones, Henry R	Florence SC	12/3/1942	1/1/1946
Jones, John W, Jr.	Florence SC	8/4/1944	10/15/1945
Jones, Lora, Jr.	Florence SC	11/21/1945	2/27/1947
Jones, Ludie	Pamplico SC	4/1/1943	1/5/1946
Jones, McKeever	Timmonsville SC	12/6/1945	1/21/1947
Jones, Robert Lee	Florence SC	1/10/1946	2/7/1947
Jones, Roscoe	Florence SC	5/11/1944	3/9/1946
Jones, Sammie Lee	Timmonsville SC	4/27/1945	10/11/1946

★ ★ ★ ★

NAME	CITY	ENTRY DATE	DISCHARGE
Jones, Saul	Florence SC	5/16/1944	12/15/1944
Jones, Spurgeon W	Pamplico SC	11/29/1939	9/6/1945
Jones, Willie (Junior)	Florence SC	7/5/1943	1/27/1946
Jordan, Arthur	Baltimore MD	3/23/1943	3/18/1946
Jordan, Isaac	Timmonsville SC	3/5/1946	12/1/1946
Jordan, James	Florence SC	2/17/1942	7/7/1945
Jordan, Joel B, Jr.	Florence SC	12/5/1942	12/27/1945
Jordan, Robert Cleney	Florence SC	5/27/1944	2/11/1946
Jordan, Thaddues	Philadelphia PA		
Jordan, Vyrle D	Florence SC		
Joseph, Clarence	Florence SC	6/4/1941	11/1/1945
Joseph, Ervin Alonza	Florence SC	3/4/1942	7/29/1946
Joseph, John	Florence SC	11/10/1943	2/8/1946
Josey, McKinley	Timmonsville SC	6/7/1945	8/20/1946
Joye, David Bunton	Florence SC	3/23/1943	2/26/1946
Joyner, David E	Wilmington NC		10/30/1944
Joyner, Jack Harrington	Scranton SC	11/21/1945	12/15/1944
Joyner, Jack Harrington	Scranton SC	11/21/1945	12/15/1944
Joyner, Richard Lafay	Timmonsville SC	8/8/1942	2/14/1946
Joyner, Thomas Edison	Florence SC		
Judge, Abraham, Jr.	Pamplico SC	7/14/1943	3/15/1946
Judson, Darrell	Florence SC	10/1/1940	10/23/1945
June, George Charlton	Florence SC	6/24/1942	12/18/1945
June, William C	Florence SC	10/5/1942	
Jupiter, Ernest	Florence SC		12/17/1943
Jupiter, James Junior	Baltimore MD		12/15/1944
Jupiter, Lee	Florence SC	9/6/1943	10/6/1945
Jupiter, Nelson	Florence SC	3/6/1942	11/28/1946
Justice, Charles Donald	Hendersonville NC	12/5/1942	
Kafer, John Barnwell	Florence SC	4/18/1942	12/26/1945
Kale, Nathan Chalmas	Florence SC	9/21/1944	6/26/1946
Kastel, Francis J	Florence SC		11/11/1944
Kea, Frank Willard	Timmonsville SC	4/3/1945	10/19/1946
Kea, Ray Acey	Florence SC	1/28/1944	5/24/1946
Keefe, Guy	Florence SC	11/4/1939	9/26/1945
Keefe, Guy	Florence SC		11/4/1939
Keefe, Harrell Finklea	Florence SC	10/23/1942	2/21/1946
Keith, John E	Pamplico SC	9/15/1942	12/14/1945
Kelley, John	Florence SC	12/30/1944	7/6/1946
Kelly, Baxter	Florence SC	7/15/1943	12/11/1945
Kelly, Benjamin Francis	Florence SC		5/14/1945
Kelly, Cephas	Timmonsville SC		1/6/1946
Kelly, Ernest Thomas	Florence SC		
Kelly, James Franklin, Jr.	Florence SC	2/12/1943	12/13/1945
Kelly, James W	Florence SC	1/13/1941	9/17/1945
Kelly, James, Jr.	Florence SC	2/2/1943	3/15/1946
Kelly, John C	Florence SC	2/9/1943	1/16/1946
Kelly, John Thomas	Florence SC	4/29/1943	2/27/1946
Kelly, Johnnie	Florence SC	2/19/1942	1/15/1946
Kelly, Manley	Pamplico SC	4/2/1941	11/8/1945
Kelly, Phillip A, Jr.	Florence SC	2/20/1943	9/10/1945
Kemmerlin, George David, Jr.	Long Branch NJ	2/14/1944	6/30/1946
Kemmerlin, Laurie	Florence SC	12/5/1942	12/11/1945
Kendall, James Russel	Charleston SC	8/29/1943	
Kennedy, Alfred L	Florence SC	5/28/1945	11/21/1945

★ ★ ★ ★

NAME	CITY	ENTRY DATE	DISCHARGE
Kennedy, Boyd	Florence SC	11/2/1945	12/25/1946
Kennedy, Carl	Florence SC	7/30/1942	1/13/1946
Kennedy, James	Pamplico SC	9/24/1942	12/5/1945
Kennedy, James Matthew	Raleigh NC		
Kennedy, John Henry	Florence SC	12/31/1942	12/21/1945
Kennedy, Lewis	Timmonsville SC	1/6/1944	3/26/1946
Kennedy, Roland E	Florence SC	12/6/1942	10/19/1945
Keretses, George Constatine	Florence SC	6/16/1943	5/7/1946
Kersey, Wesley NMN	Conway SC	4/2/1943	8/31/1945
Kershaw, Christopher	Florence SC	5/6/1944	4/25/1946
Kershaw, Frank William	Florence SC	4/23/1944	3/13/1946
Killen, Clyde Hyman	Florence SC	5/26/1944	2/16/1946
Killen, William Clifton	Los Angeles CA	7/14/1942	11/19/1945
Killingsworth, James Mayson	Denmark SC	4/17/1944	1/27/1946
Kilpatrick, Thomas J	Lynchburg SC	4/18/1942	11/25/1945
Kimley, Shelly Jene	Florence SC	11/13/1945	12/2/1946
Kinard, James E	Columbia SC	12/27/1943	12/16/1945
King, Alex	Baltimore MD	10/16/1943	4/22/1945
King, Alton L	Florence SC	1/1/1943	3/17/1946
King, Campbell	Florence SC		3/20/1943
King, James R		9/30/1942	11/17/1945
King, Levi, Sr.	Florence SC	7/12/1944	1/18/1946
King, Moses	Florence SC	4/26/1945	3/30/1946
King, Ralph	Florence SC	3/20/1943	2/28/1946
King, Townzo J W	Florence SC	1/1/1944	1/3/1947
King, Travis Peebles	Florence SC	12/2/1943	4/2/1946
King, V James	Florence SC	3/28/1941	10/21/1945
King, William Frank	Philadelphia PA	4/29/1943	
Kinley, James Alfonso	Florence SC	4/19/1944	
Kinley, Robert Lee	Florence SC	7/21/1943	12/22/1945
Kirby, Dainey T	Olanta SC	4/2/1943	1/21/1946
Kirby, Donald Clyde	Florence SC	8/12/1940	9/16/1945
Kirby, Fred Javin	Florence SC	7/26/1942	12/2/1945
Kirby, Herman Joseph	Florence SC	4/28/1943	3/15/1946
Kirby, Jack Leroy	Timmonsville SC	10/30/1944	1/21/1947
Kirby, James Elijah	Florence SC		
Kirby, James Marion	Effingham SC	4/13/1947	11/29/1945
Kirby, Larry D, Jr.	Effingham SC	1/28/1944	5/11/1946
Kirby, Samuel J	Columbia SC		9/19/1945
Kirby, Samuel J	Columbia SC		12/15/1944
Kirkley, James	Florence SC	3/4/1943	12/14/1945
Kirven, Richard Benjamin	Florence SC	4/2/1942	12/12/1945
Kirven, Rogers	Norfolk VA	2/12/1945	12/13/1946
Kirvin, Archie C	Florence SC	3/9/1944	11/26/1945
Kirvin, Wilds Wallace	Florence SC		4/12/1945
Kiser, Cecil Fono	Florence SC	5/6/1942	12/15/1944
Kishey, Toufic	Florence SC	10/15/1942	2/16/1946
Kitchens, Ralph Lewis	Florence SC	12/13/1943	12/16/1945
Kittrell, Edward Lee	Florence SC	7/19/1940	11/22/1945
Kittrell, Robert A, Jr.	Florence SC	6/28/1944	8/2/1945
Knight, Laverne M	Timmonsville SC	2/13/1945	7/24/1946
Koperna, Andrew	Schuykill Have PA	9/5/1942	2/16/1946
Korytkowski, Henry E	Detroit MI	9/2/1942	12/11/1945
Kyle, Leon E	Florence SC	12/30/1942	12/15/1944
Lackey, James Allen	Lake City SC	10/16/1941	12/15/1944

★ ★ ★ ★

NAME	CITY	ENTRY DATE	DISCHARGE
Lail, George Dougals	Florence SC	2/23/1945	7/17/1946
Lakin, Bennie David	Durham NC	5/27/1942	9/25/1945
Lambert, Ernest Carl	Effingham SC	4/18/1940	4/19/1946
Lambright, James Walter	Florence SC	10/7/1943	12/10/1945
Lane, Henry E	Florence SC	11/13/1944	2/24/1946
Lane, Peter E	Florence SC		3/31/1943
Lane, Thomas Edward	Florence SC	6/11/1945	8/20/1946
Langston, Allen Montgomery	Florence SC	4/7/1943	12/15/1944
Langston, Clifford F	Timmonsville SC	12/18/1945	8/28/1946
Langston, Gerald Foster	Florence SC	4/29/1942	11/20/1945
Langston, LeRoy Bernard, Jr.	Florence SC	9/22/1944	12/15/1944
Langston, Travis R	Florence SC	8/29/1940	8/7/1945
Lanos, Charlie	Elizabeth NJ		
Larrison, Fay Eugene	Florence SC		
Larson, Myron L	Florence SC	12/14/2013	12/15/1944
Lassiter, Joseph T, Sr.	Navy Yard SC	1/11/1945	12/15/1944
Latson, M K	Effingham SC	10/25/1945	12/13/1946
Latta, Andrew Broadfoot	Florence SC	6/30/1942	10/10/1945
Laughlin, Laurence Edward	Florence SC	2/9/1943	12/15/1944
Lawhon, Clayton Hester	Navy Yard SC	9/9/1943	4/2/1946
Lawhon, Herman O'Neil	Effingham SC	12/22/1942	11/27/1945
Lawhon, William C	Effingham SC	4/10/1945	1/17/1946
Lawhon, William McAdee	Florence SC		6/29/1945
Lawrence, Clyde	Fayetteville NC		3/3/1945
Lawrence, Daniel	Florence SC	1/1/1943	12/16/1944
Lawrence, Eugene Thomas	Florence SC	2/6/1946	12/15/1944
Lawrence, Fred Wilson, Jr.	Florence SC	1/18/1944	12/15/1944
Lawrence, George Owens	Florence SC	6/29/1941	12/15/1944
Lawrence, James E	Florence SC	9/1/1943	12/17/1945
Lawrence, Mallie	Florence SC	4/28/1943	1/2/1946
Lawrence, Theodore Moses	Florence SC		
Lawrence, Thomas Hartwell	Baltimore MD		11/4/1945
Lawrence, Wilbur Hook	Effingham SC	10/4/1945	1/14/1947
Laws, George Washington	Florence SC	9/11/1942	11/16/1945
Lawson, Edward N	Jamestown NY	11/21/1942	2/4/1946
Lawson, Victor R, Jr.	Florence SC	9/23/1942	1/25/1946
Lawson, William James	Florence SC	4/28/1943	4/9/1946
Lawton, Joesph Maner, Jr.	Myrtle Beach SC	4/18/1942	12/15/1944
Leach, Kenneth L	Florence SC	1/28/1942	9/11/1945
League, Walter h	Florence SC	5/2/1942	
LeCorno, Henry J	Florence SC	9/30/1941	12/12/1945
Lee, Charles Covington	Timmonsville SC	11/28/1945	1/31/1947
Lee, George Frederick	Memphis TN	1/16/1942	10/13/1945
Lee, Harry	Florence SC	7/13/1943	12/15/1944
Lee, Herbert	Florence SC		8/9/1945
Lee, June E	Florence SC	6/5/1945	5/30/1945
Lee, Raney C, Jr.	Mooresville NC	11/20/1941	10/13/1945
Lee, Thomas Banaman	Florence SC	8/13/1945	5/7/1946
Lee, Virgil B	Coward SC	6/8/1943	2/22/1946
Lee, Warner Lou, Jr.	Florence SC	10/17/1944	12/15/1944
Lee, Wilbur Harrison	Johnsonville SC	10/7/1946	11/25/1946
Lee, William Hillard	Scranton SC	8/16/1943	12/9/1945
Lee, Willie Theodore	Florence SC	7/1/1943	8/26/1944
Leeper, Wilbur Nathan	Florence SC	6/17/1943	8/18/1945
Legette, Frank E	Florence SC	7/3/1940	5/13/1946

★ ★ ★ ★

NAME	CITY	ENTRY DATE	DISCHARGE
Legette, Ray Gladstone	Florence SC	10/17/1944	8/6/1946
Lemm, Leonard J	Ripley MN	8/27/1942	2/4/1946
Lemmon, Dewey Milton	Starke LA		3/2/1944
Lenard, Vege George	Florence SC	12/31/1942	2/19/1946
Lesiour, Henry Joseph	Florence SC	3/21/1941	12/12/1945
Leslie, Lawrence Lowraine	Florence SC	1/3/1942	1/3/1946
Leslie, Leroy Frazier	Florence SC	1/13/1941	8/13/1945
Lester, Theodore	Florence SC	5/17/1943	11/20/1945
Lewellen, James F	Florence SC	2/10/1945	1/6/1947
Lewis, Archibald King	Mainlan FL	9/30/1942	
Lewis, Jack Ernest	Florence SC	3/24/1944	12/28/1945
Lewis, James Jefferson, Jr.	Florence SC	3/23/1943	12/15/1944
Lewis, John H	Brooklyn NY	4/23/1941	1/23/1946
Lewis, Laurie Berkely, Jr.	Florence SC	11/13/1942	3/9/1946
Lewis, Leroy B	Florence SC	6/1/1943	4/9/1946
Lewis, Luke Levi	Florence SC		10/22/1944
Lewis, Marion Joseph	Florence SC	2/26/1943	11/26/1945
Lewis, William Elliot	Florence SC	5/2/1943	11/28/1945
Lewis, William Lyde	Florence SC		8/28/1944
Linley, Owen P	Florence SC	6/30/1943	4/20/1946
Linton, Lonnie, Jr.	Florence SC	10/8/1943	12/26/1945
Liston, Fulton	Florence SC	4/19/1944	1/10/1946
Little, Ernest	Englewood NJ		
Lloyd, Thomas Edison	Florence SC		3/29/1944
Lloyd, William Henry	Lamar SC	12/23/1943	12/15/1944
Lockamy, James RG	Dillon SC		7/4/1944
Lockhart, Carl Alexander	Florence SC	3/29/1944	11/21/1945
Locklair, Woodrow William	Florence SC	8/28/1942	
Logan, Thomas, Jr.	Lynchburg SC	5/31/1945	2/13/1947
Long, Clarence Eastman, Jr.	Florence SC	3/10/1944	10/8/1945
Long, Roscoe	Florence SC	1/10/1945	10/1/1945
Lonon, George	Florence SC	3/1/1943	1/17/1946
Lonon, Mahlon H	Florence SC		10/21/1942
Lonon, Walter Thomas	Florence SC	8/31/1943	12/15/1944
Lothrop, Donald L	New Castle CA	10/22/1942	1/10/1946
Lovless, John E	Providence RI	7/27/1940	8/13/1945
Lowder, Harrington M	Coward SC	9/19/1943	12/15/1944
Lowe, Erskine Lee	Florence SC	6/25/1940	9/29/1945
Lowery, Marshall M	Timmonsville SC	1/9/1943	12/15/1944
Lowery, Moses	Florence SC		
Lowman, Ira Brown	Florence SC	1/14/1942	12/15/1944
Lucas, Hollen Lane	Society Hill SC	9/20/1944	12/15/1944
Lucas, Marion DuBois, Jr.	Florence SC	8/1/1941	2/27/1946
Lucas, Shavers	Coward SC	9/8/1942	11/2/1945
Luhrs, Herman Russell	Florence SC	12/5/1942	1/14/1946
Lundy, Billy	Florence SC		12/4/1943
Lundy, Elbert, Jr.	Bondtown VA	11/6/1942	
Lundy, George Edward	Clyde NY	10/28/1942	2/6/1946
Lung, Harold Meritt	Florence SC	11/6/1940	10/4/1945
Lunon, Bobbie	Darlington SC	2/4/1944	1/16/1946
Lyde, Dumore	Florence SC	4/1/1943	12/15/1944
Lyerly, J Q	Pamplico SC	1/24/1944	8/26/1945
Lyle, Thomas Braheam	Toldeo OH		
Lyles, Colon Walter	Columbia SC	7/17/1942	11/30/1945
Lynch, James Willard	Timmonsville SC	1/21/1941	12/15/1944

★ ★ ★ ★

NAME	CITY	ENTRY DATE	DISCHARGE
Lynch, Tommy Junior	Lynchburg SC	6/15/1943	1/11/1946
Lynch, Willie Wyly	Florence SC	12/13/1943	11/6/1945
Lynn, Charlie, Jr.	Florence SC	1/1/1943	1/8/1945
Lytle, William M	Birmingham AL	6/15/1943	12/1/1945
Mabry, Otis Oliver	Inman SC	4/9/1943	3/12/1946
Mack, Christopher Columbus	Florence SC	6/25/1942	
Mack, Horry	Florence SC	1/17/1942	12/23/1945
Mack, Junius Manning	Florence SC		6/7/1945
Mack, Levi	Timmonsville SC		
Mack, Raymond	Effingham SC	4/2/1941	8/2/1945
Mack, Robert	Florence SC	6/10/1944	1/4/1946
Mack, Roschild	Florence SC	12/31/1942	12/24/1945
Madison, Alfred Freddie	Florence SC	9/9/1942	10/29/1945
Madison, Boyd, Jr.	Florence SC	9/8/1942	12/4/1945
Madison, James Willie	Florence SC	12/11/1941	10/25/1945
Madison, John Lee	Wilmington NC		3/3/1944
Madison, Samuel	Florence SC	1/21/1944	1/18/1946
Magruder, Arthur G	Charleston SC	11/1/1943	5/15/1946
Malatin, George A	Florence SC	6/12/1941	9/18/1944
Maleye, Monroe	Darlington SC	2/11/1944	10/9/1945
Malia, Jerry	Florence SC	7/12/1944	1/13/1947
Mangum, Coit Lytell		6/1/1943	12/11/1945
Mangum, George	Charlotte NC	10/16/1941	1/8/1946
Marchett, Louis D, Jr.	Florence SC	12/11/1942	3/16/1946
Marinko, John	Florence SC		4/23/1945
Marks, Kenneth	Lamar SC	3/14/1944	6/10/1946
Marks, Willie	Florence SC	1/14/1944	12/26/1945
Marshall, Thomas R	Florence SC	4/7/1943	12/13/1945
Marshall, William	Florence SC	10/17/1944	10/16/1946
Martin, Cecil Wray	Bostic NY	5/13/1943	3/9/1946
Martin, Frank McNeil	Florence SC	2/10/1943	12/18/1945
Martin, James C	Florence SC	7/11/1945	3/12/1947
Martin, Jesse William	Columbia SC		
Martin, Lee Albert	Coward SC	12/20/1945	7/31/1946
Martin, Louis B	Florence SC	10/28/1942	10/22/1943
Martin, Oliver Edward	Lane SC	5/10/1943	12/19/1945
Martin, Preston	Florence SC		6/4/1945
Martin, Richard	Florence SC	7/27/1943	2/28/1946
Martin, Robert Earl	Lake City SC	7/4/1942	3/12/1946
Martin, Theodore Bernard	Florence SC	12/31/1942	12/24/1945
Martion, Tarpley Douglas	Florence SC	3/11/1945	11/30/1945
Mathis, Walter F	Florence SC		6/29/1945
Matney, George N	Florence SC	9/7/1943	4/29/1946
Matthews, Henry	Coward SC	3/4/1946	2/15/1947
Matthews, Horace Z	Effingham SC		
Matthews, John Wesley	Florence SC	5/27/1944	5/15/1946
Matthews, Marvin French	Timmonsville SC	10/15/1944	3/3/1946
Matthews, Marvin French	Navy Yard SC	10/16/1944	3/3/1946
Matthews, Milton	Coward SC	7/31/1940	9/17/1945
Matthews, Odie C, Jr.	Florence SC	11/1/1943	12/4/1945
Matthews, Robert Hugh, Jr.	Florence SC	9/6/1943	4/26/1946
Matthews, Wheler	Effingham SC	3/1/1943	12/31/1945
Maxwell, William J	Florence SC	12/9/1942	2/24/1946
May, Oscar Vinton	Effingham SC	1/8/1942	1/15/1946
May, Spencer	Effingham SC	7/5/1944	6/20/1946

★ ★ ★ ★

NAME	CITY	ENTRY DATE	DISCHARGE
Mayers, John L	Florence SC	11/15/1940	7/31/1945
Mayers, Thomas Cameron	Florence SC	5/18/1944	5/29/1946
Mayes, Willie James	Florence SC	5/11/1944	3/18/1946
Maynard, Ben Allen	Florence SC	4/2/1943	1/24/1946
McAlister, Abnew R	Effingham SC	3/1/1943	2/23/1946
McAlister, John Allen	Effingham SC	9/8/1945	7/24/1946
McAllister, Dice	Effingham SC	12/10/1943	4/11/1946
McAllister, James DeLeon	Scranton SC	10/28/1942	9/7/1945
McAllister, James L	Pamplico SC	4/1/1943	2/3/1946
McAllister, Quince	Effingham SC	5/20/1941	12/4/1945
McAllister, Raleigh Lee	Effingham SC	3/26/1946	2/17/1947
McAllister, Raleigh Lee	Effingham SC	3/26/1946	
McArver, Walter LeRoy, Jr.	Lumberton NC		11/10/1945
McBratney, James Thomas	Florence SC	3/26/1941	4/13/1946
McCain, Parley Walkup	Waxhaw NC	12/27/1943	3/28/1946
McCalester, Otto Pete	Effingham SC		11/5/1947
McCall, Arthur	Florence SC		5/31/1945
McCall, Clafton R	Florence SC	3/4/1943	7/9/1945
McCall, Gus Armstron, Jr.	Brooklyn NY	1/31/1942	10/10/1945
McCall, Jerome Rivers	San Francisco CA		
McCall, Julian L	Florence SC	6/24/1942	1/25/1946
McCalm, Henry Joe	Timmonsville SC	11/13/1945	12/29/1946
McCants, Herbert	Florence SC	1/19/1944	11/21/1945
McCarter, Deva Leslie	Florence SC	6/30/1944	4/5/1946
McCarty, Glenn Prestion	Savannah GA	12/6/1942	2/3/1946
McChesney, Robert S	Florence SC	6/15/1942	12/14/1945
McClain, Boston	Florence SC	3/10/1944	3/25/1946
McClain, Dave, Jr.	Florence SC	1/20/1943	12/31/1945
McClain, Hosea	Claussen SC	11/13/1942	1/25/1946
McClain, Jacob	Florence SC	11/3/1942	1/26/1944
McClain, Jeremiah	Brooklyn NY	7/17/1943	2/15/1946
McClain, John	Florence SC	3/5/1943	1/9/1946
McClain, Josiah, Jr.	Florence SC	3/18/1946	12/28/1946
McClain, Robert	Florence SC		9/29/1943
McClam, David Lee	Savannah GA	4/22/1941	10/14/1945
McClam, Richard	Timmonsville SC	5/22/1943	8/19/1946
McClary, Robert	Greeleyville SC	4/21/1944	3/21/1946
McClellan, Archibald James	Florence SC	10/10/1942	2/22/1946
McClellan, Robert L	Florence SC	2/9/1943	12/24/1945
McCormick, Ralph McKinnen	Florence SC	8/8/1942	1/12/1946
McCown, Clarence, Jr.	Florence SC	2/18/1943	1/4/1946
McCown, John Charles	Florence SC	12/22/1943	11/30/1945
McCown, Phillip Reese	Florence SC	2/22/1943	
McCown, William Jerome	Florence SC	6/2/1943	3/10/1946
McCrary, Charles Howard	Florence SC	5/9/1945	6/7/1946
McCrary, Cyril Clark, Jr.	Florence SC		10/20/1944
McCrary, Harold Glenn	Florence SC	12/15/1941	10/21/1945
McCrary, Norris Reese	Florence SC	8/3/1942	10/2/1945
McCullough, Willie Joe		12/27/1943	
McCutcheon, James I	Florence SC	8/25/1946	1/13/1947
McCutcheon, William Bayard	Charlotte NC		12/18/1943
McDaniel, Charles William	Lake City SC	11/9/1944	
McDaniel, James	Florence SC		3/3/1946
McDaniel, John Fulton	Columbia SC	3/1/1943	4/3/1946
McDaniel, Otho, Jr.	Effingham SC	11/20/1943	6/25/1946

★ ★ ★ ★

NAME	CITY	ENTRY DATE	DISCHARGE
McDaniel, Sanders Rudolph	Florence SC	4/7/1943	4/21/1946
McDonald, John R	Florence SC		2/25/1945
McDonald, Lloyd G	Florence SC	8/6/1942	1/10/1946
McDonald, Thomas L	Pamplico SC	4/15/1942	9/20/1945
McDonald, William	Florence SC	1/22/1944	4/5/1946
McDonald, Willie	New York NY	7/22/1943	
McDonald, Willie	New York NY	1/22/1944	
McDuffie, Sandy	Florence SC		
McEachin, Daniel Malloy	Florence SC	3/29/1945	4/30/1946
McElveen, Adam Paul, Jr.	Effingham SC	12/8/1943	5/10/1946
McElveen, Archie Clifford	Florence SC	8/26/1942	10/27/1945
McElveen, Arthur Richard	Florence SC	4/28/1944	3/23/1946
McElveen, Eugene		4/5/1943	4/7/1947
McElveen, Thomas	Florence SC	6/21/1944	4/16/1946
McElveen, Waldo Emerson, Jr.	Florence SC	8/21/1945	11/26/1945
McElveene, Albert	Florence SC	4/19/1944	2/20/1946
McFadden, Charles Wesley	Florence SC	5/6/1944	1/30/1946
McFarland, Earnest	Florence SC	10/24/1945	12/5/1946
McFarland, General Lee	Washington DC		
McGee, Andrew J	Coeards SC	6/16/1943	7/20/1945
McGee, Horace LaVerne	Coward SC	11/21/1945	2/15/1947
McGee, Moot Charlie	Florence SC	6/23/1944	11/23/1945
McGee, Willard M	Florence SC	2/12/1944	11/2/1945
McGlamery, William Brock	Greensboro NC	7/24/1944	10/20/1945
McGowan, James Francis	Florence SC	10/17/1942	
McGowan, William John	Denver CO		
McIntosh, Harry M		9/2/1942	1/15/1946
McIntosh, James C	Florence SC		3/30/1945
McIntyre, Richard Howard	Florence SC	10/28/1942	12/30/1945
McIntyre, Richard Howard	Florence SC	10/15/1943	12/30/1945
McIver, Adam	Florence SC	10/16/1943	1/30/1946
McIver, Clyde Edward	Pittsburg PA		10/2/1944
McIver, Preston	Florence SC		11/29/1943
McKain, Richard Franklin	Florence SC	4/7/1943	1/31/1946
McKay, Billy LaRue	Florence SC	7/20/1946	10/11/1946
McKay, James J	Florence SC	1/1/1944	10/5/1945
McKay, Seare Dewey, Jr.	Timmonsville SC	5/25/1943	
McKenzie, George David	Florence SC	4/28/1944	4/17/1946
McKenzie, James Lewis	Florence SC	10/13/1944	7/11/1946
McKenzie, Robert S	Loris SC	3/6/1942	11/26/1945
McKinney, John T	Florence SC		
McKinzie, Albert J	Johnsonville SC	3/17/1944	1/6/1946
McKinzie, John Gary	Florence SC	2/6/1940	9/11/1945
McKissick, Audward R	Florence SC	4/24/1942	9/21/1945
McKissick, Barney J	Florence SC	10/22/1946	1/22/1947
McKissick, James Francis	Florence SC	4/7/1943	12/28/1945
McKissick, Ludie M	Florence SC	8/21/1945	
McKnight, Wilbert	New York NY	9/28/1944	5/25/1946
McLaughlin, Frank L	Florence SC	6/26/1941	10/7/1945
McLaughlin, Gordan Carrol	Florence SC	4/29/1944	4/13/1946
McLaughlin, Isham J L, Jr.	Florence SC	5/25/1942	12/7/1945
McLaughlin, William A	Florence SC	4/16/1942	9/21/1945
McLaughlin, Williard P	Florence SC	11/23/1945	7/4/1946
McLaurin, Edwin Layton	Florence SC	12/29/1943	2/6/1946
McLaurin, Gilliam Richard	Bethune SC	2/23/1942	12/28/1945

★ ★ ★ ★

NAME	CITY	ENTRY DATE	DISCHARGE
McLellan, Milton Hubert	Florence SC	3/27/1946	4/16/1947
McLellan, Osborne Norfleet	Florence SC	9/14/1942	
McLellan, Samuel C	Florence SC	1/27/1941	8/26/1945
McLellan, William Archie	Florence SC		11/22/1944
McLemore, Preston D	Florence SC	3/19/1942	11/3/1945
McLendon, James E	Florence SC	4/2/1941	10/17/1945
McLendon, James Jimmie	Florence SC	9/16/1943	3/4/1946
McLendon, Lucas	Florence SC	2/26/1943	11/21/1945
McLendon, Walter Jerome	Florence SC	6/28/1944	1/10/1946
McLeod, Billy Franklin	Timmonsville SC	9/22/1945	11/10/1946
McLeod, Earl Emmett	Florence SC	7/1/1944	3/17/1946
McLeod, Frank Hilton		6/27/1944	10/7/1945
McLeod, James C	Florence SC		1/20/1945
McLeod, John G	Timmonsville SC	8/14/1941	12/3/1945
McLeod, Joseph Brunner	Sumter SC	5/17/1943	12/6/1945
McMillan, David	Florence SC	3/20/1941	
McMillian, Bert A	Hartsville SC	12/7/1943	10/12/1945
McNair, Thomas	Fayetteville NC	8/25/1942	11/2/1945
McNeil, John Moultry	Florence SC	1/31/1945	5/3/1946
McNeil, Legett	Florence SC	2/19/1942	1/11/1946
McNeil, Smith	Florence SC	2/26/1943	2/15/1946
McNeil, Willie C	Florence SC	11/14/1942	12/14/1945
McNulty, Raymond Francis	Heleke MA	12/15/1939	10/15/1945
McPherson, Charles Joseph	Florence SC	9/22/1945	11/5/1946
McPherson, Frank Hilton, Jr.	Florence SC	5/31/1942	11/19/1945
McPherson, John D	Florence SC	5/9/1942	11/5/1945
McPherson, William Francis	Florence SC	3/13/1941	12/16/1945
McRae, James Alton	Florence SC	7/20/1942	1/22/1946
McSween, Samuel C, Jr.	Florence SC	10/18/1941	10/26/1945
McVeigh, Homer Jackson	Marion SC	4/21/1943	11/18/1945
McWhite, James Leroy	Florence SC	1/21/1943	1/7/1946
McWhite, John	Pamplico SC	1/17/1942	1/15/1946
McWhite, Sam	Pamplico SC	12/31/1942	12/20/1945
McWhite, Sam	Pamplico SC	12/31/1942	12/20/1945
Meekins, Harold T	Florence SC		4/23/1945
Meerritts, Abraham Cornelius	Florence SC	1/20/1943	1/17/1946
Meggs, Wallace Nat	Florence SC	1/20/1945	3/29/1946
Melett, Wayne Durant	Florence SC	1/19/1941	11/18/1945
Melette, Russell Eugene	Florence SC	11/7/1944	8/31/1945
Mellette, Charles W, Jr.	Florence SC	4/28/1943	1/10/1946
Melton, Carey B	Florence SC	6/26/1941	11/4/1945
Melvin, Lee	Florence SC	12/31/1942	
Merrill, James Raymond	Florence SC	12/10/1940	11/10/1945
Merriman, Hugh Gross	Florence SC		4/27/1946
Merriman, Russell Preston	Florence SC		5/23/1945
Merritt, Milton J	Florence SC		8/9/1943
Miles, Cully NMN	Florence SC	1/9/1940	9/3/1945
Miles, Raleigh J	Florence SC	1/13/1941	8/5/1945
Miles, Willie L	Coward SC		11/12/1945
Milford, Otis	Florence SC	4/12/1944	7/12/1946
Miller, Allen, Jr.	Florence SC	10/3/1940	9/28/1945
Miller, Arthur	Florence SC		
Miller, Bernard Heyward	Leads SC		9/17/1945
Miller, David Smith	Florence SC	6/17/1943	12/27/1945
Miller, Ernest NMN	Florence SC		12/30/1944

★ ★ ★ ★

NAME	CITY	ENTRY DATE	DISCHARGE
Miller, Gilberts Franklin	Florence SC		9/29/1945
Miller, Harold Edward	Florence SC	2/5/1943	10/20/1945
Miller, Hyman	Williamsburg SC		6/20/1941
Miller, Karl Frank	Florence SC	8/4/1943	2/16/1946
Miller, Lawrence Hamby		4/4/1945	2/10/1946
Miller, Melvin T	Greeleyville SC		
Miller, Richard P	Pamplico SC	2/24/1942	11/20/1945
Miller, Thaddeus Freeman	Florence SC	5/6/1943	2/1/1946
Mills, Benjamin Arthur	Florence SC	10/17/1944	11/27/1945
Mills, Jack	Florence SC	10/29/1940	10/2/1945
Mills, Woodrow Joseph	Florence SC		12/21/1944
Mimms, Robert Earle	Florence SC		
Mims, Fred Pete, Jr.	Florence SC	12/7/1942	11/2/1945
Mims, George William	Florence SC		9/7/1944
Mims, James Allen	Florence SC	4/8/1943	10/20/1945
Mims, Louis Marion	Florence SC	9/22/1944	
Mims, Paul Silas, Jr.	Florence SC	12/15/1942	2/3/1946
Mims, Thomas Williard, Jr.	Florence SC	9/21/1944	11/20/1946
Mims, Wyman Harding	Florence SC	6/17/1943	2/25/1946
Mitchell, Christopher	Florence SC	9/8/1942	11/8/1945
Mitchell, Cole Blease	Florence SC		
Mitchell, Frank Leon	Baltimore MD	7/20/1942	12/6/1945
Mitchell, Willie Lee	Florence SC	3/11/1943	2/22/1946
Mitchum, Hampton Lee	Florence SC		3/23/1943
Mixon, Milton L	Florence SC	9/24/1939	
Mixon, Rufus Lee	Florence SC	8/4/1942	12/28/1945
Mobley, Marion B	Florence SC		9/22/1944
Monore, Albert Lee	Wallas TX		7/5/1943
Monroe, Samuel Walter	Florence SC	12/27/1943	12/17/1945
Montrose, Swan Dan	Florence SC	10/6/1942	10/13/1945
Moody, John Willard	Florence SC	12/31/1942	1/21/1946
Moore, Albert		5/8/1943	2/20/1946
Moore, Bernard Emerson	Florence SC		6/29/1944
Moore, Douglas B	Florence SC	11/3/1943	4/16/1946
Moore, Fred Muldrow	Florence SC	2/9/1943	11/25/1945
Moore, Harry Montague	Effingham SC	2/24/1944	5/24/1946
Moore, Harvey	Pamplico SC	3/8/1944	1/30/1946
Moore, Henry	Florence SC	7/28/1943	3/4/1946
Moore, Johnnie Wilber	Effingham SC	9/3/1942	3/4/1946
Moore, Leon Brooks	Florence SC		5/25/1943
Moore, Nedd	Florence SC	6/5/1941	12/23/1945
Moore, Ralph Hill, Jr.	Florence SC	6/21/1945	11/25/1946
Moore, Span	Florence SC	8/21/1942	11/30/1945
Moore, Thomas Flourney, Jr.	Florence SC		4/9/1945
Moore, Thomas Vincent, Jr.	Florence SC	12/13/1943	5/17/1946
Moore, William J, Jr.	Timmonsville SC	3/7/1946	3/1/1947
Moore, Woodrow Wilson	Florence SC	5/5/1942	1/1/1946
Moorer, Daniel Norman	Florence SC	10/6/1942	
Moorer, Hughes A, Jr.	Florence SC	9/5/1944	10/26/1945
Moorer, William G, Jr.		10/15/1941	11/24/1945
Moreck, Wensel V	Florence SC	8/6/1942	9/8/1945
Morgan, Charles B	Detroit MI	2/3/1944	3/29/1946
Morris, Eldon Dewie	Lake City SC		
Morris, Frank		11/26/1943	3/11/1946
Morris, Friendly Liston	Florence SC	2/14/1944	5/21/1946

★ ★ ★ ★

NAME	CITY	ENTRY DATE	DISCHARGE
Morris, James Ellison	Florence SC	10/29/1942	
Morris, James Martin	Florence SC	1/31/1944	2/5/1946
Morris, Levern	Florence SC	3/26/1946	1/9/1947
Morris, Richard Jessie	Florence SC		
Morris, Walter Lee	Huntersville SC	1/8/1942	11/18/1945
Morris, Willie M	Florence SC	6/3/1943	12/4/1945
Morris, Woodrow	Coward SC	10/5/1945	2/20/1947
Mosby, Lane S	Glendale CA	2/18/1943	4/1/1946
Moses, Andrew	Florence SC	10/12/1945	12/6/1946
Moses, Booker T	Florence SC	9/9/1943	11/22/1945
Moses, Ceaser	Florence SC	9/5/1943	2/25/1946
Moses, Ernest Eston	Florence SC		10/20/1945
Moses, Henry	Cleveland OH	5/9/1945	8/20/1945
Moses, James	Florence SC	7/19/1943	3/15/1946
Moses, Mack	Florence SC	3/9/1944	12/16/1945
Moses, Robert	Florence SC	11/13/1942	2/16/1946
Moses, Robert, Jr.	Florence SC	12/31/1942	1/9/1946
Moss, Robert Allen	High Points NC		12/5/1946
Moss, Robert T	Florence SC	10/9/1942	11/20/1945
Motte, Harold Whitton	Florence SC	12/23/1943	10/29/1945
Mouzon, Edward, Jr.	Florence SC	2/23/1943	2/3/1946
Mouzon, Ervin	Florence SC	9/10/1942	2/1/1946
Mouzon, George Elijah	Florence SC		6/24/1944
Mouzon, Woodrow	Florence SC	12/31/1942	12/20/1945
Muldroe, Thomas	Florence SC	1/1/1944	4/11/1946
Muldrow, Ira High	Florence SC	6/2/1943	2/6/1946
Muldrow, James	Florence SC	2/19/1943	1/22/1946
Muldrow, James Carol, Jr.	Florence SC	12/6/1946	3/4/1946
Muldrow, Robert, Jr.	Florence SC	1/15/1943	1/15/1946
Muldrow, Thomas	Florence SC	12/31/1942	3/10/1946
Mungo, Anderson	Florence SC	8/11/1945	6/11/1946
Munn, Alma M	Florence SC	3/25/1943	12/3/1945
Munn, Charles Dewey, Jr.	Pamplico SC	8/10/1944	6/6/1946
Munn, Dallas A	Effingham SC	1/14/1941	9/24/1945
Munn, Frank M	Pamplico SC	10/30/1942	2/1/1946
Munn, Jack Youmons	Florence SC	3/26/1942	
Munn, Jesse Edward	Effingham SC	5/25/1944	2/25/1946
Munn, Neil Benj	Florence SC	8/6/1940	8/28/1945
Munn, Samuel Alfred	Florence SC	5/28/1944	5/8/1946
Munn, Steele	Pamplico SC	7/31/1942	11/27/1945
Munn, Wilbert B	Florence SC	4/19/1944	9/25/1945
Munn, Wilson H	Florence SC	9/17/1942	12/15/1945
Munnerlyn, Joe Clarke	Marion SC	4/22/1944	2/11/1946
Murchison, John D, Jr.	Florence SC	12/6/1943	10/8/1945
Murphy, Douglas	Florence SC	1/20/1943	3/1/1946
Murphy, Joseph, Jr.	Florence SC	3/25/1943	2/14/1946
Murphy, Otic E	Florence SC	10/22/1943	7/19/1945
Murray, James	Florence SC	2/17/1944	3/24/1946
Myers, Clarence Dudley	Effingham SC		9/24/1945
Myers, Dalton Cecil	Florence SC	10/23/1939	8/6/1945
Myers, Edward Eddie	Florence SC	10/4/1943	1/16/1946
Myers, James Otis	Florence SC	7/15/1943	2/24/1946
Myers, Paul B	Effingham SC	2/6/1945	4/26/1946
Myers, Richard Adrian	Florence SC	5/27/1944	2/8/1946
Myers, Woodrow	Buffalo NY		6/10/1944

★ ★ ★ ★

NAME	CITY	ENTRY DATE	DISCHARGE
Najjar, Basil Edward	Florence SC	2/14/1944	5/21/1946
Nance, Claude E	Florence SC	8/9/1945	9/12/1946
Nance, John P	Florence SC	6/28/1941	11/8/1946
Nance, Leory	Florence SC	5/23/1944	4/16/1946
Neely, William Joseph	Rock Hill SC		12/11/1944
Nelson, Fred T	Florence SC	4/11/1941	10/8/1945
Nelson, Guilford Lemuel	Scranton SC	9/10/1940	10/31/1945
Nelson, Lewis Clement	Florence SC	11/29/1939	12/7/1945
Nettles, James	Florence SC		11/27/1943
Nettles, Jesse	Barlington SC	7/19/1943	2/17/1946
Nettles, Robert Maxy	Florence SC		
Newak, Robert Jacob	Florence SC	9/6/1939	9/30/1945
Newell, David Beasley	Charleston SC	4/29/1944	5/28/1946
Newell, Robert Harper	Scotland Neck NC	10/30/1942	3/16/1946
Newsome, Thomas C	Florence SC	12/6/1942	3/16/1946
Nickols, John E	Timmonsville SC	12/20/1944	11/22/1946
Nielson, Kirk Perkins	Bluff UT		3/4/1946
Nissen, Adolph Allen	Timmonsville SC	10/2/1939	10/8/1945
Nissen, Albert DuBose	Timmonsville SC	4/7/1943	10/5/1945
Nissen, George Frederick	Florence SC	7/21/1945	1/17/1947
Nixon, Robert Bod	New York NY		10/18/1945
Nofal, George Joseph	Florence SC	10/16/1942	12/1/1945
Norton, Royal E	Florence SC	10/16/1941	9/11/1943
Norwood, George E	Florence SC		
Norwood, Leonard E	Florence SC	8/10/1942	10/28/1945
Oakley, Odell Wallace	Effingham SC	1/30/1947	4/30/1947
O'Connor, Timothy Jerome	Florence SC	7/21/1946	
O'Doherty, John K	Florence SC	8/13/1943	10/13/1945
Odom, Woodrow	Florence SC	2/24/1942	10/22/1945
O'Hara, William Elijah, Jr.	Florence SC	6/26/1942	2/10/1946
O'Harra, Robert Lee	Florence SC		
Olasov, Sanford	Marletta GA	8/31/1944	
Oliver, Henry V	Florence SC	7/12/1940	9/11/1945
Oliver, John Ivey	Timmonsville SC	8/25/1943	3/16/1946
Oliver, Marion Parks	Rocky Mount NC	6/28/1944	3/12/1946
Oliver, Russell T	Florence SC	1/13/1941	9/28/1945
Olsen, Joseph Ellis	Salisbury NC	10/27/1942	11/17/1945
O'Neal, Charles Monroe	Florence SC		
O'Neal, Leo Burch	Florence SC		5/29/1945
Orjala, Alfred David	San Deigo CA		
Outlaw, Wilson Truesdale	Florence SC	11/13/1944	3/15/1946
Overton, Howard E, Sr.	Florence SC	9/3/1943	12/14/1945
Owens, Elliott	Florence SC	11/17/1942	1/3/1946
Owens, Jampsey G	Florence SC	11/1/1937	
Owens, John Leonard	Florence SC	9/18/1940	7/8/1945
Owens, Louis Andrew	Florence SC	5/6/1943	
Owens, Robert Guy	Florence SC	4/8/1943	3/18/1946
Pace, Leander James	Orlando FL		12/9/1945
Packer, Neil	Florence SC		12/6/1944
Page, Henry Dobson Reese	Columbia SC	7/2/1943	1/29/1946
Palles, Mitchell Chris	Florence SC	4/3/1943	1/10/1946
Palles, Mitchell DeBerry	Florence SC	12/22/1944	2/7/1946
Palmer, Ralph A	Florence SC	11/7/1942	1/25/1946
Parker, Aubrey Theodore	Florence SC	6/1/1943	9/22/1945
Parker, Carl Davis	Florence SC	12/7/1942	1/22/1946

★ ★ ★ ★

NAME	CITY	ENTRY DATE	DISCHARGE
Parker, Curtis M	Miami FL	4/14/1943	2/22/1946
Parker, Edward Harley	Effingham SC	1/7/1944	6/5/1946
Parker, Ervin Hannah, Jr.	Florence SC	6/3/1943	2/5/1946
Parker, Franklin William	Florence SC	6/28/1944	
Parker, James Claude	Florence SC		12/15/1944
Parker, James Marion	Florence SC	3/12/1941	10/4/1945
Parker, James William, Jr.	Florence SC	5/9/1942	4/1/1946
Parker, John Nicholas, Jr.	Florence SC	3/2/1942	2/26/1946
Parker, Richmond Millard, Jr.	Polkton NC		10/13/1944
Parker, William Quitman	Florence SC	4/23/1942	9/25/1945
Parker, Woodrow W	Florence SC	2/1/1942	9/18/1945
Parkins, Grover Cleveland, Jr.	Florence SC	12/5/1944	11/28/1946
Parrish, Monroe	Florence SC	11/27/1940	7/6/1945
Parrott, Eugene William, Jr.	Florence SC	8/6/1943	
Parrott, James Sutton	Florence SC	6/12/1943	2/8/1946
Pate, Amay Judson, Jr.	Florence SC		11/6/1944
Pate, Jerome NMN	Florence SC	8/18/1942	11/10/1945
Pate, Marvin	Florence SC		8/10/1946
Pate, Marvin NMN	Florence SC		1/17/1945
Pattillo, Ned Wallace		10/8/1942	2/10/1946
Patton, Robert Alexander	Florence SC		9/17/1943
Paul, Otto	Florence SC	1/21/1944	2/1/1946
Paxton, Pickett D	Florence SC	6/14/1939	9/3/1945
Peanard, Albert	Cameron SC	1/13/1943	2/2/1946
Pearson, Newton Walker, Jr.	Sumter SC	12/21/1945	6/1/1943
Peck, Edwin W	Augusta GA	3/14/1945	10/12/1945
Pendergrass, William Roper	Bristol MD	10/3/1943	2/4/1946
Perkins, Lewis	Florence SC		5/31/1943
Perkins, Henry Ford	Florence SC	8/4/1942	2/21/1946
Perkins, Woodrow Wilson	Florence SC	1/22/1941	12/23/1945
Perrin, Clark Wardlaw	Union SC		11/28/1942
Perry, Lee Roy	Jonesboro NC	12/5/1942	9/19/1945
Perry, Lordell	Florence SC	10/28/1942	2/20/1946
Peterson, Elliott (Mutt), Jr.	Florence SC		
Pettigrew, John Lake	Florence SC	7/11/1944	5/7/1946
Pettigrew, Keith Alexander	Florence SC	7/25/1945	11/12/1946
Philippi, Patrick a	Marshfield WI	8/17/1942	2/8/1946
Phillips, Cletus Earl	Florence SC	6/8/1942	12/29/1945
Phillips, Herbert Leroy	Sellers SC	9/27/1943	3/3/1946
Phillips, James C	Florence SC	1/13/1941	10/23/1945
Phillips, James C	Florence SC	1/31/1941	10/23/1945
Phillips, L R	Fair Bluff NC	4/7/1943	1/22/1946
Phillips, L R	Fair Bluff NC	4/7/1943	1/22/1946
Phillips, Thomas Wallace	Florence SC		6/6/1944
Phillips, Thomas Wallace	Florence SC	6/22/1944	6/6/1944
Pickens, Claude	Effingham SC	2/15/1946	4/19/1947
Pierce, James Allard	Timmonsville SC	10/20/1945	11/24/1946
Pigate, Charlie Herbert	Florence SC		6/19/1945
Pigate, Charlie Robert	Florence SC		6/19/1945
Pigatt, Boyd Rockfellow	Effingham SC	4/27/1945	10/30/1946
Pigatt, Edward	Effingham SC	10/26/1945	12/18/1946
Pinckney, Carl	Florence SC	1/7/1943	2/11/1946
Pinckney, George	Florence SC		7/4/1945
Pinkard, Tom	Florence SC	8/17/1942	1/9/1946
Pitte, Edward Clifton	Florence SC	6/4/1942	10/2/1945

★ ★ ★ ★

NAME	CITY	ENTRY DATE	DISCHARGE
Pittman, Harold Franklin	Florence SC		3/12/1945
Pitts, Edward Clifton	Florence SC	6/4/1942	10/2/1945
Pizzuti, Nicola D	Detroit MI	9/5/1942	1/30/1946
Planter, Elmore, Jr.	Florence SC	12/24/1942	12/21/1945
Player, Charles Montgomery	Florence SC	1/27/1941	10/16/1945
Player, Henry LeRoy	Darlington SC	9/30/1944	11/26/1946
Player, Willie	Florence SC	12/31/1942	2/12/1946
Plowden, George, Jr.	Florence SC	5/3/1945	12/15/1945
Plowden, Samuel Theodore	Florence SC	10/21/1943	11/21/1945
Polston, Carl Clifton	Florence SC	8/14/1943	12/21/1945
Pope, Lee Jackson, Jr.	Florence SC	6/28/1944	2/28/1946
Porterfield, Robert L	Florence SC		9/10/1943
Poston, Benjamin S	Florence SC	12/20/1942	12/15/1945
Poston, Clemson A	Scranton SC	1/27/1944	10/29/1945
Poston, Eddie	Florence SC	11/25/1940	1/4/1946
Poston, Edward B, Jr.	Navy Yard SC	10/30/1942	1/1/1946
Poston, Edward Clye	Florence SC	12/13/1943	11/24/1945
Poston, James E	Florence SC	4/10/1945	11/10/1945
Poston, Jesse L	Florence SC	1/14/1941	9/26/1945
Poston, Jethro	Hyman SC	2/12/1945	12/14/1946
Poston, Joseph Norman	Pamplico SC	4/10/1945	12/8/1946
Poston, Leegal Lauren	Hyman SC	3/31/1946	2/24/1946
Poston, Louie Oscar	Florence SC	12/3/1943	11/6/1945
Poston, Marvin Burt	Effingham SC	10/12/1940	2/1/1945
Poston, Melvin	Florence SC		
Poston, Palion Sulion	Hyman SC	9/9/1942	11/27/1945
Poston, Richard Austin	Hyman SC	12/29/1939	7/24/1945
Poston, Thomas Eli	Johnsonville SC	11/11/1944	10/27/1946
Poston, Wilbur, F	Florence SC		1/2/1945
Poston, Wilson Benjamin	Johnsonville SC	6/14/1944	2/18/1946
Potts, William Sylvester, Jr.	Timmonsville SC	3/3/1946	12/27/1946
Powell, Aurices Lynwood	Florence SC	8/19/1941	11/4/1945
Powell, Johnnie Elfred	Effingham SC	4/22/1944	3/6/1946
Powell, Joseph Chesney	Hyman SC	2/4/1943	11/9/1945
Powell, Lofton T	Johnsonville SC	1/27/1941	9/1/1945
Powell, Lonnie Eugene	Effingham SC	4/1/1941	
Powell, Remier Joseph	Florence SC		
Powell, Vesper	Effingham SC	3/28/2006	9/11/1944
Powell, Willie David	Scranton SC		11/20/1945
Powers, Dewey William, Jr.	Effingham SC	11/6/1943	3/26/1946
Powers, Eugene Russel	Florence SC	11/10/1945	12/14/1946
Powers, Thomas Robert	Timmonsville SC	8/23/1945	10/8/1946
Pressley, Willie Swails	Florence SC	10/9/1942	12/3/1945
Presson, Bill Charles	Florence SC	2/18/1943	2/11/1946
Price, Charles, Leroy			12/1/1944
Price, George	Cameron SC	1/31/1944	4/5/1946
Price, Junius Chaimous	Florence SC		10/12/1945
Price, V George	Cameron SC	1/31/1944	4/5/1946
Pridgen, Carlton Larue	Florence SC	12/6/1943	4/5/1946
Pridgen, Early Quiten, Jr.	Florence SC	4/2/1943	12/6/1945
Pridgen, George W	Florence SC	10/26/1945	11/14/1946
Pringle, Elerby	Effingham SC	3/3/1946	1/3/1947
Pringle, James Devandua	Lake City SC	10/28/1942	12/3/1945
Privette, Charles Thomas	Lake View SC	9/5/1942	2/8/1946
Privette, Ernest Henry, Jr.	Florence SC	10/28/1942	11/28/1945

★ ★ ★ ★

NAME	CITY	ENTRY DATE	DISCHARGE
Proctor, George H	Olanta SC	3/24/1944	12/6/1945
Prosser, Cullen Lavern	Florence SC	4/28/1943	11/12/1945
Pruitt, Alexander Bennett	Florence SC	4/18/1942	1/2/1946
Purvis, Davis Eugene	Florence SC	1/9/1946	1/21/1947
Purvis, Gerald E	Florence SC		
Purvis, Hallie	Florence SC	1/14/1941	10/12/1945
Purvis, James Alvin	Florence SC		1/27/1945
Purvis, John	Florence SC	1/21/1943	1/16/1946
Purvis, Trize V	Florence SC	6/7/1943	12/4/1945
Putman, Glenn William, Jr.	Florence SC	7/3/1945	1/17/1947
Quarles, Robert Eugene, Jr.	Florence SC	6/28/1944	
Quick, Malcomb Francis	Florence SC	2/7/1944	1/15/1946
Quillens, Hosea boy	Florence SC	8/13/1945	8/13/1945
Rafus, James O	Florence SC	12/28/1944	3/28/1947
Rainey, John Edward, Jr.	New York NY	11/3/1942	11/7/1945
Rainey, Michell Henry	New York NY	10/27/1943	11/21/1945
Rainge, Jimmie L	Florence SC	10/26/1943	11/18/1945
Rainwater, Ira Sidney	Florence SC	3/25/1944	12/2/1945
Ranson, Arthur Jones, Jr.	Florence SC	6/16/1942	11/15/1945
Ratcliffe, James	Montgomery Al	1/18/1942	11/27/1945
Ratliff, James Hamer, Jr.	Florence SC	5/26/1945	5/13/1946
Rawlinson, Charles Richard	Florence SC	3/4/1942	
Rawlinson, Harold Lauren	Florence SC	7/24/1942	10/30/1945
Rawlinson, Linwood Way		6/28/1944	4/1/1946
Rawlinson, Louis LeGrand	Florence SC	12/6/1942	12/11/1945
Rawlinson, Oscar Hawley	Goldsboro NC	12/23/1942	1/16/1946
Rawlinson, William Henry	Florence SC	10/20/1943	4/2/1946
Readdin, Laurence	Florence SC	1/21/1943	11/6/1945
Reaves, Earl Gibson	Florence SC		9/28/1945
Reaves, George	Dillon SC	7/1/1944	5/1/1946
Reaves, Oscar Layyet	Mullins SC	1/6/1943	12/17/1945
Reaves, Powell Hubert		6/21/1943	2/28/1946
Reese, Henry W	Florence SC	8/13/1942	1/24/1946
Reese, Marshall Johnnie	Florence SC	6/23/1943	4/5/1946
Reese, Robert Saverance	Florence SC		12/4/1944
Reese. Clyde Lowanie	New York NY	2/27/1945	7/29/1946
Reeves, Floyd V	Florence SC	1/14/1942	9/26/1945
Reeves, Marion Hillis	Florence SC		1/23/1945
Regin, General Lee	Florence SC		
Regina, Bobbie Lee	Florence SC	5/14/1946	1/8/1947
Register, Samuel J	Florence SC	6/7/1943	2/14/1946
Renfro, Leon S	Florence SC	6/6/1942	1/16/1945
Revell, John P, Jr.	Florence SC	8/19/1943	
Revell, William James, Jr.	Florence SC	12/31/1941	11/5/1945
Revelle, William E	Florence SC	1/7/1941	12/7/1945
Reville, James Heyward	Florence SC	12/6/1944	
Reynolds, James Elijah	Florence SC	8/10/1940	11/25/1945
Rhames, William J, Jr.	Timmonsville SC		10/26/1945
Rhodes, Mike	Florence SC	8/16/1943	
Rice, Quay DeBure	Spartanburg SC	5/23/1941	12/2/1945
Rich, Carlie	Florence SC	4/1/1944	3/9/1946
Rich, Eaton, Jr.	Florence SC	12/14/1945	10/31/1946
Rich, Ernest	Florence SC		
Richardson, David Linwood	Lake City SC	11/8/1943	1/31/1946
Richardson, Francis F	Johnsonville SC	4/7/1943	1/5/1946

★ ★ ★ ★

NAME	CITY	ENTRY DATE	DISCHARGE
Richardson, Haggod O'Neil	Johnsonville SC		7/27/1945
Richardson, Hughes	Florence SC	11/26/1942	
Richardson, John Junior	Florence SC		12/10/1944
Richardson, Johnnie	Florence SC	4/19/1944	3/11/1946
Richardson, Johnny	Norfolk VA	5/17/1943	11/11/1945
Richardson, Joseph F	Jamaica NY	1/7/1943	2/9/1946
Richardson, Lee	Johnsonville SC	4/2/1945	
Richardson, Lonnie NMN, Jr.	Florence SC	3/4/1943	10/6/1945
Richardson, Moses	Florence SC	5/12/1944	4/14/1946
Richardson, Orville L, Jr.	Orlando FL	12/4/1942	3/13/1946
Richardson, Theodore	Florence SC		6/18/1943
Richburg, Bevis Maurice	Florence SC	1/30/1942	10/10/1945
Richburg, Clyde Mitchell	Florence SC	2/14/1944	2/22/1946
Richburg, Dewey Merritt	Florence SC	8/20/1941	8/11/1945
Riddick, Alton T	Florence SC	5/3/1943	1/6/1946
Rivers, Charlie David	Florence SC	11/1/1944	11/30/1946
Rivers, Frank	Florence SC		8/27/1943
Rivers, Howard Luther	Morehead City NC	9/4/1942	12/9/1945
Rivers, James D	Florence SC	1/14/1943	8/23/1945
Rivers, Marion	Florence SC	11/18/1943	2/18/1946
Robertson, James Poindexter	Florence SC	4/18/1942	11/19/1945
Robinson, Arthur	Florence SC	3/3/1945	11/21/1946
Robinson, Calvin Coolidge	Florence SC	12/20/1943	11/10/1945
Robinson, Chester Lee	Florence SC	1/20/1943	2/27/1946
Robinson, David	Florence SC	2/18/1942	2/13/1946
Robinson, David Samuel, Jr.	Florence SC	2/14/1944	4/22/1946
Robinson, Dorsey	Florence SC	3/20/1940	10/26/1945
Robinson, Edward	Florence SC	3/11/1943	6/11/1946
Robinson, Ellis	Newport News VA	11/18/1943	3/8/1946
Robinson, Frank E	Florence SC	9/28/1942	2/26/1946
Robinson, Garfield	Florence SC	11/26/1943	4/24/1946
Robinson, George	Florence SC	1/21/1943	2/16/1946
Robinson, Irvin	New Brunswick NJ		12/16/1944
Robinson, Isiah	Florence SC	8/23/1944	8/23/1946
Robinson, John Charles	Sumter SC	3/4/1943	2/1/1946
Robinson, Joseph B	Florence SC	1/20/1942	11/26/1945
Robinson, Lavette	Florence SC	12/24/1942	1/18/1946
Robinson, Lawrence Edward	Florence SC	3/3/1943	12/26/1945
Robinson, Mingo Lee	Florence SC	1/15/1944	6/12/1946
Robinson, Thomas	Florence SC		
Robinson, Vander B	Florence SC	2/20/1942	12/12/1945
Robinson, Wilbur	Florence SC		
Robinson, William (Bill)	Florence SC	3/12/1943	1/14/1946
Robinson, William McKinley	Florence SC	5/5/1943	3/19/1946
Robinson, Willie James	Florence SC	8/18/1943	12/12/1945
Rodgers, Morgan Webber	Olanta SC	3/21/1940	3/25/1946
Rodrigue, Ernest Louis	Florence SC	6/17/1943	3/28/1946
Rogers, Cyrus Elmore	Belmont NC	12/9/1942	1/27/1946
Rogers, David Oliver	Hyman SC	2/12/1945	12/13/1946
Rogers, Frank Mandeville III	Florence SC	4/9/1943	3/29/1946
Rogers, John Lewis	Sumter SC	4/9/1943	8/19/1946
Rogers, Karl Leon, Jr.	Florence SC		
Rogers, Malcolm Paul	Florence SC	12/16/1943	11/23/1945
Rogers, Nathaniel	Florence SC	10/12/1942	10/27/1945
Rogers, Patrick H, Jr.	Columbia SC	1/27/1944	1/5/1946

NAME	CITY	ENTRY DATE	DISCHARGE
Rogers, Richmond	Florence SC	9/2/1943	3/1/1947
Rogers, Richmond	Florence SC	9/10/1943	12/3/1945
Rogers, Roy Newton	Lake City SC	10/21/1943	2/27/1946
Rogers, Thomas James	Hyman SC	9/18/1943	4/15/1946
Rolfe, Albert C	Florence SC	2/18/1943	1/27/1946
Rolfe, Hubert Isadore	Florence SC		
Rollins, William Benjamin, Jr.	Florence SC	3/25/1944	12/5/1945
Roney, Jackson Lee	Florence SC	8/6/1943	4/7/1946
Roney, Samuel Daniel	Florence SC		10/24/1944
Rose, Brantly Frank	Florence SC	4/21/1943	3/27/1946
Rose, Harry S	Florence SC		4/25/1945
Rose, Henry Samuel	Florence SC		3/2/1945
Rose, John G, Jr.	Timmonsville SC	11/1/1945	
Rose, Powell W	Florence SC	12/31/1942	12/21/1945
Rose, Robert Wilson, Jr.	Florence SC	11/10/1945	1/30/1947
Ross, Alfonza Emerson	Florence SC	2/4/1943	6/26/1946
Ross, Charles A	Florence SC	10/2/1939	11/2/1945
Ross, Harry Keith	Florence SC	5/23/1941	9/16/1945
Ross, Roland B	Florence SC	6/8/1940	8/22/1945
Ross, Wilbur Carl	Florence SC	8/9/1943	9/5/1945
Rouse, Hiram NMN	Florence SC		11/5/1944
Rouse, James	Florence SC	1/27/1944	1/2/1946
Rouse, Monroe	Atco NJ	9/25/1943	5/30/1946
Rowell, Caesar, Jr.	Florence SC	1/29/1944	4/23/1946
Rowell, Claude Edward	Florence SC	9/18/1939	11/7/1945
Rudd, Elmer B	Hemmingway SC	9/17/1943	9/12/1945
Rumph, Fred Leroy	Florence SC	10/28/1942	12/20/1945
Rush, Bennie, Jr.	Florence SC	1/20/1943	11/27/1945
Rush, Charles William	Timmonsville SC	3/18/1946	4/13/1947
Rush, Cleveland	Florence SC	4/27/1945	8/15/1946
Rush, Ralph	Florence SC	1/21/1943	12/10/1945
Rush, Seymore	Sumter SC	4/28/1944	1/8/1946
Rush, William B	Belton SC	2/21/1944	9/11/1946
Rushing, Willie Stevenson	Charlotte NC	11/26/1945	11/26/1945
Russell, Albert Marion	Florence SC	3/2/1943	12/20/1945
Russell, Samuel O, Jr.	Florence SC	11/20/1944	9/21/1945
Ruth, Willie Lee	Baltimore MD	8/28/1944	11/6/1943
Saleeby, Edwin George	Florence SC	4/12/1943	3/26/1946
Saleeby, Mitchell Nick	Florence SC		
Saleeby, Nicholas Sam	Florence SC	10/21/1943	4/16/1946
Sample, Thomas G	Florence SC	8/19/1942	1/24/1946
Samra, Nicholas	Florence SC	7/10/1943	9/17/1945
Sams, Thomas	Florence SC	10/25/1943	11/16/1945
Samuel, David Edward	Timmonsville SC	5/1/1945	10/25/1946
Samuel, David Ellison	Florence SC	3/7/1942	11/20/1945
Samuel, Herbert H	Florence SC	4/27/1945	6/28/1945
Samuel, Willie	Timmonsville SC	11/3/1943	1/19/1947
Samuels, Albert	Florence SC	12/31/1942	12/8/1945
Sanders, Edgar	Florence SC	4/28/1944	4/29/1946
Sanders, Elijah	Florence SC	11/13/1945	10/30/1946
Sanders, Henry, Jr.	Florence SC	10/9/1942	1/18/1946
Sanders, James	Florence SC	12/10/1943	5/22/1946
Sanders, James William	Florence SC	2/23/1943	3/20/1946
Sanders, Luther James	Florence SC	6/7/1943	12/15/1945
Sanders, Maxie	Florence SC	12/9/1943	

NAME	CITY	ENTRY DATE	DISCHARGE
Sanders, Monroe	Florence SC	11/3/1942	1/14/1946
Sanders, Norman	Florence SC	3/3/1943	12/31/1945
Sanders, Oliver	Alcolu SC	11/2/1942	10/14/1945
Sanders, Robert	Florence SC	8/5/1944	10/29/1946
Sandifer, Phillip Randolph	Florence SC	8/19/1942	12/1/1945
Sansbury, Baron Everett	Effingham SC	2/6/1941	10/31/1945
Sansbury, Frederick E	Florence SC		
Sansbury, Herman Bland	Florence SC	12/6/1943	11/8/1945
Sansbury, Justin W	Timmonsville SC	10/30/1943	12/22/1945
Sargon, Thomas Henry	Philadelphia PA	5/29/1941	11/20/1945
Sauls, David Rogers	Florence SC	7/8/1944	2/14/1946
Sauls, Melvin Jimmy	Florence SC		11/14/1944
Saunders, Allen, Jr.	Florence SC		
Saunders, William Manning	Florence SC		3/2/1943
Savage, Roy L	Goldsboro NC		
Saverance, Gleen Edwin	Effingham SC	9/22/1942	11/14/1945
Saverance, Hope Reedy	Timmonsville SC	11/11/1944	12/22/1946
Sawyer, Albert Preston	Marion SC		6/24/1945
Sawyer, Walter Zack	Florence SC	12/6/1944	4/3/1946
Scaffe, Frank	Florence SC	11/13/1944	11/7/1946
Schaible, John A, Jr.	Florence SC	9/26/1940	8/30/1945
Schindell, Herman H	Brooklyn NY	1/29/1943	2/17/1946
Schipman, John Kenneth	Florence SC		11/23/1944
Schofield, Charles S	Florence SC	7/1/1943	12/31/1945
Schuler, Edwin Denby	Berkeley CA		10/8/1945
Schuler, George A	Florence SC	12/6/1942	2/13/1946
Schuyler, Jack	Florence SC	12/3/1942	5/23/1944
Scipio, Evans	Florence SC	5/8/1944	1/11/1946
Scipio, isaac	Timmonsville SC	8/2/1944	10/24/1946
Scipio, Jeffery	Florence SC	3/11/1944	2/7/1946
Scipio, Moses	Florence SC	12/24/1942	1/21/1946
Scott, Bert	Florence SC	3/4/1943	2/17/1946
Scott, Charlie Henry	Florence SC	4/22/1944	1/29/1946
Scott, Cleveland	Elliott SC	8/28/1943	11/10/1945
Scott, Eddie	Washington DC	3/8/1946	3/3/1946
Scott, Leroy	New York NY		2/15/1944
Scott, Major	Florence SC	7/11/1945	10/20/1945
Scott, Quincy	Florence SC		1/29/1944
Scott, Raleigh	Florence SC	7/14/1943	11/23/1945
Scott, Silas Henry	Brooklyn NY		11/17/1944
Segars, James	Boston MA	7/17/1943	12/7/1945
Segars, James Burrell	Bishopville SC	2/8/1941	11/14/1945
Self, James Alfred	Florence SC	8/20/1941	9/28/1945
Sellers, Lawrence Lee "Son"	Florence SC	3/20/1944	3/5/1946
Sellers, Robert James	Florence SC	11/12/1943	1/22/1946
Sessions, George Quinton	Florence SC	11/28/1942	12/11/1945
Sessions, Joseph C	Florence SC	10/15/1940	9/4/1945
Sex, Juel Eskeuw	Fayetteville NC	10/27/1943	11/12/1945
Shannon, Douglas	Florence SC	8/14/1943	3/8/1946
Shannon, Horace, Jr.	Florence SC	6/10/1944	12/15/1945
Shannon, Jenis Calvin	Florence SC	11/8/1945	1/31/1947
Shattles, Claud	Florence SC	2/1/1944	3/21/1946
Shaw, Alton Buren	Florence SC	8/9/1943	3/7/1946
Shaw, Charles Milton	Florence SC	11/18/1944	8/4/1946
Shaw, Tom	Florence SC	5/19/1944	

★ ★ ★ ★

NAME	CITY	ENTRY DATE	DISCHARGE
Shepard, Robert Louis	Florence SC	1/5/1945	7/24/1946
Shields, Wallace	Florence SC	7/13/1944	3/7/1946
Shinholster, Paul	Savannah GA	10/25/1939	8/20/1945
Sidler, Leonard Oscar	Florence SC	1/5/1945	1/26/1946
Sills, Leroy	Washington DC	4/2/1941	12/20/1945
Simmons, Fred, Jr.	Florence SC	3/4/1943	1/12/1946
Simmons, Henry W	Florence SC		7/23/1944
Simmons, John Thurmon	Florence SC	4/7/1943	1/10/1946
Simmons, Sam	Florence SC	11/26/1943	10/12/1945
Simpson, Charlie	Florence SC	11/1/1945	1/21/1947
Simpson, Johnny Wesley	Florence SC	12/31/1942	12/5/1944
Simpson, William Sinkler	Florence SC	12/17/1941	8/27/1945
Sims, Bennie Alexander	Florence SC	1/13/1942	12/19/1945
Sims, Guymon W	Sumter SC	5/26/1942	11/29/1945
Sims, Harley	Florence SC		
Sineath, Wesley S	Timmonsville SC	5/22/1945	9/28/1946
Singletary, James Durant	Florence SC	1/6/1936	12/15/1945
Singletary, Jetter LaCue			
Singletary, John	Florence SC		
Singletary, Raymond	Florence SC	10/13/1942	2/15/1946
Singletary, Sammie	Florence SC		12/1/1943
Singletary, Verdell (Mack)	Florence SC	7/2/1943	11/21/1945
Singletary, Wattie McNeil	Florence SC		
Singletary, Willie	Florence SC		
Singletary, Woodrow	Florence SC	9/2/1943	11/26/1945
Singleton, Freddie	Florence SC		
Singleton, James	Florence SC		11/30/1944
Singleton, Nathaniel Earl	Florence SC	11/3/1942	10/7/1945
Skinner, Eugene	Florence SC	8/12/1942	1/9/1946
Skinner, James	Florence SC		11/11/1945
Skinner, Ralph Trey	Darlington SC	11/21/1945	7/15/1946
Small, Eugene	Philadelphia PA	2/8/1945	8/26/1946
Small, Herbert	Florence SC	5/27/1944	
Small, James	Florence SC	5/5/1943	12/27/1945
Small, James	Florence SC	11/3/1942	2/14/1946
Small, James Curley	Florence SC	5/15/1944	6/23/1946
Small, Moses	Florence SC	2/19/1943	1/15/1946
Small, Willie Edward	Florence SC		5/10/1943
Smalls, Albertus	Florence SC	9/29/1942	1/14/1946
Smalls, Jerry	Florence SC	11/3/1942	1/8/1946
Smart, Clyde Sylvester	Florence SC	2/25/1944	2/13/1946
Smart, Jesse W	Florence SC	11/4/1942	4/26/1946
Smart, Robert Milvard	Brooklyn NY	1/21/1946	1/4/1947
Smith, Archie	Florence SC	3/25/1943	2/18/1946
Smith, Charles Linwood	Florence SC	12/18/1945	3/4/1947
Smith, Charlie H, Jr.	Florence SC	6/27/1945	8/28/1945
Smith, Claiborne Pendleton	Savannah GA	8/2/1943	4/20/1946
Smith, Claude Boye, Jr.	Florence SC	12/27/1943	5/15/1946
Smith, Edward	Florence SC	3/30/1945	6/19/1946
Smith, Elliott, Jr.	Florence SC	6/19/1944	5/16/1946
Smith, Everette Vernon	Florence SC	3/13/1944	4/24/1946
Smith, Forest	New York NY		4/11/1942
Smith, Frederick Ligen	Laurenburg SC		7/25/1945
Smith, George	Florence SC	3/13/1944	4/11/1946
Smith, George Covington	Florence SC	3/1/1941	11/30/1945

★ ★ ★ ★

NAME	CITY	ENTRY DATE	DISCHARGE
Smith, Henry C	Florence SC	11/15/1945	11/8/1946
Smith, Henry Vereen	Fairfax SC	3/5/1942	2/5/1946
Smith, Hugh M	Florence SC	8/10/1945	7/16/1946
Smith, Ida cole	Florence SC		4/17/1945
Smith, James Bryan	Florence SC	6/1/1943	3/16/1946
Smith, James L	Florence SC	7/23/1942	1/25/1946
Smith, James P	Florence SC	8/7/1941	11/14/1945
Smith, James Preston, Jr.	Florence SC	2/1/1945	12/6/1946
Smith, Joe E	Florence SC	7/20/1943	2/6/1946
Smith, Kenneth L	Florence SC	9/8/1943	8/9/1945
Smith, Lenyard	Florence SC	5/15/1944	12/17/1945
Smith, Leroy	Florence SC		1/15/1946
Smith, Leroy	Henderson NY	5/18/1944	5/17/1946
Smith, Marion Claude	Florence SC	1/3/1942	11/27/1945
Smith, Mendel Lewis	Florence SC		
Smith, Monte Bernard, Jr.	Charlotte NC	4/6/1943	12/12/1945
Smith, Oliver Carlton	Bennettsville SC	4/14/1943	1/13/1945
Smith, Otis LaBorde	Florence SC	1/26/1943	2/19/1946
Smith, Richard Sessions	Florence SC	2/7/1941	12/10/1945
Smith, Robert Boyd, Jr.	Florence SC	4/15/1942	1/3/1946
Smith, Robert, Jr.	Motte WC	10/12/1942	11/25/1945
Smith, Roy E	Florence SC		6/25/1945
Smith, Rufus	Norfolk VA	5/24/1944	4/13/1946
Smith, Staley	Conway SC	9/9/1942	3/16/1946
Smith, Thomas, Jr.	Florence SC	3/3/1945	8/26/1946
Smith, Walter Powell	Latta SC	6/25/1945	11/17/1946
Smith, Willaim Edward	Florence SC	4/20/1943	3/15/1946
Smith, William Frank	Florence SC	2/4/1942	2/3/1946
Smith, William Henry, Jr.	Summeville SC	12/14/1942	9/21/1945
Smith, Willie Edward	Florence SC	6/29/1941	12/21/1945
Smith, Willie Raymond	Florence SC		11/24/1944
Smith, Willie Wesley	Florence SC	12/27/1941	9/28/1945
Smoot, Charles Leroy, Jr.	Florence SC	3/9/1944	5/6/1946
Smoot, Edmond, Jr.	Florence SC	6/11/1943	4/3/1946
Smoot, Lewis	Florence SC	9/23/1943	12/30/1945
Smoot, Tom	Florence SC	12/31/1943	12/20/1945
Snipes, Archie Cilchrist	Florence SC	1/13/1941	1/6/1946
Snipes, Benjamin Robert	Florence SC	9/11/1944	8/25/1946
Snipes, Joe Harry	Florence SC		
Snyder, Charles William	Florence SC		3/8/1945
Snypes, Milton E	Florence SC	7/24/1942	9/26/1945
Sole, Earsel C	Florence SC	7/18/1945	8/7/1945
Soloman, Willie Lee	Florence SC	11/5/1945	10/24/1946
Solomon, James Robert	Montverdo FL	2/16/1943	1/5/1946
Spake, Joe Wilson	Florence SC	1/19/1942	1/25/1946
Sparrow, Harlie G, Jr.	Florence SC	2/2/1943	1/17/1946
Spears, Gordon Hinson	Florence SC	6/8/1942	12/11/1945
Spears, Henry Athol	Florence SC	4/18/1942	1/2/1946
Spears, Johnnie Elijah	Florence SC	7/27/1943	3/22/1946
Spears, Jonnie	Brooklyn NY	1/20/1943	10/10/1945
Spears, Pearson Frederick	Florence SC		2/16/1945
Spears, Wade	Baltimore MD		5/7/1943
Spellar, Frank	Florence SC		10/18/1944
Spencer, Lawrence W	Florence SC	10/16/1943	10/19/1945
Sports, Julian Dan	Florence SC	2/21/1944	2/3/1946

★ ★ ★ ★

NAME	CITY	ENTRY DATE	DISCHARGE
Sports, Robert E L	Florence SC	1/7/1942	1/1/1946
Sports, Rupert Wallace	Florence SC	6/21/1943	2/12/1946
Sports, William Franklin, Jr.	Florence SC	6/17/1940	1/7/1946
Spriggs, George Boosier	Hanford WA		3/3/1943
Springs, Bennie Buster	Timmonsville SC	9/27/1943	7/17/1946
Springs, Richard F	Florence SC	1/30/1941	7/31/1945
Springs, Walter	Marlboro SC	3/4/1942	11/5/1946
Stackley, John Frederick	Florence SC	1/4/1945	8/15/1946
Stafford, William Walker, Jr.	Florence SC	12/29/1940	9/22/1945
Stanley, Archie McIntyre	Florence SC	10/31/1942	9/27/1945
Stanley, Archie McIntyre	Florence SC	10/31/1942	9/27/1945
Stanley, Jay Bion, Jr.	Florence SC		7/3/1946
Stanton, John Thomas	Florence SC	1/13/1941	10/13/1945
Stanton, Lawrence B	Florence SC	4/7/1943	2/22/1946
Stanton, Morris Howard, Jr.	Florence SC		12/8/1944
Stanton, Thomas Woodrow	Dillon SC	1/17/1945	5/2/1946
Stavenhagen, Monroe "S"	Florence SC	6/15/1945	8/21/1946
Steagall, William Paul, Jr.	Florence SC	3/9/1944	
Steel, John L, Sr.	Pamplico SC	10/29/1943	12/14/1945
Steele, Joseph Grisby	Huntington WV	1/9/1942	10/30/1946
Steen, John William	Florence SC		10/29/1945
Stephens, Charles Wesley	Florence SC		1/24/1946
Stephenson, Davis	Florence SC	12/31/1942	12/20/1945
Stephenson, Joseph Paul	Clemson SC	6/18/1943	12/13/1945
Stevens, Chester Burlington, Jr.	Florence SC	10/16/1944	3/23/1946
Stevenson, David Richard	New York NY	5/28/1941	11/28/1945
Stevenson, Robert McKenley	Warm Springs GA		
Stevenson, Woodrow	Florence SC	12/11/1941	3/23/1947
Stewart, Abraham Jerome	Florence SC	1/12/1943	11/16/1945
Stewart, Dewight L	Florence SC	10/30/1942	2/1/1946
Stewart, Franklin L	Effingham SC	10/24/1940	8/23/1945
Stewart, John E, Jr.	Pamplico SC	7/14/1943	3/15/1946
Stewart, Robert NMN	Darlington SC		
Stewart, Samuel Edward, Jr.	Georgetown SC	8/19/1942	10/17/1945
Stewart, Uriah Winslow	Florence SC		4/7/1943
Stewart, Willie	Florence SC	1/6/1943	10/21/1945
Stokes, Austin	Darlington SC	12/7/1942	2/11/1946
Stokes, Bennie William	Florence SC	12/5/1942	12/29/1945
Stokes, Dalton Rembert	Florence SC	10/17/1944	11/2/1946
Stokes, Hazel Garison	Florence SC		
Stokes, Isiah Malachi	Florence SC		7/20/1944
Stokes, James William	Florence SC	1/13/1941	10/26/1945
Stokes, Joseph Franklin, Jr.	Florence SC	4/7/1943	10/28/1945
Stokes, Lottie O	Florence SC	9/1/1942	1/23/1946
Stone, Forrest Moultrie	Hyman SC	2/26/1944	12/18/1946
Stone, Gren Lee	Florence SC		11/16/1943
Stone, Raymond Calvin	Florence SC	1/1/1943	10/15/1945
Stone, Robert H	Lake City SC	3/24/1944	1/4/1947
Stone, Vernon L	Florence SC	12/13/1941	10/8/1945
Stone, Walter, Jr.	Florence SC	12/31/1943	2/6/1946
Stone, William J	Raleigh NC		7/28/1945
Stonescypher, Roy Thomas	Atlanta GA		2/10/1945
Straughan, James A	Florence SC		9/3/1944
Strawn, William Keith	Florence SC	8/5/1942	3/11/1946
Street, Abraham	Florence SC	1/28/1944	5/18/1946

★ ★ ★ ★

NAME	CITY	ENTRY DATE	DISCHARGE
Street, Albert Earl	Florence SC	12/6/1942	11/5/1945
Street, Charles, Weldon	Florence SC	9/8/1942	11/4/1945
Street, Ernest Harrington	Florence SC	6/27/1944	12/16/1945
Street, George DeForest	Florence SC	9/9/1941	10/23/1945
Street, Herbert Terrell	Florence SC	3/4/1942	10/11/1945
Street, Ross Edgar	Florence SC		5/1/1944
Strickland, Harlan Emerson	Florence SC		11/27/1944
Strickland, Harvey	Sellers SC	9/23/1941	11/19/1946
Strickland, James Eugene	Lake City SC	4/5/1944	12/24/1945
Strickland, William A	Florence SC	3/28/1944	8/13/1945
Stricklin, Malcolm McCaskill	Florence SC	7/12/1941	12/21/1945
Strother, Henry	Florence SC	6/12/1944	4/11/1946
Stubbs, Benjamin	Florence SC	5/17/1941	4/6/1946
Stubbs, Otto Wright	Florence SC	8/9/1943	11/18/1945
Stuckey, Benjamin Franklin	Florence SC	1/19/1942	10/27/1945
Stuckey, France	Johnsonville SC	8/14/1945	10/20/1945
Suber, Herbert C	Florence SC	1/20/1944	7/4/1945
Suber, Heyward E	Florence SC	8/31/1943	2/25/1946
Summerford, Curtis Kershaw, Jr	Florence SC	6/23/1945	8/4/1946
Summerford, Major, Jr	Florence SC	7/6/1944	7/19/1946
Summerford, Thomas Kenneth	Florence SC	7/23/1943	3/4/1946
Summerford, Waverly Clyde	Florence SC	10/27/1942	5/3/1946
Summerford, Winifred Eugene	Florence SC	4/7/1943	11/10/1945
Sumter, James	Florence SC	1/14/1943	
Sumter, Richard S	Florence SC	5/5/1943	9/8/1945
Surles, Herman Gregg	Florence SC	4/17/1944	6/3/1946
Surls, Ruffin Lewis	Florence SC	6/18/1943	5/16/1946
Sutton, William W, Jr	Fayetteville NC		9/26/1945
Swann, Thomas Baxter	Florence SC	11/26/1945	11/23/1945
Sweet, Ernest Edward	Florence SC	01/09/194_	12/18/1946
Swinton, Clarence	Florence SC	12/8/1943	1/2/1945
Swinton, Laverne	Florence SC	1/15/1944	2/13/1946
Syracuse, Robert J	Chicago IL	6/15/1942	1/9/1946
Tallevast, William DeKalb, Jr		6/10/1943	11/14/1945
Tallon, Clyde Theo	Florence SC	6/1/1943	4/9/1946
Tanner, Roland L	Johnsonville SC	12/11/1940	1/4/1946
Tanner, Walter Way	Florence SC	2/2/1943	11/27/1945
Tanner, Wilber P	Florence SC	11/4/1942	12/3/1945
Tarpley, Ernest R	Florence SC	12/12/1941	9/1/1945
Taylor, Bennett Wilson	Balmont NC	4/7/1944	10/11/1945
Taylor, Charles William	Florence SC	8/22/1944	2/1/1946
Taylor, Curtis Stanclor	Florence SC	6/28/1944	1/8/1946
Taylor, Frank Flem	Timmonsville SC	2/15/1944	1/4/1946
Taylor, George G	Florence SC	6/14/1941	12/15/1946
Taylor, Harding	Florence SC	10/1/1942	1/18/1946
Taylor, James F	Florence SC	5/27/1944	2/6/1946
Taylor, John Leroy	Florence SC	2/22/1945	2/14/1947
Taylor, Joseph Albert	Florence SC	2/23/1942	11/14/1945
Taylor, Julins NMN	Florence SC		11/29/1944
Taylor, Marvin Hampton	Florence SC	5/22/1943	2/24/1946
Taylor, Marvin Lee	Rock Hill SC		3/8/1946
Taylor, Milton Eric	Florence SC		
Taylor, Thomas Scott	Florence SC	6/4/1942	11/14/1945
Taylor, William Carter	Florence SC		
Taylor, William F	Florence SC	4/20/1943	10/16/1945

★ ★ ★ ★

NAME	CITY	ENTRY DATE	DISCHARGE
Taylor, William W	Florence SC	8/23/1943	12/29/1945
Tedder, Gary Eugene	Coward SC	9/24/1945	7/14/1946
Temple, James	Florence SC	12/31/1942	1/9/1946
Tennant, Franklin G	Abraham UT	1/20/1941	10/29/1946
Teskey, Robert Howe	Florence SC	4/21/1942	10/1/1945
Testruth, John F	Florence SC	1/15/1941	9/4/1945
Thames, Ducan Allen	Florence SC	6/7/1943	10/26/1945
Thames, John Olin	Florence SC		
Thames, Robert Lee	Washington DC	2/2/1943	11/23/1945
Thames, Wilbur Ross	Lane SC	10/17/1944	7/29/1946
Thigpen, Bartan	Cades SC	10/5/1942	2/8/1946
Thigpen, John Leroy	Florence SC	2/21/1944	1/14/1946
Thigpen, Kathlyn D	Florence SC		2/4/1945
Thomas, Charles Harris	Florence SC	5/8/1942	11/20/1945
Thomas, Elijah Pate	Florence SC	5/6/1941	10/18/1945
Thomas, George Wells	Florence SC	7/30/1942	1/4/1946
Thomas, Harrell Wallace	Cheraw SC	2/20/1941	11/8/1945
Thomas, Harry E, Jr	Florence SC	8/23/1942	8/23/1945
Thomas, Henry	Florence SC	3/13/1944	1/10/1946
Thomas, Jack Clinton	Chicago IL		6/26/1943
Thomas, James Richard	Lake City SC	5/26/1943	5/1/1946
Thomas, James Valentine	Florence SC		
Thomas, John, Jr	Lake City SC	1/7/1943	10/23/1945
Thomas, Johnnie	Florence SC	1/9/1943	1/8/1946
Thomas, Richard Allan	Florence SC		
Thomas, Robert	Florence SC	8/6/1943	4/19/1946
Thomas, Robert L	Florence SC	1/4/1943	12/17/1945
Thomas, Samuel	Florence SC	10/15/1942	12/12/1945
Thomas, Santee	Florence SC	7/10/1945	8/11/1945
Thomas, Whisman	Pamplico SC	4/5/1940	2/24/1946
Thompson, John Price	Davidson NC	5/6/1942	1/31/1946
Thompson, John Wiles	Effingham SC		
Thompson, Roy	Pamplico SC	8/25/1942	2/13/1946
Thornhill, Marvin James	Olanta SC		10/24/1944
Tiller, Randolph Morgan	Florence SC		3/26/1946
Tiller, Woodrow Wilson	Florence SC	4/20/1943	12/15/1945
Timmons, Curtis William	Timmonsville SC	8/21/1945	1/29/1947
Timmons, Dorsey R	Florence SC	12/10/1943	10/26/1945
Timmons, Forest	Florence SC	8/3/1943	4/14/1946
Timmons, Harley	Florence SC	5/11/1944	2/18/1946
Timmons, Hubert Elgin	Effingham SC	3/7/1946	1/7/1947
Timmons, James Earl	Florence SC	1/18/1944	12/24/1945
Timmons, James Preston	Florence SC	10/14/1942	11/14/1945
Timmons, Lee Roy	New York City	9/26/1942	1/25/1946
Timmons, Oscar	Florence SC	11/3/1942	12/1/1945
Timmons, Ray	Johnsonville SC		6/8/1945
Timmons, Morgan	Effingham SC	4/21/1941	12/30/1945
Tindall, Alexander	Florence SC		11/10/1945
Tindall, James	Florence SC		7/1/1944
Tindall, Preston	Florence SC	5/30/1944	5/15/1946
Tindall, Roodrow	Florence SC		
Tinsley, Edward Diskin, Jr.	Florence SC	10/8/1942	2/5/1946
Tippett, Guy A, Jr.	Florence SC	2/14/1944	10/3/1945
Tisdale, James	Albany NY		7/1/1943
Tisdale, Wilbur G	Florence SC	6/21/1943	12/16/1945

★ ★ ★ ★

NAME	CITY	ENTRY DATE	DISCHARGE
Tomlinson, Carl William	Timmonsville SC	3/25/1946	1/6/1947
Tomlinson, Charles Franklin	Olanta SC	1/3/1942	11/20/1945
Tomlinson, Liston D	Effingham SC	3/20/1940	3/29/1946
Treatt, James F, Jr.	Florence SC	7/21/1941	8/30/1945
Truesdale, Maulsin Hilton	Florence SC	10/15/1943	12/25/1946
Trutte, James Dowling	Florence SC	4/17/1944	1/31/1946
Tucker, James Andrew	Deceased	3/1/1943	
Turbeville, Byron Gay	Florence SC	9/24/1940	8/2/1945
Turner, Dallace Otto	Florence SC	1/31/1941	4/8/1946
Turner, Davis NMN, Jr.	Florence SC	8/21/1944	4/25/1946
Turner, Ernest	Florence SC	2/9/1943	1/13/1946
Turner, Lonnie Hite	Florence SC		9/29/1944
Turner, Mathis	Florence SC		9/27/1944
Turner, Norwood	Effingham SC	1/7/1941	9/17/1945
Turpin, John Henry	Florence SC	5/11/1944	1/29/1946
Tyler, Jack Stevenson	Florence SC	8/9/1943	2/16/1946
Tyler, Walter Dixon, Jr.	Florence SC		2/18/1946
Tyner, Joel O, Jr.	Florence SC	4/1/1941	12/13/1945
Tyner, Joseph Wallace	Florence SC	6/4/1942	12/10/1945
Tyner, Foster Esward	Florence SC	8/18/1942	8/17/1945
Tyson, Uncan Wright	Florence SC	3/27/1943	7/14/1946
Vaught, Robert W	Florence SC	8/27/1942	8/5/1945
Vause, Don Cornelius			
Vereen, Willie James	Pamplico SC	1/16/1946	4/14/1947
Waddell, Alton William	Effingham SC	8/18/1944	6/12/1946
Waddell, Lester Roland	Florence SC	8/30/1943	4/2/1946
Waddell, Ted Theodore	Effingham SC		9/20/1945
Wade, Donald B	Jacksonville Fl	1/7/1944	
Waiters, James NMN	Mars Bluff SC	9/10/1943	1/3/1946
Waiters, John Allen	Florence SC		5/11/1944
Wakefall, Ben	Florence SC	3/4/1943	1/14/1946
Walden, Billie	Timmonsville SC	9/12/1940	10/17/1945
Walden, Casual L	Timmonsville SC	12/21/1943	1/10/2016
Walker, Butler A	Florence SC	7/1/1944	12/20/1945
Walker, Clovie R	Florence SC	9/12/1942	12/20/1945
Walker, Franklin	Florence SC	7/17/1943	1/30/1946
Walker, Hugh Grady, Jr.	Florence SC	11/9/1945	1/30/1947
Walker, Robert P	New York City	9/28/1939	8/21/1945
Wallace, Curtis Marion	Florence SC	6/17/1944	2/8/1946
Wallace, Ernest Edwin	Florence SC		4/18/1945
Wallace, George Gary, Jr.	Florence SC		9/29/1944
Wallace, George, Jr.	Florence SC	9/8/1942	11/18/1945
Wallace, Howard James	Florence SC	7/27/1942	10/9/1945
Wallace, John Barnwell	Florence SC	6/30/1943	3/12/1946
Wallace, Vernon Malley	Marion SC	4/2/1945	10/7/1945
Waller, Joe Henry, Jr.	Florence SC	4/28/1943	1/11/1946
Walsh, Albert, Jr.	Miami Fla	10/21/1943	1/21/1946
Walsh, Eugene Porter	Florence SC	1/3/1942	12/3/1945
Walters, Joseph	Florence SC	4/2/1945	3/2/1945
Walters, Joseph	Florence SC	1/30/1945	2/2/1947
Walters, Stephen Earle	Florence SC	4/15/1943	10/13/1945
Waltes, Dan, Jr.	Florence SC	1/21/1944	1/18/1946
Ward, Charles	Florence SC	5/25/1944	1/6/1946
Ward, Chevis H	Florence SC	9/23/1941	12/29/1946
Ward, Espy Eramus, Jr.	Miami Fla	2/8/1943	10/10/1945

★ ★ ★ ★

NAME	CITY	ENTRY DATE	DISCHARGE
Ward, Horace J	Florence SC	9/26/1941	9/28/1945
Ward, Jesse Lee, Jr.	Florence SC	3/6/1945	12/23/1945
Ward, Mack William	Effingham SC	8/23/1945	2/21/1947
Ward, Robert E	Timmonsville SC	2/12/1942	1/28/1946
Ward, Vernon Dalhart	Florence SC	3/30/1944	12/5/1945
Wardy, Cicore	Florence SC	7/26/1942	7/17/1945
Wardy, Willie J	Effingham SC	12/31/1942	2/5/1946
Warr, Andrew James	Florence SC	3/13/1941	9/8/1945
Warr, George Franklin	Florence SC	6/2/1943	11/9/1945
Washington, Dozier	Florence SC	4/19/1944	12/17/1945
Washington, Paul A	Albany NY		
Washington, Vann	Florence SC	4/27/1945	11/22/1946
Waters, Washington Marion	Florence SC	1/24/1944	5/4/1946
Waters, William Frederick, Jr.	Sumpter SC	5/29/1943	1/12/1946
Watford, Clifton P	Timmonsville SC	4/7/1943	2/10/1946
Watford, John Russell	Lamar SC	8/21/1941	12/9/1945
Watkins, Harry C	Florence SC	6/27/1943	1/10/1946
Watkinson Warren Murray	Vernon Washington		9/18/1945
Watson, William Ivey	Raleigh NC	6/29/1944	4/4/1946
Watts, Thomas McDuffie	Florence SC	2/1/1956	12/6/1945
Weatherford, Charles Emery	Florence SC	3/16/1943	4/16/1946
Weatherford, Gordon E	Florence SC	4/3/1943	11/25/1946
Weatherford, James Lucian	Florence SC	1/20/1943	4/3/1946
Weatherford, John Howard	Florence SC		6/9/1945
Weatherford, Leslie Carter	Florence SC		11/15/1943
Weatherford, Ollie Allen	Florence SC	5/13/1944	2/2/1946
Weatherford, Paul Everett	Effingham SC	7/23/1944	7/4/1946
Weatherford, William Henery	Florence SC	10/17/1940	7/1/1945
Weatherford, Willie Eugene	Florence SC	9/8/1944	10/29/1946
Weaver, Elbert	Timmonsville SC	10/17/1944	7/17/1946
Weaver, George Cleatus, Jr.	Florence SC		10/17/1944
Weaver, George Cleveland	Greenville SC		
Weaver, Henry Grady, Jr.	Florence SC	4/8/1943	2/22/1946
Weaver, Thomas Benny, Jr.	Hampton VA		12/20/1944
Webb, John William	Florence SC	5/27/1944	3/21/1946
Webb, Thomas Cooke	Florence SC	11/13/1942	2/26/1946
Weeks, Louis	Florence SC	12/31/1942	1/15/1946
Weeks, William Lloyd	Florence SC	9/12/1941	8/29/1945
Weigel, Robert M	Navada	3/5/1942	11/8/1945
Welch, Joseph Howard, Jr.	Florence SC	5/27/1944	5/11/1946
Welch, Richmond	Walterboro SC	5/25/1944	2/20/1946
Weldon, Russel Cirtus	Florence SC	12/21/1942	1/6/1946
Wells, Emmette Gordon	Laurenburg NC	3/23/1943	1/6/1946
Wells, William Pope	Laurenburg NC	10/28/1942	3/17/1946
West, Ollie Long	Florence SC	3/25/1943	9/24/1945
Whaley, Bernard Clyde	Florence SC		10/9/1945
Wheeler, John McGill	Charleston SC		
Wheeler, Mark H		1/27/1941	7/31/1945
Wheller, Robert Peirce	West Barnstable MA	12/17/1941	10/17/1945
Whisonant, Lowery Meek	Marion SC		4/8/1943
Whistnant, Grayson David	Florence SC		5/2/1944
Whiswnhunt, Fredrick S	Florence SC	3/27/1945	2/6/1947
Whitaker, Gerald D	Owensboro Kentucky	9/11/1942	4/25/1946
White, Author	Florence SC		11/25/1944
White, Charles Raymond	Florence SC	1/8/1943	11/21/1945

★ ★ ★ ★

NAME	CITY	ENTRY DATE	DISCHARGE
White, Ernest, Jr.	Florence SC	10/31/1942	1/9/1946
White, Frank	Florence SC	12/23/1942	1/13/1947
White, George Huges	Florence SC	1/29/1945	1/30/1946
White, Harlod Reaves	Otlanta SC	9/19/1942	11/7/1945
White, Louis	Florence SC	4/15/1941	10/15/1945
White, Randolph Isom	Florence SC	9/17/1943	2/24/1946
White, Thoman Hicks	Church St City	4/21/1943	2/5/1946
White, Thomas	Florence SC	4/23/1941	12/30/1945
White, Thomas	Florence SC	4/23/1941	12/30/1945
White, Thomas H	Florence SC	12/31/1942	11/11/1945
White, William Thurman	Dargan St City	9/22/1943	2/3/1946
White, Willie	Hummingway SC	7/10/1941	9/30/1945
Whitfiels, James "Pepper"	Florence SC		
Whitley, Ervin Lee	Florence SC	6/2/1943	2/7/1946
Whitley, James Judy	Blandenbro NC	9/22/1944	3/28/1946
Whittington, Prentiss Benjamin	Florence SC	5/5/1944	5/7/1946
Whitton, Thomas J	Florence SC	6/13/1943	2/19/1946
Wiggens, Clavin W, Jr.	Pamplico SC		
Wiggens, Edward Gregg	Charleston SC	1/11/1941	12/5/1945
Wiggens, Leo W	Florence SC	7/1/1941	8/31/1945
Wiggens, Patrick, Zingale	Darlington SC	1/5/1945	1/21/1946
Wike, Fred A	Pamplico SC	8/20/1941	6/28/1945
Wike, James David	Florence SC	12/1/1943	12/22/1945
Wilds, Sherman	Florence SC	8/5/1944	9/10/1946
Wilhoit, Cecil Thornton	Palmetto St City	3/27/1944	3/17/1946
Wilhoit, Clarence Richmond	Florence SC	10/20/1943	11/11/1945
Wilhoit, E Q		10/20/1943	1/18/1946
Wilhoit, Monty Rea	Florence SC	5/26/1943	11/26/1945
Wilkes, George Thomas	Lynchburg SC	8/19/1942	1/30/2008
Wilkes, Martin Manroe	Florence SC	1/20/1944	3/5/1946
Wilkins, Cirtus	Florence SC	3/4/1943	11/24/1945
Wilkins, Richard Irwin		3/30/1945	11/9/1945
Willcox, Henry St Gworge Carson	Florence SC	2/1/1942	4/20/1946
Williams, Adam	Florence SC	6/23/1943	2/15/1946
Williams, Adolph Lamar	Florence SC	4/18/1942	9/11/1945
Williams, Bartow	Florence SC	12/11/1941	11/17/1945
Williams, Benjamin Franklin	Effingham SC	4/26/1945	10/20/1946
Williams, Carl Sheppard	Conway SC	12/1/1943	2/8/1946
Williams, Cary Eugene	Florence SC	8/28/1942	1/17/1946
Williams, Charlie P	Pamplico SC	1/17/1942	2/13/1945
Williams, Clarence Vivian, Jr.	Florence SC		9/21/1945
Williams, Duncan McLinsy	Baltimore MD		
Williams, E C, Jr.	Pamplico SC	5/7/1941	10/5/1945
Williams, Eddie Junius	Topeka Kansas	4/24/1946	12/30/1946
Williams, Eddie S	Florence SC		10/21/1945
Williams, Edward H	Bainbridge GA	4/10/1942	9/10/1945
Williams, Edward H	Florence SC	4/10/1942	9/10/1945
Williams, Ernest L	Florence SC	11/16/1939	6/29/1944
Williams, Frank	Florence SC	5/20/1944	3/9/1946
Williams, Frank	Brooklyn NY		
Williams, Herdon F	Florence SC	5/24/1943	8/18/1945
Williams, James	Florence SC	7/24/1942	12/10/1945
Williams, James Harding, Jr.	Florence SC	12/31/1942	1/28/1946
Williams, James K	Florence SC	10/28/1944	2/26/1946
Williams, Jesse Junior	Florence SC	10/28/1944	7/26/1946

NAME	CITY	ENTRY DATE	DISCHARGE
Williams, John H	Florence SC	2/24/1944	12/13/1945
Williams, Johnnie Byrd	Florence SC	9/28/1943	10/16/1945
Williams, Joseph Henery	Florence SC	7/14/1942	3/29/1946
Williams, King	Florence SC	6/3/1943	1/20/1946
Williams, Levern	Florence SC	7/11/1945	11/16/1946
Williams, Levy	Florence SC	4/18/1942	12/21/2005
Williams, Richard General	Florence SC	11/26/1940	9/22/1945
Williams, Robert	Florence SC	1/28/1944	1/18/1946
Williams, Robert Fulton	Florence SC	9/8/1942	11/19/1945
Williams, Robert W	Florence SC	7/9/1940	9/24/1945
Williams, Ruben	Coward SC	5/11/1944	1/22/1946
Williams, Sunny	Columbus OH	11/30/1945	1/31/1946
Williams, Thomas	Effingham SC	2/20/1943	5/24/1946
Williams, Thomas Cecil	Florence SC		6/19/1945
Williams, Tommie Louis	Baltimore MD	8/13/1943	4/17/1946
Williams, Walter	Florence SC	12/31/1942	2/6/1946
Williams, Walter	Timmonsville SC	11/11/1943	12/29/1945
Williams, Wilbur	Augusta GA	4/2/1941	8/21/1941
Williams, Willie NMN	Florence SC		4/9/1945
Williams, Willie NMN	Brooklyn NY	9/1/1943	3/4/1946
Williamson, Ivory, Jr.	Coward SC	7/1/1943	2/19/1946
Williamson, Jessie	Florence SC	7/11/1945	
Williamson, Johnnie	Florence SC	7/17/1942	1/8/1946
Williamson, Somers H	Florence SC	9/23/1943	4/4/1946
Williamson, Walter P	Loris SC	12/6/1942	10/4/1945
Willis, Charles William	Florence SC	9/26/1945	4/30/1946
Willis, Frank Bound	Florence SC	10/24/1944	7/12/1946
Willis, James N	McCall SC	12/15/1942	8/15/1945
Willis, William Crawford	Florence SC	2/9/1943	2/28/1946
Wilson, Cleo	Florence SC	7/7/1942	1/11/1946
Wilson, Isaac	Florence SC	1/21/1943	11/17/1945
Wilson, James	Florence SC	1/7/1942	12/15/1945
Wilson, James	Florence SC	1/22/1944	1/10/1946
Wilson, James M	Timmonsville SC		1/19/1942
Wilson, James Raymond Jr.	Florence SC	12/22/1939	12/26/1945
Wilson, John Lucious	Philadelphia PA	12/22/1945	12/7/1946
Wilson, Leslie L	Morristown Tenn		12/16/1945
Wilson, Nathaniel	Florence SC		11/4/1944
Wilson, Neil Lyddell	Effingham SC	8/18/1944	6/14/1946
Wilson, Ray L	Effingham SC	7/17/1941	9/28/1945
Wilson, Ray NMN	Florence SC		12/5/1944
Wilson, Robert Leland	Florence SC		11/5/1944
Wilson, Roscoe Jerome	New York City	9/11/1942	1/16/1946
Wilson, Sylvester Lee	Florence SC	4/15/1944	11/27/1946
Wilson, Walter	Florence SC	2/22/1946	5/19/1947
Wilson, William Dainel	Washington DC	1/19/1942	12/29/1945
Wilson, William Francis	Florence SC	4/26/1945	11/21/1946
Wilson, Willie Jr.	Florence SC	11/17/1943	1/29/1946
Windham, Allen Lester	Florence SC	1/7/1941	2/4/1946
Windham, Burnice DeLee	Timmonsville SC	6/11/1937	7/18/1946
Windham, Harold Thomas	Florence SC	6/27/1944	4/3/1946
Windham, James Lawrence, Jr.	Florence SC	12/5/1942	12/29/1945
Windham, Leonard Wallace	Florence SC	1/31/1941	9/21/1942
Windham, Wesley Eugene	Florence SC	12/18/1941	1/4/1946
Windham, Willie	Florence SC	3/24/1943	2/20/1946

★ ★ ★ ★

NAME	CITY	ENTRY DATE	DISCHARGE
Wines, V James	Florence SC	1/15/1944	6/28/1946
Winfield, Wallace W	Florence SC	10/20/1942	1/17/1946
Wingate, Charlie	Florence SC	3/23/1945	4/22/1946
Wingate, Henry	Darlington SC	12/29/1945	4/7/1947
Wingate, Robert	Darlington SC	11/3/1942	
Wingate, Victor	Florence SC	1/20/1943	11/2/1945
Winter, Phillip	Columbia SC	5/23/1941	9/11/1945
Wison, Charles Montgomery, Jr.	Effingham SC	1/7/1942	12/24/1945
Witherspoon, Charles F	Florence SC	5/21/1945	12/17/1946
Witherspoon, Cleveland	Florence SC	3/3/1943	3/7/1946
Witherspoon, Douglas	Florence SC	1/21/1943	1/14/1946
Witherspoon, Goerge, Jr.	Florence SC	9/4/1943	12/31/1945
Wolfe, Robert Gray	Florence SC	6/20/1945	8/2/1946
Wolfe, Thomas E, Jr.	Florence SC	3/30/1943	4/22/1946
Woodard, Ted Roosevelt	Agust, GA	4/16/1943	3/14/1946
Woodburry, Isaac	Johnsonville SC	3/19/1945	5/22/1946
Woodbury, James A	Johnsonville SC		
Woodbury, James Thomas	Florence SC	3/5/1943	2/7/1946
Woodbury, John DeWitt	Florence SC	3/12/1943	12/30/1945
Woods, Eugene	Florence SC	4/22/1941	11/15/1945
Woods, Henry Leaboy	Florence SC	3/31/1943	1/13/1946
Woods, James	Effingham SC	1/27/1942	5/23/1946
Woods, Larry	Florence SC	7/30/1942	12/1/1945
Woods, Theo, Jr.	NY	5/11/1943	5/31/1946
Woodside, Hubert F, Jr	Florence SC	6/17/1943	10/1/1945
Worrell, Carl Robert	Florence SC		1/11/1944
Worrell, Dozier W	Florence SC	9/11/1941	
Worrell, Luther Willard	Florence SC	6/4/1942	
Worrell, Robert James	Florence SC	10/5/1942	8/9/1945
Wright, Author Dixon	Ladson SC	1/22/1944	1/26/1946
Wright, Bert	Florence SC	11/26/1943	11/1/1945
Wright, David Martin	Florence SC	3/31/1944	12/12/1945
Wright, Isia	Florence SC	11/3/1942	1/30/1946
Wright, James	Timmonsville SC	3/18/1946	3/9/1947
Wright, Joseph,	Florence SC		11/27/1943
Wright, Louis Lurinzo	Florence SC		9/4/1944
Wright, Norman Earl	Florence SC	9/4/1942	2/14/1942
Wright, Roland	Florence SC	11/26/1942	1/5/1946
Wright, Roscoe	Florence SC	6/24/1946	12/10/1946
Wright, Willie	Florence SC	1/5/1946	12/12/1946
Wysong, James Ermey	Florence SC	11/29/1944	8/27/1946
Yopp, Herbert	Florence SC		10/9/1943
Youmans, Robert Lannis	Florence SC	7/8/1944	
Young, Bennie James	Florence SC	1/14/1943	1/16/1946
Young, Edward Hames	Florence SC		1/6/1945
Young, George N	Florence SC	8/25/1942	1/20/1946
Young, George Nataniel	Florence SC	8/25/1942	1/20/1946
Young, John Frederick	Florence SC	7/21/1945	12/1/1945
Young, Nathan	Florence SC	4/23/1944	6/22/1946
Young, Parish, Jr.	Elizabeth NJ	7/31/1945	9/24/1945
Young, Sam	Timmonsville SC	1/3/1943	10/1/1945
Young, Thomas Benton, Jr.	Florence SC		12/9/1946
Young, Willie Blease	Florence SC	3/30/1945	11/28/1945
Zandies, Richard	Grier SC	4/19/1941	9/23/1945
Zeigler, Edwin Deanes	Florence SC	4/29/1944	10/11/1945
Zeigler, James, Jr.	Timmonsville SC	7/9/1945	2/5/1947